Cowboy Up!

The History of Bull Riding

Cowboy Up!
THE HISTORY OF BULL RIDING

By
Gail Hughbanks Woerner

Illustrations by
Gail Gandolfi

EAKIN PRESS Fort Worth, Texas

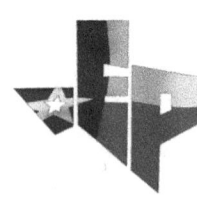

Copyright © 2001
By Gail Hughbanks Woerner
Published in the United States of America
By Eakin Press
An Imprint of Wild Horse Media Group
P.O. Box 331779
Fort Worth, Texas 76163
1-888-982-8270
www.EakinPress.com
ALL RIGHTS RESERVED
1 2 3 4 5 6 7 8 9
ISBN-10: 1571685316
ISBN-13: 978-1571685315

Library of Congress Cataloging-in-Publication Data
Woerner, Gail Hughbanks, 1936–
   Cowboy up! : the history of bull riding / by Gail Hughbanks
Woerner; illustrations by Gail Gandolfi.– 1st ed.
     p.   cm.
   Includes bibliographical references and index.
   ISBN 1-57168-531-6 (PB)
   ISBN 1-57168-615-0 (HB)
   1. Bull riding—United States—History. I. Title
GV1834.45.B84 W64   2001
791.8/4–dc21   2001040532

Contents

Preface	v
Acknowledgments	vii
Introduction	ix
1. Exhibition or Competition?	1
2. Diaper Days of Rodeo	15
3. Cowboys Unite!	29
4. Trial & Error	47
5. Cowboys Are Too Tough to Kill	64
6. The Golden Years of Rodeo	78
7. School Daze	104
8. The Mighty Sponsors and the '70s Era	137
9. The Feminine Touch	164
10. Doctor! Doctor!	177
11. Athletes: The Four-Legged Variety	199
12. The Twenty-first Century	223
13. Competition—The American Way	241
Appendix	255
Champion All-Around Cowboys	255
Champion Bull Riders	257
PRCA Bull of the Year	259
Linderman Award Winners	260
PRCA Resistol Rookie of the Year	261
PRCA Bull Riding Rookie of the Year	262
PRCA National Finals	263
NFR Average Bull Riding Champion	263
NFR Top Bucking Bulls	264
PRCA Dodge National Circuit Finals Winners	265

Circuits Competing	265
All-Around	265
Bull Riding	266
Professional Bull Riders	266
World Champions	266
World Champion Event Winners	267
Rookie of the Year	267
Bull of the Year	267
Stock Contractor of the Year	267
High Money Bull Before PBR Finals	268
PBR Bucking Bull of the Finals	268
PBR Prize Money Increase	268
PBR Ring of Honor	269
Professional Women's Rodeo Association Champions	269
All-Around	269
Bull Riding	269
National Cowboy Hall of Fame Honorees	270
ProRodeo Hall of Fame Honorees	274
Rodeo Organizations	276
Glossary	277
Resource Materials	283
Index	289

Preface

A 2,000-pound bull, gray in color, with loose skin that seems to slide up and down and to and fro as he kicks, jumps, twists and gyrates his body, tries to rid himself of the 140-pound rider. The rider works in opposition to the bull's manipulating just long enough to stay aboard until the eight-second bell rings. As the bull shakes his head, adorned with fierce, pointed horns that jut from his skull, his nostrils flare and snot shoots up and lands on the rider. The bull's eyes have a glaze to them; his mouth is open as if he is trying to bellow for help, but not a sound is heard. The ferocious beast has one agenda: to be free of the person mounted on his back, *at any odds*.

Meanwhile, the bull rider is working just as hard sitting on a four- to five-inch square directly behind the bull's withers, holding on to a rope pulled tautly under the bull's belly and wrapped tightly over the cowboy's hand. The rider's hand is close to his crotch, with the end of the rope, rosined to keep it from slipping, twisted around his fingers. To hold this rope in place as the bull jerks and shakes takes a tremendous amount of strength on the part of the rider. The bull rider's mental state is one of total concentration on the movements of the bull, trying to anticipate the next move the two-ton mountain of fury will make.

Who wins? If the bull is successful in his attempt to throw his rider, the bull does. If the rider maintains his seat on the bull, without touching the bull, the rope, or himself with his free hand, until the whistle blows at eight seconds, the rider wins.

It is an exciting event that tops the charts in rodeo interest today, but it has not always been so. In fact, bull riding is one of the only rodeo events that did not evolve from the life of a ranch cowboy and his everyday work. Now it is one of the most exciting events because of the danger involved. It pits the rider against a bull, an animal that is mean by nature, and not only wants to dump his rider but will try to use his horns to hook or gore him or anyone else the bull might see. The rider may get stepped on, if he falls and can't get out of the way of the two-ton menace.

Do audiences want to see someone get gored, hooked, stomped, or killed? It's a hard question to answer. If spectators are asked, they will say, "Of course not!" But there is always that slight possibility that death or injury might happen. And if it does, spectators are there to witness it.

Man versus beast. The hunter and the hunted. The challenge is to be pitted against the most dangerous of beasts. The rider must prove to himself and others that he has the strength, talent, and expertise to overcome the most dangerous adversary.

As the western frontiers disappeared in our country, and more and more people began to live in urban areas, there was an increasing need for people to get outside and enjoy themselves. A logical way to do this was to play sports, such as baseball or football, and those not so inclined to play could enjoy watching as spectators. In less inhabited areas, mainly the American West, people from ranches, farms, and local communities would gather on a Sunday or a holiday, such as the Fourth of July, when everyone could enjoy a day of rest. Covered-dish dinners were always the fare, as were ballgames, horse races, or making a few wagers pitting a couple of cowboys against each other, to see who could ride or rope the best.

Out of this early-day entertainment eventually came the sport of rodeo. A competition between cowboys; a competition between cowboys and the animals they tried to ride or rope. The cowboy competing against some of his best friends, an animal, or the clock. Rodeo has become the only true western American sport.

Acknowledgments

This book has been a joy to create because in doing so I have met and worked with some of the most wonderful people I have ever known. This is my third book related to the history of rodeo, and with each book my world has been expanded greatly because of the people I have met in gathering the information to complete this history.

First of all, I must thank my husband, Cliff, for his continual support and input on my project. He corrects all my silly mechanical mistakes and encourages me to take control of the computer (even though I crashed the first one and had to get a second one). He never complains when I take off for some rodeo or cowboy reunion somewhere in this country and leave him for weeks at a time. He rarely mentions the huge telephone bills I incur just contacting my many sources across the nation. And most of all, he never has a discouraging word for me.

I want to thank my friend Imogene Beals, who is a great traveling partner to many of these events. She is part of a four-generation rodeo family and knows practically everyone in the rodeo world. She helps me remember all the different directions I plan to go to gather information once we arrive at our destination. I do appreciate her patience and interest. Friends Bob McKenzie and Bill Roberts have helped me with various sources of information. Bill's extensive library of rodeo videos, magazines, scrapbooks, etc., were always available to me. June and Buster Ivory have supported my projects from the beginning. They have such vivid memories of their rodeo days, and have been so willing to share with me. Their friendship has been invaluable.

I couldn't do a project without my dear friend and college roommate, Gail Gandolfi, who always comes up with illustrations that depict so well various stories in the history. She is always willing to stop in the midst of her extremely busy schedule to accommodate me with her talent.

And thanks to photographers Arthur Frank, Gene Peach, Dan Hubbell, Randall Wagner, Matt Johnson, Ferrell Butler, and Bern Gregory, who have allowed me to use their photographs in this book. Without visual history the project would not be complete and would lack so much. These talented people have freely given me their photographs, and I hope rewards for doing so come back to each and every one of them tenfold.

Because the subject of bull riding is one riddled with injury, I asked cartoonists I know to share their abilities and humor so we can all get a chuckle now and then. True to the cowboy way, they all came through for me. Thank you so much for sharing your comical insight into this injury-riddled event, Bonnie Shields, Daryl Talbot, M. C. Tin Star (*aka* Wally Badgett), and Boots Reynolds.

There are cowboys and cowgirls, past and present, who have taken their time to talk with me about this event. Stock contractors who own or owned the bulls that made this sport truly great have shared special information. Employees of producers, rodeo volunteers, announcers, doctors, staff members of the ProRodeo Hall of Fame, the National Cowboy Hall of Fame, Professional Bull Riders and the National Cowgirl Hall of Fame, and of course, bullfighters have been so generous to share knowledge or search for specific information needed.

A very special friend of mine, Jack Long, was tremendously encouraging and never hesitated to help me with research in his personal rodeo archives or brainstorm with me regarding the project. Jack passed away before the book was finished. I miss him very much, but I know he would be pleased with the finished product.

Introduction

"Cowboy" is a word that immediately brings to mind a mental image of a hero who saves the day, does whatever needs to be done (in his own way), and looks great in the doing.

Children and grown-ups alike across the world—whether it be in Cheyenne, Wyoming; Beijing, China; Kiev, Ukraine; or Maun, Botswana—fantasize about being a cowboy. Some have never even seen one, but the persona has been visualized or talked about in movies and storybooks around the world.

What is the appeal of the cowboy? Is it the glamour of wearing boots, chaps, a big hat, and colorful shirts? Or going just where the cowboy wants to go, not having to be somewhere from 8:00 A.M. to 5:00 P.M.? Always being the "good guy" and being able to ride off on a beautiful horse, into the sunset, when the deed is done? It all sounds quite enticing, not only to children but to people of all ages.

In reality, cowboys come in all kinds of packages. They are definitely not always the persona described above. The cowboy may be short in stature or extremely tall, a little on the homely side or ruggedly handsome, or maybe he talks too much or too little. But regardless of the build or demeanor, put him in cowboy garb and he seems to take on a glow like nothing else.

Historically, a first reference to the word "cowboy" was used during the Revolutionary War days about Tories, who rang cowbells to lure farmer patriots with lost cows into the brush—where the Tories could ambush them.[37] Certainly not the heroic image we think of as a cowboy.

Later the word "cowboy" was used to signify Texas bandits who stole cattle from Mexicans. Again, not the vision we have in mind for this bigger-than-life western hero. After the Civil War, however, the reference signified anyone who worked with cattle in the West. By 1876, Texas longhorn cattle, brought to America by the early Spanish explorers, were being rounded up and driven to the Kansas railheads, shipped back to the beef-hungry East, or trailed to ranches on the northern plains for grazing. In twenty years, more than 5.5 million cattle were driven up the trail by cowboys.[37]

By the beginning of the twentieth century, the cowboy was tending cattle, breaking horses, building corrals, and encroaching on the frontier as it moved farther and farther west. He could have homesteaded a plot of ground and developed it into a ranch, or he may have been hired by a rancher to do work involving cattle and horses. On occasion he would enter a competition of bucking broncs or roping to show his capabilities, which were constantly called upon in his daily work. People everywhere enjoy proving their abilities against their peers—whether it be cowboying, racing, or chopping wood.

Around the turn of the century, some cowboys spent as much time as possible competing at rodeos, which had developed into major events. In time they found that if they won an event they could make as much money at it as they could make working on a ranch for a month. Plus they were able to travel. By the 1950s, the sport was in its heyday. Rodeos were being held at the Cow Palace in San Francisco, Calgary, Madison Square Garden in New York, Kissimmee, and Fort Worth, and many points in between, too numerous to mention.

The bull-riding cowboy didn't learn his skill on the ranch, but at the rodeo, western festival, or whatever they called the local event. He was a cowboy who was challenged by the ability to ride an animal ten to fifteen times his weight for a required period of time. Whether successful in his ride or not, he then had the crucial test to see if he could make it to a nearby fence before the wild, frenzied bucker could get to him and injure the fleet-footed rider by knocking him down, goring him with his horns, or stomping him with sharp hooves. The challenge of the bull-riding cowboy and the wild, bucking bull with fight in his eyes has produced the most exciting event in rodeo. Since the first exhibition or competition pitted man against bull, the cowboy has improved his ability to ride the beast. At the same time, however, the people who breed and raise bucking bulls have improved the bucker.

Before and during the bull ride, the cowboy mentally and physically readies himself. It is evident that there is a tremendous surge of adrenaline that races through a cowboy's veins in anticipation. Likewise, it must also be racing through the bull's body as he tries his best to unseat the rider. The spectator has a surge of adrenaline, too, just watching the cowboy as he throws himself into this very dangerous sport.

Man versus beast. Both have tried over time to outwit each other. Then they practice their skill over and over. Will there be injury? Blood? Hospital stays? Death? It happens. No one can know until the event is over.

A bull-riding cowboy is a special breed. He is challenged by a beast capable of wrath and fury. He is challenged by his own ability to ride and the ability to best his bull-riding friends. And he gives his friends, even when competing against them, the benefit of his past experiences on various bulls, so they can do their very best.

There is no other sport like it. A rider pays to get on a killer bull, tells his competitor everything he knows about the bull his competitor is going to ride, and often travels from one rodeo to the next with his closest competitor. If he gets bucked off or doesn't score well, he walks away empty handed. But if the ride works, and he keeps his seat until the whistle blows, and the judges mark the rider and the bull high enough to get in the money—it's worth it! A job well done.

1
EXHIBITION OR COMPETITION?

Texas cowboys moved the Texas longhorn cattle up the trail to either sell them as beef or to pasture them on the lush meadows of the high plains. A trail drive presented many dangers along the way, but it could also be boring and tedious. Once the cattle were delivered to their destination, the cowboys were paid and released from their responsibilities. With money in their pockets and nothing to do, some of the more adventuresome often headed to the nearest local saloon.

With a little liquor to loosen the tongue and build confidence, there were many incidents just like the event that happened in Cheyenne, Wyoming Territory, July 4, 1872. The citizens were treated to a spectacle of steer riding by the Texas cowboys who had just arrived from a trail drive.[11] It was reported that the steer or cow critters ridden were unreliable buckers and more often than not acted like pussycats.[12]

At the second year of the Prescott cowboy contests (1889), Jeff Young climbed aboard various roping steers as they were released and rode them back to the herd. This diversion was strictly for fun, but brought laughter and applause from the audience. Tot Young, Jeff's brother, was a steer rider at the Prescott event in 1901.[5] Foghorn Clancy, an early-day rodeo announcer and historian, reminiscing in his "Memory Trails" column for *Hoofs & Horns* magazine, wrote: "Once in a while at a roping and riding contest, some cowhand, on a wager or through bantering by his friends, would attempt to ride a steer or bull with a saddle. These animals were generally gentle to handle, but there are few steers or bulls that will not buck when saddled."[22] However, in 1906 at the popular Cheyenne Frontier Days, the daily program for August 17 listed "Event No. 7: *Bucking Cow.*" The cow had never been successfully ridden and had thrown all previous riders. There was much rivalry between the potential riders, and many friendly wagers were made.[12]

The first rodeo at the Calgary Stampede was held September 2, 1912, and produced by Guy Weadick. He advertised $20,000 in purses. Tickets were $1.00, plus 50 cents to sit in the grandstand. Approximately 80,000 people watched the parade, and 25,000 saw the show. Seventeen events and exhibitions were listed on the program, including steer riding.[39]

By 1913, the Prescott, Arizona, two-day rodeo held eight or nine events per day, including trick riding and fancy roping, wild horse racing, goat roping, a cow pony race, and steer riding became a contest instead of an exhibition, which it had been since 1889. The rules for the steer riding contest were: "the steer will be allowed to buck with head free and most will be ridden without a saddle, reins or surcingle." Tom Mix, western movie star of the silent screen, decided to enter the new steer riding event. Mix was known for his athletic ability and flare for showing off. He won the first event.[5]

That same year (1913) the Pendleton RoundUp also brought in a new attraction—

Tom Mix, silent screen movie star, but also a cowboy.—Photographer unknown. Courtesy of Jack Long.

Sharkey, the 1913 black bull, notorious for his bucking prowess.
—Photo by Howdyshell Photos, Matt Johnson, Pendleton, OR.

Sharkey, billed as the world's greatest bucking bull. Happy Jack Hawn sold Sharkey to the Pendleton RoundUp. Sharkey had previously thrown thirty-six riders in three days at Salinas, California. No one stayed on longer than two or three seconds. The Pendleton RoundUp Association offered to pay anyone $5.00 for getting on Sharkey, the famous 1,925-pound black menace, and $100 to anyone who could stay aboard the invincible bull for ten seconds. He was ridden with a saddle. No one rode him past the first jump. However, the following year Charles Wellington Furlong did ride Sharkey. He was a college professor from the East, who was doing research and writing a book called *Let 'er Buck, A Story of the Passing of the Old West,* which was published in 1923.

When Furlong asked a cowboy what the difference was between riding a bronc and a bull, the cowboy answered, "The best way to find out the difference between the way a hoss bucks and a bull bucks is ter git on th' bull." Furlong decided to take the challenge. He was assigned a bull named "Henry Vogt" for the next afternoon. Furlong's review of the ride was, "I grabbed for the horn of the saddle and picked up a handful of dirt!" Furlong determined the bull's back was so much broader than a horse's back, and there was very little opportunity to get a grip with the legs. He also found the saddle was back where the bull could concentrate his strongest buck. The saddle skidded with his hide over the backbone, and his movements were difficult to anticipate.

The following year Furlong arrived in Pendleton, and when he stepped from the train a nearby cowboy said, "Hey Furlong, you going to ride Sharkey this year?" When Furlong said he had not been asked, the cowboy said that it could be arranged. "Furlong versus Sharkey" was planned for Saturday afternoon. Sharkey had deposited all comers with clocklike regularity. Furlong surprised everyone by lasting twelve and a half seconds and only sustaining a broken wrist.[8] A certificate attesting to the ride hangs in the Let 'Er Buck Room on the Pendleton RoundUp Rodeo Grounds. Sharkey was inducted in to the Pendleton RoundUp Hall of Fame in 1978, the first bull to be given the honor. He was described by the local paper as "being a ton of living dynamite."[97]

As the years passed, the Pendleton RoundUp continued to own a string of bucking horses and a few specialty bulls, such as Sharkey and Sharkey, Jr. But they began depending more and more on stock contractors. Notable among them were Ed McCarty, C. B. Irwin, and George Drumheller.[6]

In Australia, the first of their most famous buckjumping (bronc riding) competitions took place in 1906. Martin Breheny, better known in those parts as "Martini," set up the grounds at Christchurch School on Pitt Street, in Sydney, opposite the entrance of the new Central Railway Station. He had a record run of twenty-two weeks with 4,000 in the audience each night. Many of these events were part of vaudeville or circus performances and were considered part of carnival life until 1924. A high-profile international competition was to take place in Wembley, England, so a number of roughriding competitions were held "down under" to select Australian representatives. Since the promoter refused to pay passage to the England contest, no one could afford to go. At the last minute Snowy Thompson was picked to attend. The international event stirred up a lot of interest with Australian cattlemen, horsemen, and the public, and roughriding was raised in status to a sport. The year 1924 was also the first time the term "rodeo" was used in conjunction with a "buckjumping."[93]

Buck Steiner, the first of a four-generation rodeo family, remembered that his love for bull riding and the sport of rodeo probably saved his life. As young men were enlisting for World War I, Buck was spending every weekend going to country picnics. "I rode mules with a loose rope, since they didn't have bareback riggin's then ——— and I was making $25 for riding bulls backwards. The bull riding gave me a running sore on my leg, and when I got drafted they didn't take me because of that sore."[43]

Most of the steer riding events were exhibitions, using any kind of a bovine that was suspected to buck—cows, steers, or bulls. The event was originally included for audience entertainment, not as a contest.

In early rodeo if only a few cowboys showed up and only a few entry fees were received, it was predetermined that only "mount money" would be paid. The rodeo producer would pay $1.00 to mount either a bucking horse or bull. When mount money was paid, some riders would just bail off after the first jump or two. Then producers began paying $1.00 mount money and $1.00 to ride ten seconds or until they were bucked off. These cowboys were referred to as "scab riders." Sometimes the same rider would ride three or four different horses or bulls in the same rodeo, under different names. The audience was generally none the wiser.[19]

The 1916 Fort Worth Rodeo was managed by Lucille Mulhall, early-day cowgirl, and offered steer riding, along with roping, bronc riding, and bulldogging.[7] The first indoor rodeo, also at Fort Worth, was produced by Lucille Mulhall and Homer Wilson in 1917. Lucille's father, Colonel Zack Mulhall, who was semi-retired from the Wild West game but still traveled with Lucille, used a chemical on the steers called "High Life" to make sure all the steer riders got a good ride. "High

First indoor rodeo in Wichita, Kansas, staged by Tex Austin and called the MidWinter Championship Contest, January 23-28, 1918. Left to right: Fred Beeson; kneeling, Johnnie Judd; 4th standing, Foghorn Clancy; Tex Austin; Idaho Bill, a promoter; Guy Shultz; behind is Ed Bowman; next six men unknown; Sammy Garrett, with rope; Toots Griffith; Curley Griffith; Hank Darnell; unknown; and Leonard Stroud.—Photographer unknown. Courtesy of Jack Long.

Life," made of bisulfate of carbon, caused a burning sensation. Colonel Zack, getting a little overzealous, practically saturated a steer with the stuff, so much so that the rider, Calgary Red, got a good share of it. "It was hard to tell which bucked the harder, the steer or Calgary Red," said Foghorn Clancy.[1]

Foghorn Clancy not only had the distinction of being rodeo's very first announcer, he also managed and produced rodeos as well. He commented on a rodeo in Waco, Texas, where he was responsible for providing the stock: "I decided to buy stock instead of renting, and since it was only a two day show I decided to use the same steers for bull dogging and steer riding. But when I got started on the job of picking steers that were big enough for bucking and yet small enough for bull dogging and had good horns, I really found myself 'on the horns of a dilemma.'"[1]

By 1918 more and more steer riding competitions started to appear. It may have been the result of Ed McCarty and

Exhibition or Competition? 7

Verne Elliott, who formed a partnership in 1917 to produce rodeos and provide the stock. This union lasted until 1940. They developed crossbred Brahmans to get an animal that would buck. The Brahmans were raised on their own ranches, but the partners also purchased potential good bucking animals from other producers and ranchers. In 1919 the Cheyenne Frontier Days daily program for the second day listed "Riding Bucking Cows, Bulls, Steers . . . for purse." Neither the amount of the purse nor the rules were given, and winners in the bull riding were not listed. Hoping to add more thrills, stock contractors experimented with Brahma crossbred steers in the event. This was also the same year that Cheyenne began to use chutes.[12] More Brahma bulls were being used for bucking events because they were larger, and had a meaner

Taken at Soldiers Field in Chicago are stock contractors and partners Verne Elliott (left) and Ed McCarty (right); with Prosser Martin (middle), standing next to famous bronc, Midnight, wearing jeweled feedbag, given to him by prize fighter of the day, Jack Dempsey.
—Photographer unknown. Courtesy of Jack Long.

disposition, quicker movements and loose hide, making it more difficult for the rider to keep his seat and stay on. They were also faster and would fight with little encouragement, which added lots of thrills to the rodeo.[19] Jean Dearinger, daughter of Ed McCarty, remembered that when she was a young girl, she and her sister would accompany their dad and other cowboys in the early morning when they would herd the Brahma bulls to the Cheyenne Frontier Days grounds on horseback. The girls were always told not to get too close to the Brahmas. Dearinger remembered one morning, for no reason, a Brahma bull charged a cowboy on horseback. What changed this docile bovine to a Brahma with an attitude is not easy to define. Perhaps it was the cross-breeding that was done once they arrived in the United States, or maybe just that so many had escaped and lived as wild animals for generations in the Gulf Coast marshes, full of insects, snakes, alligators, and bushes filled with thorns, which caused their disposition to sour. Whatever the reason, by the time they reached a rodeo arena, they definitely were mean-spirited and willing to fight.

It was a hard chore for cowhands to stay aboard the huge, wide-horned Brahma bulls that leaped and snorted across the arena, spinning and turning like a tornado. Any rider who got bucked off found himself in the dilemma of being the instant target of the angered bull's lowered head and horns. Some of the riders were injured, and limped off the field to the cheering of the audience in the grandstand.[12]

Brahmas originally came from India and were called the *Bos indicus* (cattle from India). The first recorded importation of cattle from India was in 1849 by Dr. Z. B. Davis of South Carolina.[3] The government of Great Britain gave a few *Bos indicus* bulls to Richard Barrow, a cotton and sugar farmer from St. Francisville, Louisiana, around 1861, for teaching British officials sugar cane and cotton production to be used in the deltas of India.[95] After the first few were imported, their offspring were bought by others in the southern states. Later, throughout the Gulf Coast area, stock-grade cattle showing Brahman blood were popular because of their environmental adaptability and the capability to survive and thrive where other types didn't fare as well.[3]

At the MidWinter Championship Contest at Wichita, Kansas, in January 1918, the outside temperature dropped to around zero, but it didn't bother the contestants or the stock. The event was held in a steam-heated building. Bronc riding would pay $500; steer riding, $200; trick riding, $200; trick roping, $200; bulldogging, $300; and goat roping, $400. Curley Griffith won first in the steer riding, Jack Garrett won second, and Guy Shultz, third.[1]

In 1918 steer riding started appearing as an event at more rodeos. It was sometimes still an exhibition at some rodeos, but was growing into more of a competition. At Prescott, Clarence Stewart, of the Cross Triangle Ranch, furnished the bulls. John Matli, a fifteen-year-old kid, rode a Hereford bull.[5] At the first indoor rodeo in Fort Worth, 1917, with 23,000 spectators attending, contests included Junior Steer Riding; Men's Steer Riding, along with Men's Bucking Bron-

Red Sublett, famous rodeo clown and one of the first bullfighters, and Leonard Stroud, famous trick roper of the day, 1917.
—Photographer unknown. Courtesy of Jack Long.

cos; Ladies Bucking Broncos; Negro Bucking Broncos; and Wild Horse Races.[7] In Cheyenne both bull riding and bareback riding were exhibition events. Riders were paid from $3.00 to $5.00 per ride. Soon, as cowboys began to take less pride in actually riding the animal and were only interested in the money they would receive, the event became mundane. As a result, the committee decided to pay only when a qualified ride was made.[14]

At the Magdalena, New Mexico, RoundUp in 1918, Tex Austin and Foghorn Clancy had hired Tex Parker to clown as they had seen him work at Las Vegas, New Mexico, a few weeks before. He worked very hard at clowning—but he just wasn't funny. Curley Griffith was getting the same amount of money as Parker to bulldog a steer from an automobile. Clancy and Parker decided to switch the two. Griffith's ability as a rodeo clown was unknown, but the two producers decided he wasn't going to be any worse than Parker. Red Sublett was hired to assist Griffith, and to everyone's surprise they stole the show! Sublett became a full-time rodeo clown for the rest of his working career. He would do trick riding on his mule, and on bucking Brahma steers. Riding a steer backwards was always a star performance.[1]

At Oskaloosa, Iowa, in 1920, John A. Stryker and Lou Cogger produced a rodeo staged by the Bar Seven rodeo outfit, remembered Foghorn Clancy.

> Lou Cogger owned the stock, and in his string of bucking steers there was one called Teddy that was one of the greatest bucking steers of that time. No one had ever been able to make a qualified ride on this steer. He was really a bucking demon.
>
> It is strange how reputation of a bucking animal will go the rounds. Nearly everyone in the rodeo game knew the reputation of Teddy and every steer rider who had not tried riding the famous steer thought they could ride him. I remember how pleased Tommy Douglas (famous rodeo competitor and rodeo clown of the day) was at Oskaloosa when he drew this steer.
>
> Out of respect for Teddy's long, sharp horns and the fact that they turned upward, so that if he threw his head back he might impale the rider, Douglas put on a padded

Exhibition or Competition?   11

Illustration by Gail Gandolfi.

protector and a football helmet. But in spite of this he went the same route as the others—he was bucked off in short order.[1]

In 1921 Homer C. Stokes, of Burwell, Nebraska, traveled to Norton, Kansas, and witnessed a rodeo being staged by John Stryker. Stokes went back to Burwell, promoting the idea to the local townspeople that Burwell should produce their own rodeo. The first was held in a stubblefield on the John Shultz farm, and was named the Garfield County Frontier Fair Association. The third year, the governor of the state, Adam McMullen, suggested it be named "Nebraska's Big Rodeo." The name was adopted. The Warren Cummings Livestock Commission Company at Kansas City was contacted to purchase a carload of Brahma steers for the Burwell rodeo. They could only be handled by cowboys on horseback. In 1927 the Cow Riding was won in the first go-round by Johnie Schneider, and the second go-round by Paddy Ryan.[94]

In this era it was not unusual for the producers of a rodeo to attempt new competitions that, so far as they knew, had not been attempted. At a rodeo run by Tom Burnett in Iowa Park, Texas, in 1924, he conceived a "maverick bulldogging contest." Curly Griffith, popular competitor of the day, came out of it with a broken arm, but the next day he showed that brand of courage which has made the cowboy so admired. He rode a wild steer in the finals, with his arm in a cast—and won![1]

12   COWBOY UP!

New York rodeo, 1925. Left to right: Front row: Bug Yale, Jake McClure, next two unknown, Floyd Gale, next two unknown, Everett Colborn, Bob Crosby. Middle row: First two unknown, John Bowman, Rusty McGinty, Dick Shelton, Everett Bowman, Hugh Bennett, Mrs. Josie Bennett, Earl Thode, unknown, Floyd Stillings, Dick Truitt, last two unknown. Back row: First man unknown, Carl Mendes, next three unknown, Smokey Snyder, Burel Mulkey.
—Photographer unknown. Courtesy of Jack Long.

Prescott suffered its first fatality due to a steer riding accident in 1922. Frank Stephens, from Big Sandy Valley, age twenty-five, was entered in the steer riding event. He volunteered to ride a steer for exhibition, just to please the crowd. The accident happened when the steer and cowboy hit the ground together, resulting in a fractured skull for Stephens. He never regained consciousness and died on July 7 at Mercy Hospital.[5]

In 1925 Prescott began using bulls in the bull riding event. In the earlier days Hereford steers were brought in from the range. Even after 1925, animals with Spanish fighting-bull blood in the veins were introduced to the arena, and the event became a real crowd pleaser. It has always been the last event in a performance, primarily because special fencing had to be erected to keep the animals under control.[5]

In 1925 at Cheyenne Frontier Days, a Brahma steer went berserk after throwing his rider. He jumped the fence and ran toward the bleachers. Two men received broken collar bones, and one woman fainted as a result of the harrowing experience.[14]

At the Calgary Stampede in 1925 there were 61 steer riders, 68 saddle bronc riders, and 53 bareback bronc riders entered. Attendance was 178,668 and total receipts were $162,000, making a profit of $16,396.[39]

The popular column *"The Corral,"* in *The Billboard* newspaper, reported in their January 23, 1926, issue: *"The Corral was informed last week that Tommy Kirnan and Buck Lucas had recently purchased the string of 38 bucking horses owned*

Johnie Schneider rides a mean twister at Soldier's Field, Chicago.
—Photo by R. R. Doubleday. Courtesy of Jack Long,
R. R. Doubleday Collection, National Cowboy Hall of Fame.

14   COWBOY UP!

by Tom L. Burnett, also the competition saddles and the bucking steer, 'Bovolupus.' Kirnan and Lucas will be business partners in the contest field for the season of 1926."[98]

Wild West shows were still very popular during this era. An advertisement in *The Billboard* newspaper for the Miller Brothers 101 Ranch Real Wild West and Great Far East shows requested not only bronc riders but steer riders as well.[98]

Fort Worth in 1927 introduced the side-delivery chutes, which are still used today. Previously the "shotgun" chutes were used, which released animals head first. This "shotgun" design was never really liked by the cowboy, because often the bronc or bull would balk at the opening or begin to buck before getting out of the chute and injure the rider. The following year the side-delivery chute was introduced at Cheyenne Frontier Days. Eight chutes were built across the corrals. This new design allowed eight roughstock animals to be ready at once, speeding up the event.[13] That same year Calgary built permanent chutes, catch pens, and corrals and spent sums of money on improvements.[39]

The first twenty years of the century introduced rodeos to many communities across the West, and some producers even took rodeos back East to cities like Chicago, New York, and Washington D.C. Ranch cowboys were finding rodeo to be a refreshing diversion from ranch work, which could be very dull to some, and it was an exciting way to make a living while still being able to do what they loved best—riding roughstock and attempting to outride their friends and competitors. By the 1920s some cowboys had given up ranch work, except in the off season of rodeo, and were following rodeos full time. They were also making better money than they made doing ranch work. It was a new and exciting time for the cowboy!

2
DIAPER DAYS OF RODEO

As rodeos improved and cowboy complaints were heard, committees and producers looked for more continuity in rodeo. In 1928 C. W. "Doc" Pardee, arena director for the Prescott Frontier Days, submitted to the local newspaper, *The Courier,* the "Prescott Rules."

On June 12, 1928, the following information was published:

> This contest will be held in the afternoon, commencing exactly 1:30 P.M. You can dance all night, sleep and recuperate in the forenoon, but be sure to be in the parade at 12:45 P.M. every day of the show.
>
> Every contestant must have his own outfit and be ready when called and no cowboy will be entered who is not willing to wear his big hat and boots at all times. If you are ashamed of being a cowboy, stay away from here.
>
> The management assumes no responsibility for accidents or injury to contestants or stock, and each participant by the act of entry or participation waives all claims against the management for any injury they or their stock may sustain. Management has the right to withdraw any contestant's name and entry and refuse to allow stock to be used for any of the following reasons, to-wit:
>
> Rowdyism.
> Quarreling with judges or officials.
> Abusing stock.
> Failure to give assistance when requested to do so by arena director.
> Not being ready for events when called.

Being under influence of intoxicants, or attempting to take unfair advantage of rules.[5]

In 1929 the Rodeo Association of America (RAA) was formed to ensure, through rodeo committees, that rodeos be more uniform and that they provide what they advertised. One of the major complaints of the cowboy was the difference in purses as advertised and what was actually paid off when the rodeo was over. Continually the payoff was much less than the advertised amount, which caused the cowboy to feel he was being duped.

Rodeo committees could join Rodeo Association of America by paying $35, and annual dues were 2% of the purse, or a minimum of $35 per committee, with a maximum of $150 a year. The purpose of the organization was to oversee competition, protect the stock, keep integrity in advertising, oversee payment of all just and fair accounts, and set rules for honest and fair competition. Not all rodeos across the country joined RAA at first, but as time passed and it was realized this organization was adding so much integrity to the sport, many rodeos eventually joined ranks. In the RAA bull riding became a recognized event in 1929.

The association kept yearly records, from 1929 on, and only one all-around champion and one champion in each event was recognized. Points were determined by monies won—one dollar won equaled one point, just as it is today. Prior to the RAA point system for championships, different rodeos would advertise a "World Champion" bull riding event, saddle bronc event, calf roping event, and so on. The winners of these various rodeo events would boast of being the World Champion, which of course, they had won, but multiple cowboys were credited as world champions each year. It was very confusing.

Buck Steiner, of Austin, Texas, began the original Steiner rodeo company in 1930 and provided stock to rodeos in Central Texas.[23] He also traveled with rodeo producer Colonel W. T. Johnson, and later Gene Autry, learning the ropes of rodeo production. By the time son Tommy came home from the service after World War II, Steiner had bought a string of livestock from Cuff Burrell, of California, and was ready to produce rodeos throughout the country.[43]

Earl Anderson, who lived in northeastern Colorado, had Texas longhorns in the late 1920s that he used for bucking stock at area rodeos until a blizzard in the early 1930s wiped out nearly all of his herd. Shortly after the blizzard he and his family moved to a ranch west of Grover, Colorado. He was determined to continue in the rodeo business. He sent to Texas for a carload of Brahma bulls. Anderson provided stock for the Greeley, Colorado, rodeo, trailing the stock from his ranch. The trip took two days to complete. As they took the stock down the streets of Greeley, worried housewives would stand on their lawns in front of their homes shooing those big Brahma bulls with their aprons.[42]

E. H. "Emil" Marks of Barker, Texas, just west of Houston, had more than 10,000 people coming to his rodeos by the 1930s. He had a good bull called Poison Ivy that was bucked 179 times and was never ridden.[23]

In the early days, bucking stock for the Rowell Rodeo, at Hayward, California, was provided by Harry Rowell; however, the wild steers and bulls came from a San Ramon stockman, Fred Weidemann. Later Rowell began buying and raising his own Brahmas. The *Oakland Tribune* in 1933 reported that a $25.00 prize was offered to anyone who could ride one of Rowell's bulls.[18]

Leo Moomaw and Tim Bernard formed their stock contracting company around 1933, and were the first to bring Brahma bulls to the northwest. They crossed them with native cattle. Their best bucking bull was called "Droopy."[23]

Before the days of Brahma bulls, Leo Cremer, Montana stock contractor and rancher, had his notorious "Old Black Steer" and several Texas longhorn and shaggy-haired Scotch Highlander steers which had such wide horns that they had to force their heads sideways through the old shotgun chutes. Red Murphy attempted to ride Cremer's tough bucking black steer, renamed "Texaco," but stopped a hoof with the bridge of his nose.[9]

In 1931 at the Fort Worth Rodeo the prize list was $60,000. The steer riding event didn't get the highest prize monies, but was somewhere in the middle, at $1,662.50. Dick Griffith, age eighteen at the time and in his first compe-

18   COWBOY UP!

Dick Griffith, champion bull rider of early rodeo, won his first contest at age eighteen in Fort Worth, 1931.
—Photographer unknown. Courtesy of Jack Long.

tition since he traveled with his dad, Curley, as a kid, won the Brahma bull riding. He finished second in the trick riding contest as well. He went from this event to become one of the greatest bull riders and trick riders of the rodeo world.[1]

For the *Wild Bunch,* a magazine published by the Rodeo Hall of Fame in Oklahoma City, Almon Bates of Longmont, Colorado, submitted the following remembrance in 1982:

In the 1930s an outfit called Fort Peck Rodeo Company, of Scobey, Montana, had two very large bucking steers named Herbert Hoover and Al Smith, popular politicians of the era. They may have been Brahma-Longhorn crosses. They had wide high horns tipped with brass harness hame balls and they wore long, sad faces. Brindles, they looked to me like a yoke of matched super powerful work oxen.

Looking awkward, slow and clumsy they stood in the catch pen nonchalantly chewing their cud. But when they were mounted and the chute gate opened, they were lightning fast. The most agile, high jumping, high kicking, fast spinning, head-fighting, twistingest, buckingest, two critters I ever saw before or since.

They both systematically unloaded their riders and ambled back to their pens to continue calmly chewing their cud.[34]

Black cowboys rode only as exhibition in most rodeos during the 1930s. No matter how good they could ride, they didn't qualify, according to judges. But on occasion there was the exception. In a book entitled *Black Cowboys,* Alonza Petty told that injury never bothered him when he rode. He took first place for riding a bull in 1929 at Odessa, Texas, although he had a broken shoulder.

Lewis Daniels, Jr., told of a 1938 rodeo in Dewey, Oklahoma: "I was the only one to ride a bull at all and I rode him all the way over in front of the viewing stand, then got bucked off, and still finished low man on the totem pole."

Marvel Rogers, born in 1924 at Idabel, Oklahoma, founded the American Black Cowboy Association, and put on rodeos for black cowboys. He said that when money at rodeos for white cowboys was denied him, he merely passed the hat and rode as an exhibition. He remembered one prize was $353, and he won a $100 belt buckle at a 4-H fair.[4]

In an article written for *Boots & Saddles* in the 1970s, Jack Long penned:

> I'd like to catch the dirty rascal that coined the phrase "The good old days." I want to talk about the early days of rodeo and they should be called "the bad old days."
>
> Back in the beginning of the 1930s when I started my bronc and bull riding career the Depression was in full

swing, money was scarce and rodeo was still in the "diaper" stage here in south Texas. No cowboy association had been formed yet and the advertising was poor in most areas. A truck driver going through town might stop at a saddle shop and spread the word about a big rodeo coming up in some other town. So out to the edge of town I'd go, thumb a ride and may find out when I got there, he had the wrong town, or the wrong weekend! But, if you were lucky there was a rodeo.

The books were never closed ahead of time because they needed all the cowboys they could get, and the rough riding events were mostly mount money, instead of contests. Mount money meant you could sign up for a bareback bronc, wild mule, saddle bronc, bull or wild steer, and you would usually get one head in each event at each performance. All the events paid two dollars a head, except saddle bronc, which paid three to five dollars. If the producer didn't skip town you got your mount money. Some rodeos paid an extra five or ten bucks for the best ride, in addition to the mount money.

Illustration by Gail Gandolfi.

I'll never forget one trip, I was on the side of the road waiting for some kind soul to pick me up and since my little mother had bought a Hoover vacuum cleaner a few weeks previously, I had confiscated the fine cardboard box it came in for a suitcase. It was really a choice piece of traveling gear and I had proudly packed my loose rope, spurs, chaps, a small bottle of Sloan's liniment and my other shirt. It starts raining and my suitcase comes apart at the seams. Lucky for me I found enough bailing wire on a fence to get me in to some drier weather.

Back then many of the prominent local people were asked to judge, such as the sheriff, mayor or the banker. Now, that far back you could find an honest sheriff, and sometimes even an honest mayor, and everyone knows the banker is a nice guy. But none of them knew the finer points of bucking stock. If the audience clapped more for a hometown dude, he won the money, and a great rider like myself won second.

The stock was so uneven it was pathetic. They seldom ever branded with numbers and you got whatever they run in the chute when it was your time.

Even with all the adverse conditions it was great contesting with many real good cowboys and I developed some lifelong friendships from those times. I guess it really is like Grandma, or whoever, said, "Those were the good old days." But Grandma never rode bucking stock.[92]

Colonel W. T. Johnson of San Antonio became a rodeo producer in the late 1920s, and by the early 1930s he was the premier producer in the country, acquiring some of the largest rodeos, including Madison Square Garden Rodeo and the Boston Garden Rodeo. Colonel Johnson had amassed a fortune prior to his rodeo-producing days in banking and ranching. Stepping into the rodeo business, he brought a fresh approach to rodeo with ideas which were innovative and successful. He used entertainers to perform for the rodeo crowd, in addition to the competing cowboys. His publicity stunts were unique. He took one of his colorful paint horses to the top of the Empire State Building in New York City and had photographers take publicity shots of him. Johnson seemed to know all the right people. He invited them to barbecues and encouraged many dignitaries and "movers and shakers" of the East to attend his rodeo extravaganzas.

Colonel W. T. Johnson, innovative producer of the day, and cowgirls at Madison Square Garden, 1935. Front row, left to right: Grace White, Alice Adams, Mary Parks, Mildred Mix Horner, Colonel Johnson, unknown, Florence Randolph, Reine Hafley Shelton, two unknown cowgirls. Back row: Peggy Long, Pauline Nesbitt, Mary Keen Wilson, Claire Belcher Thompson, Vaughn Kreig, Vivian White, Brida Gafford, Velda Tindall, Tad Lucas, Alice Greenough, Myrtle Compton Goodrich, Iva Del Jacobs Draeksler. —Photo by E. J. Kelty. Courtesy of Jack Long.

Creative ideas were always being attempted in rodeo. In 1932 at Cheyenne Frontier Days it was recounted, "Things had been tough and we were trying something new, we opened all the chute gates for the Brahma bull riding event at once—not one at a time. It was the worst mess you can imagine. The arena was a madhouse of jumping bulls and scared cowhands either trying to stay on or get out of the way. Fortunately no one was killed but they all could have been. We never tried that again."[12] In 1933 at the Butte, Montana, rodeo the show opened with Leo Cremer's Mad Scramble. The bucking chutes were loaded with Brahma steers, broncs, Scotch Highland steers, and a wild mule named "Rastus" that always tried to bite the boots off riders in the chutes. On Cremer's command, all the chute gates were flung open at once and out

Elliott & McCarty bull does his job as he downs his rider into the dirt, Sidney RoundUp, 1931.—Photo by R. R. Doubleday. Courtesy of Jack Long, R. R. Doubleday Collection, National Cowboy Hall of Fame.

poured the wild assortment of kicking, spinning, snorting animals and their hopeful riders.[9]

That same year Prescott, Arizona, added something new. Brahma steers were brought in for use in the bull riding event for the first time. They were tougher and meaner than the Herefords used previously in the event. As a result the rodeo crowds started staying longer—until the Brahma bull riding was over.[5]

Denver's National Western Stock Show began in 1906, and it took another twenty-five years before a rodeo was added. Rodeo added excitement and western tradition to the January venue. From the very first rodeo, top cowboys seldom missed Denver, as it was considered for many the debut of each new season.[61] Ed McCarty and Verne Elliott provided the stock. One hundred and one cowboys entered the competition. All entry fees were kept by the rodeo committee, which paid different amounts for each event. Day money was $10 to $40 per event. The prize money for calf roping was $1,875, while bareback riding and steer riding paid $840.[61]

Not everything that happened in the rodeo arena was for the better in the early thirties. The Depression was making an impact on the country. It was necessary at that time for the Calgary Stampede to become more thrifty. In 1932 the prize list was cut from $17,000 to $10,000, and expenses were cut $6,000. Guy Weadick was concerned and thought the board of the Stampede, which made this decision, was making a major mistake. He lived by the rule that when business slackened you brought in bigger and better attractions. Although entries from the United States were down, Weadick learned that the cowboy would be challenged by a bucking horse or any rodeo competition for "pennies, marbles or chalk!"[39]

The rodeo in Sidney, Iowa, was important on the circuit. Herman Linder of Cardston, Alberta, Canada, entered his first Sidney rodeo in 1933. He won the steer riding championship there and collected $186. In the next five years at Sidney he won three All-Around Champion titles and four more event championships, including another steer riding title in 1934. He was a top cowboy during this era in both Canadian and United States rodeos, winning twenty-two championships at Calgary and nine at Sidney. He competed in saddle bronc riding, bareback riding, calf roping, and bull riding.[2]

At North Platte, Nebraska, Lou Cogger provided the stock and John Stryker was the announcer. Cogger owned a steer called Teddy Roosevelt, who had gained the reputation of being a great bucker that would buck off all the top hands. By the 1930s the steer was too old to compete, but was still on exhibition.

In 1932 the North Platte rodeo committee was unable to pay off the cowboys. It created a great deal of concern; in fact, the newspaper reported an actual physical assault on announcer Stryker. Several prominent North Platte businessmen made sure the cowboys were paid in full before leaving town. Stryker left North Platte in 1937 and moved to Fort Worth, where he announced rodeos and became one of the most famous early-day rodeo photographers.[40]

Will Rogers was sitting on top of the bucking chutes at the Prescott rodeo in 1933 when a large Brahma bull busted loose and jumped the fence into the grandstand. He ran around snorting and scaring people, bellowing all the while. As he charged into the grandstand, he spread green manure as he went, scattering it over the seats and aisles. Rogers tried to soothe the crowd. "No harm done! Green is beautiful, prettiest color in the world—green comes from grass. Animals eating plenty of green grass will get fat, and fat is really the most beautiful color in the world!" This made the people laugh and forget how scared they had been.[5]

One of the favorite rodeos of the East was Boston Garden, produced by Colonel W. T. Johnson, the most innovative rodeo producer of the time. At the November 1933 event the official program for the "Third Annual World's Championship Rodeo" was a thirty-plus-page magazine. It gave people unfamiliar with rodeo educational information about the sport, and had many stories about the evolution of rodeo and the people involved. One article was on the Brahma steers used:

> One of the things that causes amazement to the "first-nighter" at the Rodeo is the type of "critter" that is seen in the steer-wrestling and steer-riding contests.
> He sees an animal with wide, sharp horns, a pronounced hump on his back, and a waving, loose-hanging bit of flesh beneath his neck; an animal that seems to be packed full of dynamite, and with more gyroscopic evolutions, twists and squirms than is seemingly possible; an animal that is constantly "on the prod" as the cowboy says, and "goes" for any unmounted cowboy, with lowered horns and death in his eye.

The program goes on to explain that the Brahma used in rodeo was a cross-breed of the "sacred" cow of India and the longhorn of old Texas.

The "Cowboys' Steer-Riding Contest" for a championship purse of $840 was defined in the program:

> Steer riding provides a lot of the comedy—and also a lot of the mishaps—at a rodeo. Cowboys have always ridden

steers at the round-up, "just for fun." Then they took to riding the "critters" at rodeos, just to provide fun and thrills for the public.

A lot of pep was injected into steer riding when cattlemen down in the Southwest began raising a new kind of steer. Brahmas they were called—a cross between the "sacred cattle" of India and our own range cattle. The Brahma is distinguishable by the big hump on his shoulders—a mark of his oriental paternity. Also by his wide, sharp horns, and his disposition, the latter being anything but the gentle sort which naturally would be associated with the word "sacred."

A Brahma steer, to describe him briefly, is fast as a deer, mean as a wolf, and can jump as if his legs were made of a combination of springs and India rubber.

When the gate opens on a Brahma steer, he bounces out of the chute, writhing, gyrating and trying to hook everything and everybody in sight. He is "sure on the prod," in cowboy parlance, which means that a naturally sour disposition is suffering from the added effects of a brainstorm.

The contestant who rides a Brahma is out to stay nine seconds on the back of this unnamable and uneasy product of India and Texas.

The Brahma steer ride is made bareback.

All the contestant has in the way of a handhold is a loose rope, passed around the steer just behind the shoulders. The rope is grasped tightly by the contestant. If his grip relaxes, the rope is loosened and the rider is thrown.

Just to give the rider a little more of a handicap, a cowbell is attached to the rope beneath the steer. At every jump the bell rings and the steer responds by jumping a little higher and adding a twist that would rouse the envy of a boa-constrictor.

If the rider stays on for nine seconds, thus completing a ride, the next problem is to get off the steer, which is now headed for the gate at the far end of the arena.[47]

The cowboys entered in the Cowboys' Steer Riding Contest, Saturday evening, November 11, 1933, at Boston were: Smokey Snyder, Pat Woods, Frank Sharp, Eddie Curtis, M. Lund, Hughie Long, Luther Marsh, Al Hobson, Johnnie Williams, Tom Bride, and Bill Liland.[47]

Smokey Snyder, World Champion bull rider and bareback rider of the 1930s.
—Photographer unknown. Courtesy of Jack Long.

Another famous eastern rodeo began in 1931, at Cowtown, New Jersey. It provided a rodeo each weekend during the summer, and was begun by Howard Harris, Sr. Through the years, his son, Howard III, then grandson, Howard Grant, became the producers. It is still one of the longest running rodeos in the East.

In faraway Australia, "bushmen's carnivals" were well established in New South Wales and Queensland by the 1930s. A bushmen's carnival was an extended sports day with more time for the four main bushmen's contests: 1. cattle drafting in particular, which was well trained and bred horses working cattle in various ways; 2. bullock throwing (by the tail from horseback) and tying was a stockman's method for catching wild or intractable cattle; 3. riding buckjumpers (broncs); 4. bullock or steer riding. Bullock riding by the 1930s was a one-handed contest, but once the bullock, or steer, was ridden it was left in the arena until all were ridden. Extra points were awarded if the rider could release and take his surcingle with him.[92]

The 1934 Fort Worth Rodeo program announced, "Watch the Wild Bulls," but the event was still billed as "steer riding."[7] San Angelo added rodeo to their Stock Show in 1934.

28   COWBOY UP!

The rodeo's historic book *Fifty Years at San Angelo* quotes, "The 1935 Brahma bulls dumped riders with speed."[20] At Cheyenne Frontier Days, Brahma bull riding and bareback riding were exhibitions, not contests, until 1935. Bull riding, considered the most deadly event of the three roughstock categories, featured the mean Brahmas, which wore large brass knobs fitted over their sharp horns to protect riders.[50]

Foghorn Clancy and members of his family. He was the first rodeo announcer, and also produced rodeos and wrote articles on rodeo.
—Photographer unknown. Courtesy of Imogene Veach Beals.

3
Cowboys Unite!

The Depression years took their toll on rodeo audiences across the West. As the committees sought contests that would put new excitement in the rodeo, Cheyenne turned to Brahma bull riding. There was no entrance fee; they would buck out of the chute with a surcingle, for ten seconds, and a qualified ride would be given $3.00. The following year, 1936, bull riding was a contest and offered a purse. The official program from the second day of the show, Thursday, July 23, 1936, read:

> Event No. 4—Out of Chutes. BRAHMA STEER RIDING CONTEST. Purse $300.00 and all entrance fees. Entrance fee $10.00. 60 per cent of the total purse will be split into two day moneys and divided 50, 25, 15 and 10 per cent. Final money or the remaining 40 per cent of purse divided 50, 25, 15 and 10 per cent.

Riders that day were:

77–Junior Caldwell	114–Ken Hargis	130–Harold Piper
89–Al Wilkinson	115–Chick Hannon	146–Ray Hannon
92–Shorty Hill	125–Dan Fernamburg	155–Jimmy Wallace
93–Art Casteel	126–Paul Crain	

The Boston Garden official program for the Sixth Annual World Championship Rodeo, 1936, had the following rules for its Cowboys' Steer-Riding Contest:

> The steer rider will receive no marking if he is not ready to ride when called upon.

Any cowboy who does not make an honest attempt to ride will be disqualified.
Steers to be numbered and drawn for daily.
This is a one-handed contest.
Rider must leave chute with both spurs against steer's neck.
Rider must "scratch" mount during the ride.
Whistle is the signal to dismount.

Rodeo was developing and improving year by year. However, there were still problems afoot. Cowboys, even those who were winning on occasion, were still having financial trouble getting from rodeo to rodeo because purses were not substantial. They traveled as a group, split expenses, shared rooms and food, and attempting to save money as much as they possibly could, but the results were still meager.

There were plenty of cowboys complaining about the circumstances in rodeo, but few knew what to do about it. Those more inclined to speak out were soon trying to make rodeo producers understand the dilemma all the cowboys were experiencing, even though their complaints fell on deaf ears. By late summer of 1936 rumors were afoot that Colonel Johnson was having some opposition from other producers as well as the competing cowboys. However, Johnson ignored all complaints and put out notices regarding the prize money and the rules for the Madison Square Garden Rodeo in October, which read: "If you are not willing to dress in highly colorful shirts, boots and big hat every performance—DON'T COME. Every contestant coming to this contest will be given a square deal and if you are good. THIS IS THE PLACE FOR YOU TO COME AND PROVE IT. If you follow the rules you will be GLAD YOU CAME. If you do not want to do this—DON'T COME. Strikers will not be tolerated."

The total prize money was $30,225 for the Madison Square Garden Rodeo. More than 200 cowboys and cowgirls arrived in New York for the event. But this did not discourage the cowboys from their mission. Something had to be done! A plan was put into effect. Hugh Bennett, Everett Bowman, Herman Linder, Richard Merchant, and others met secretly each day, sometimes two and three times each day, during their New York stay. By-laws were written, rules made, offi-

Cowboys heavily involved in the forming of the Cowboys Turtle Association, 1936. Front row, left to right: Dick Truitt, Rusty McGinty, Eddie Curtis, Hub Whiteman, and Hugh Bennett. Back row: Everett Bowman, Bug Yale, E. Pardee, Jake McClure, and Everett Shaw. —Photographer unknown. Courtesy of Jack Long.

cers elected, all in preparation to approach Colonel W. T. Johnson the first day of the Boston Garden Rodeo, which followed on the heels of the Madison Square Garden event.

The petition the cowboys prepared read: "For the Boston Show, we the undersigned demand that the Purses be doubled and the Entrance Fees added in each and every event. Any Contestant failing to sign this Petition will not be permitted to contest, by order of the undersigned." Signatures of sixty-one cowboys followed. To no avail, Colonel Johnson ignored their requests and proceeded to make ready for that night's performance. The Cowboys Turtle Association, which the striking

World Champions of the 1938 Madison Square Garden Rodeo, left to right: Dick Truitt, steer wrestling; Eddie Curtis, bareback bronc riding; Vivian White, cowgirl's bronc riding; Col. John Reed Kilpatrick, president of Madison Square Garden Corp.; Burel Mulkey, saddle bronc riding and 1938 All-Around Cowboy; Frank Marion, steer riding; and Jake McClure, calf roping.
—Photographer unknown. Courtesy of Jack Long.

cowboys had named themselves, walked out, with photographers and reporters witnessing this monumental moment in rodeo that changed the sport forever.

The rodeo went on with grooms, pick-up men, actors, and roustabouts instead of cowboys. Colonel Johnson had contacted cowboys at a rodeo in Chicago to come and compete, but only two arrived. Meanwhile the Turtles sat in the audience and jeered. Finally, George Brown, manager of the Boston Garden, stopped the show, gave refunds to the spectators, and told Colonel Johnson to get right with the cowboys or forfeit his contract. Herman Linder, remembering the important time in a 1994 letter, wrote, "Mr. Brown and his whole group were wonderful people." But Linder's feelings toward Johnson were not good. Much negotiating was done, and Colonel Johnson finally reluctantly agreed to add the additional prize money and satisfy the cowboys' requests. The Cowboys Turtle Association (CTA) was born. The confrontation took its toll on Colonel Johnson and he sold his rodeo company to Mark Clemens, Everett Colborn, and Harry Knight early in 1937. Johnson never produced another rodeo. He died in 1943.

Probably no group is more carefree and individualistic than rodeo cowboys, and thus they proved difficult to organize.[24] The Cowboys Turtle Association elected the following to be their first officers: Everett Bowman, president; Hugh Bennett, secretary-treasurer; Rusty McGinty, steer wrestling representative; Smokey Snyder, bareback riding representative; Dick Griffith, bull riding representative; Clyde Burk, calf roping representative; Roscoe Shaw, steer roping representative; and Herman Linder, saddle bronc representative.

World Champions of the 1939 Madison Square Garden Rodeo, left to right: Mitch Owens, steer riding; Paul Carney, bareback riding; Harry Knight, assistant manager of rodeo; Mildred Mix Horner, cowgirl's bronc riding; Col. John Reed Kilpatrick, president of Madison Square Garden Corp.; Everett Colborn, managing director of rodeo; Lizzy Minnick, sponsor girl title winner; Mark Twain Clemens, president, World Champion Rodeo Corp.; Fritz Truan, saddle bronc; Everett Shaw, calf roping; and Harry Hart, steer wrestling.
—Photographer unknown. Courtesy of Jack Long.

Rusty McGinty called Rocky Reagan on the telephone from back East, during the finalization of plans for the newly formed Cowboys Turtle Association. Reagan was a rancher in the Three Rivers area in South Texas, and producer of the rodeo in Beeville, Texas, that always took place the first week in November. McGinty said, "Mr. Rocky, you are going to have to start paying one hundred dollars an event at Beeville, according to our Turtle Association rules," recalled Bob Reagan, Rocky's son. When Reagan assured him he had already been paying that much per event at Beeville, the Rocky Reagan and Sons, rodeo producers, began having CTA-approved rodeos—Beeville, Kingsville, and Corpus Christi. Bob Reagan said the cowboys came to Beeville on the rodeo train as far as San Antonio, directly from the Boston Garden Rodeo. He said they had more than 100 cowboys entered at Beeville, and more spectators than they could handle. Also, proceeds went to the needy.

"We brought in a chuckwagon from the ranch and fed all the cowboys," remembered Reagan. "We had a cook, named Rafael Gonzales, that probably weighed over 300 pounds, and you shore didn't want to get between his chuckwagon and his fire or he'd run over you," Reagan chuckled. "We fed all the cowboys at the rodeo. If we told the cook he'd have ten men to cook for he could end up feeding fifty." Reagan said they were using Brahma bulls to buck in those days. They bought some of their broncs from Heard and Heard, a transport company from San Antonio, whom Colonel W. T. Johnson sold some of his bucking horses to when he went out of the rodeo business. They in turn used them as teams on the hauling wagons. Reagan recalled they were good buckers.

The Reagans continued to produce rodeos throughout the 1940s. Rocky Reagan died at the age of ninety-three, but was herding cattle horseback six weeks before he died. His son, Bob, still works in Three Rivers on the Paisano Ranch.

At some rodeos the prize money in the bull or steer riding event was not comparable with the other roughstock events. In June 1937 Everett Bowman, CTA president, wrote a letter to Fred McCarger, president of the Rodeo Association of America, saying, "Bull riding is classified in the RAA as a major event and we feel therefore it should be paid as a major event."[22]

The Pendleton RoundUp in 1937 refused the CTA demand that judges of the rodeo be Turtles. The Turtles were working out the kinks, but a rival group called Northwest Cowboys Association was formed at Pendleton. That year a sign was hung in the RoundUp office: "No Turtles Need Apply." The president of the Northwest Association said, after Pendleton's rodeo, that the RoundUp had not suffered without the Turtles "because of the fine performances of the cowboys from our own ranges." By 1939 the RoundUp committee and the Turtles had resolved their differences, and Turtle members were competing at the Pendleton annual event.[6]

From 1930 to 1938 at Prescott only day money was paid in bull riding. Champions were determined in the early years by which rider had won the most day money. In 1939 at Prescott, bull riding, even though Brahma steers were used, became a regular contest event including day money and finals. A champion was declared at the end of the show. Brahma bulls were used in 1940 and have remained ever since.[5]

In 1939 Mitch Owens, a one-handed bull rider, showed up at the Madison Square Garden Rodeo. He had lost his hand several years before, and while the rules required only one

Cartoon by Bonnie Shields.

hand be used, it seemed unlikely that a fellow who had only one hand and could not grasp with the other in a tight spot could handle this dangerous riding very well. But the one-handed Californian showed that he was equal to the job by winning the championship in this event. His total score on eleven steers was nearly 200 points greater than his nearest rival, Kid Fletcher. Hoyt Hefner won third, and Frank Marion and Dick Griffith split fourth.[1]

"You bet! That ticket gets you the best seat in the house!"
Cartoon by Daryl Talbot.

Cowboys Unite! 37

At the Las Vegas 1937 Helldorado Rodeo the Brahma riding was tough. Two of the big bulls, owned by stock contractor Jack Dew, "Sonora Red" and "The Spinning Wheel," came through three days without a rider staying on them. The final day was a day of spills, with the ambulance working at top speed. Sonora Red bucked off Wesley Walls and knocked him out, Steve Heacock went off a Brahma and broke his arm, Alvin Gordon caught his foot on the chute as he came out and threw a toe out of joint, and Jimmy Jackson had six stitches taken in his cheek after his bout with a Brahma.[22]

In an article in *Hoofs & Horns* Weldon Bascom referred to injury by Brahma as "Brahma-Ritis." His report said: "notice the number of cowboys who are walking on crutches, carrying an arm in a sling—chances are most of them suffer from 'Brahma-ritis.' It is almost impossible to get off them without a fall. There is no kindly pickup man to take the rider off when the time comes. He is left to his own resources and when he jumps there is usually a race for the nearest fence."[22]

More and more injuries were happening in the bull or steer riding event at rodeos across the country. The *Hoofs & Horns* magazine, often referred to during this era as the rodeo "Bible," was full of injury reports:

> At Preston, Idaho, 1937, Ross Lunc was bucked off, the bull turned on him, caught him on his horns, and tossed him two or three times before anyone could reach him. Ross broke a couple of ribs, but was back riding the next night.[22]
>
> Providence, Rhode Island, the second night of the rodeo Bob Matthews was bucked off of one of Colonel Eskew's greatest bucking Brahmas and hit the ground so hard that he suffered a concussion and was carried from the arena on a stretcher and rushed to the hospital where he remained unconscious for about three days. He was so near death that his family was called to Providence to be at his bedside. He did recover.[1]
>
> Buck Killough broke his leg in the bull riding at San Angelo in 1939.
>
> At the Treasure Island, California, rodeo Duward Ryan was pinned against a gate by a Brahma and received a broken leg. Carl Dykes was knocked out by a Brahma that

38   COWBOY UP!

tossed him off it's back and gored him. Joe Burrell was thrown and the Brahma fell on him severely bruising his leg. John Bartram was gored behind the ear.[22]

Tragically, not every bull rider survived. In 1937 at Madison Square Garden, Walter Cravens, a twenty-nine-year-old cowboy from Butler, Oklahoma, died from injuries he incurred when he was thrown by a steer. As he fell the steer's hooves got him, then the steer circled and came back and trampled him. By the time nearby cowboys could get the steer off of Cravens, he had five fractured ribs, and one had punctured his lung. He managed to get up and limp to the side of the arena, then collapsed. Friends took him to the hospital, but he died the following morning.

A funeral for Cravens was held in Madison Square Garden after the Tuesday night performance, open only to cowboys. Approximately 350 attended. The casket was placed in the center of the arena, where cowboys filed past the body dressed

Cowboys waiting for the rodeo action in Billings, Montana, 1938. Left to right; Buttons Yonnick, Frank Quirk, Scrap Iron Patch, Louis Quirk, last two unknown.
—Photographer unknown. Courtesy of Louis Quirk.

in cowboy regalia. A cowboy quartet sang "The Last Roundup" and "Nearer My God to Thee," and Dr. Nathan Seagle, rector of Saint Stephens Episcopal Church, officiated. The body was sent home to Oklahoma at the expense of the Garden, and Cravens was buried in the Butler cemetery. Cravens had been a rodeo contestant for many years and had won the bull riding at Fort Worth and Amarillo prior to his demise.

Handy Anderson, an Oklahoma contestant, was killed in a Brahma steer riding accident at Houston in 1938, shortly after he had taken a new bride. In 1939 Carl Dykes died as a result of a burst appendix caused from riding a Brahma at the Great Falls, Montana, rodeo a few days earlier.

In January 1938 at the Ogden, Idaho, convention, the RAA announced that rules for the bull and steer riding would change to read *"eight seconds, instead of 10."*[22]

Ben, the well-known rodeo tailor of Philadelphia, Pennsylvania, was at the 1938 Woodstown, New Jersey, rodeo kibitzing with Tommy Horner. Horner told Rodeo Ben that he wouldn't be a real cowboy until he rode a bucking steer. Ben shucked his fancy jacket, climbed over the chute gate, settled himself on a Brahma, and the gate flew open. And Ben, wonder of wonders, rode that old ox until the whistle blew![22]

Through the 1930s the bull riding event, previously called steer riding, became a full-fledged rodeo event with prize money comparable to other roughstock events. The timing was changed from ten seconds to eight seconds. The cowboys, in general, finally joined ranks and formed the Cowboys Turtle Association, which demanded better payoffs and consistent rules. Their work was not done, but cowboys were well on their way to improving conditions in the rodeo world. Several stock contractors were beginning to be known for their outstanding Brahma bulls, who were pitching riders consistently. Bull (or steer) riding, formerly an exhibition included merely to entertain audiences, had developed and grown to become one of the most exciting competitive events in rodeo. It had also become an event that caused the most injuries to the cowboy. It was evident some solution had to be found to keep bull riders from continuing to suffer the breaks, cuts, bruises, and bumps they were incurring on a regular basis. The solution came through the development of the bullfighter, which ironically became part of the rodeo clown's job description.

Early-Day Bull Riders

JOHNIE SCHNEIDER

Born in Stockton, California, May 3, 1904, he began working on cattle ranches at an early age, trying out all the spoiled horses he heard about. He became a superb athlete and soon found a place for himself in rodeo, both as a race rider and contestant at nearly all events. He went to Australia to compete in 1935 with a group of rodeo cowboys.

His all-around championship was taken in 1931; his bull riding championships included 1929, 1930, and 1932. In 1932 he split the year-end honors with another famous bull rider, Smokey Snyder.

Schneider managed to buy a ranch with his rodeo winnings, which was his goal. Even during the Depression years he averaged $8,000 a year in winnings, a great income for that time.

In a 1939 Livermore, California, rodeo the announcer told the audience Johnie Schneider would attempt to ride a Brahma that had never been ridden. The ride was rough, complete with spinning, twisting leaps by the bull, but Schneider hung on until the eight-second horn blew. He jumped off as the crowd broke out in screams of approval. The bull turned and scraped the rider, knocking him down, and Schneider spun around, protecting himself with his feet. Homer Holcomb, bullfighter, came in to distract the Brahma, allowing the downed cowboy to get to safety.

Schneider became a California brand inspector in the early forties until his retirement in 1969. Livermore rodeo grounds displays a statue of this rodeo champion. Inducted into both the National Cowboy Hall of Fame and the ProRodeo Hall of Fame, his plaque in Colorado Springs reads: "Schneider had the soul of a poet and the heart of a cowboy."

Through the Rodeo Historical Society, Schneider kept up with the sport past and present. In 1974, when the RHS dis-

At the National Finals Rodeo in 1963, newly honored Bull Riding World Champion, Bill Kornell, and Smokey Snyder, Champion of 1931, 1932, 1935, 1936, and 1937, get together.
—Photograph by Devere Helfrich. Courtesy of Imogene Veach Beals. Devere Helfrich Collection, National Cowboy Hall of Fame.

tributed a ballot for election of a single honoree in the Rodeo Hall, Johnie returned the ballot without voting. On the ballot he wrote, "I am not going to vote . . . because somewhere along the line during the past 50 years, each of these great cowboys and fine gentlemen has been a roommate, splitting partner, or special friend for one reason or another. I love them all. I cannot choose between them." [34]

He died on April 20, 1982.

SMOKEY SNYDER

Albert Edward Snyder was born June 1, 1908, in Cripple Creek, Colorado. His family moved to Washington, then on to British Columbia, Canada. He entered his first rodeo in 1923 at Hussar, Alberta, Canada, and spent the next twenty-three years in the rodeo arena. He competed in all three roughstock events in the United States and Canada.

Multi-talented cowboy Kid Fletcher rides bull at Strong City, Kansas, 1940.—Photographer unknown. Courtesy of Imogene Veach Beals.

Instrumental in helping to form the Cowboys Turtle Association, he was one of its first representatives. Titles included World Champion Bull Rider in 1931, 1932 (when he split the championship with Johnie Schneider), and again in 1935-1937. He also won the Bareback Bronc Riding world titles in 1932 and 1936. He was Calgary Champion Brahma Bull Rider in 1931 and 1932, and won the Bareback Riding in 1932 as well, indicating Kimberley, British Columbia, as home.

Snyder was only 5'6, weighing 145 pounds, with a size 42 chest and 28-inch waist, and he was very strong. His last ride was at San Diego, California, in 1946, on an Andy Jauregui bareback horse, Miss Newhall.

He was killed in an automobile accident on October 24,

1965, on the highway between Taft and Maricopa, California, while returning from a rodeo in Taft.[35]

FRANKIE SCHNEIDER

Schneider was born in 1912 in Stockton, California. Older brother Johnie had become a top hand in rodeo. Frankie followed by competing in his first rodeo when he was thirteen years old at Salinas. Soon he went to work for Cuff Burrell, a stock contractor from Hanford, California. Schneider helped with the bucking stock, race horses, and also worked at rodeos.

Schneider competed in all three roughstock events and bulldogging, plus he also competed in races. At age twenty-one, he took some bucking horses on a rodeo circuit back east for Burrell, going to St. Louis, Missouri, Chicago World's Fair, and Cinncinati, Ohio. At the World's Fair there were seventeen days of rodeo, with two performances each day. Schneider and Dick Griffith were the only competing bull riders that rode all their bulls at this rodeo.

Frankie Schneider won the Bull Riding Championship in 1933 and 1934. In 1935 he won the Bareback Riding Championship too.

Later in life he continued to compete in rodeos near his home, but his primary time was spent ranching. He never lost his interest in rodeo and continued to participate through the rodeo activities of his children and grandchildren.

KID FLETCHER

George Leslie Fletcher was born February 14, 1914, in Competition, Missouri. His father, Henry Fletcher, was a farmer. In 1921 the family moved to Hugo, Colorado, and eventually switched from farming and went into the dairy business. Although George could milk a cow faster than anyone in the county, it was not a labor of love. He had a strong desire to travel and seek adventure.

He and a buddy headed to Minnesota to join a thriving pulpwood industry, but they went broke and were stranded on the way. They heard Clyde Miller's Wild West Show was hiring. When Miller asked George, whom he called "Kid," if he could ride broncs, the answer was yes. After a month he hadn't stayed on even one, and Miller got worried. He asked Fletcher if he thought he could ride bulls. Again Fletcher said he would try. Miller gave him the rankest bull he had, and the "Kid" rode him, plus every bull Miller had. He later mastered bronc riding as well.

Three years later, 1937, Fletcher headed to Madison Square Garden and the rodeo world. He won the bareback riding and his first trophy saddle. In 1938 Fletcher had a big winning rodeo season and ended as the Rodeo Association of America's champion bull rider.

Kid Fletcher generally entered all three roughstock events and steer wrestling. On occasion he would enter the wild horse race or the wild cow milking contests. In 1939 he continued his winning streak until he had a bad day at Tulsa, Oklahoma. He suffered a broken neck as a result of an arena accident. Once healed, he went back to rodeo. Nearing the end of the season he was leading the RAA all-around cowboy title. He did all right at Madison Square Garden, and only the Boston Garden Rodeo was left to complete the year. By the end of the Boston rodeo he had dropped to fourth for the year. It was a big disappointment to the Kid.

After the 1941 Reno rodeo the Kid, Hubert Sandall, and Sandy Guymon headed to Elko for the rodeo. On the way their car left the road on a sharp curve and wrecked. Sandall was killed, Guymon was not badly hurt, but Kid Fletcher had a broken pelvis, a broken collar bone, and broken right arm. He wore a body cast for six months.

He joined the army in 1942 but was given a medical discharge in 1944. He went back to full-time rodeoing and was the National Rodeo Association's All-Around Champion Cowboy in 1945. He married Frances "Flaxie" Leete, who was a rodeo secretary. In 1948 at the Vernon, Texas, rodeo the Kid broke his neck again in a steer wrestling accident. After recovering he judged rodeos and eventually got a job in electrical construction. He died July 4, 1957, as a result of a head injury incurred on a construction project. He was buried at Hugo, Colorado.[57]

Felix Cooper, bullfighter, uses cape on a Brahma at Klamath Falls, Oregon. He also rode bulls for a time.
—Photo by Hawk Hyde. Courtesy of *Hoofs and Horns*.

Early-Day Bulls

TARZAN

The rodeo crowd at Sidney, Iowa, was given a thrill one Tuesday night when Felix Cooper announced that it was his lifetime ambition to ride Tarzan, the bull owned by the Sidney American Legion. Tarzan had never been ridden, and Cooper would attempt to ride him to a finish. Practically tearing down the bars of the chute before the gate could be swung open, Tarzan and Cooper emerged in a blur. Cooper appeared to be tossed about as if on a twister. After the ride was over, it was still Cooper's lifetime ambition to ride Tarzan. Tarzan still held his record of never having been ridden.[2]

In August 1937 at Phillipsburg, Kansas, Tarzan again proved his mettle, when two attempts to ride him failed dismally. One jump out of the chute, and the cowboy was through. This bull was ridden only once when he was two years old, but no one had come close to riding him since, and he had been at most of the major rodeos in the country.[22]

Tarzan's history is dotted with would-be riders, but he had tossed them all off after a short dash from the chutes. Shorty Hill held the honor of having remained seated longest on this champion tosser. So hazardous a job had it become that even getting on Tarzan made the cowboys leery, demanding payment by the footage if they managed to stick on. Numerous prizes were offered to lure prospects to ride. Money prizes went as high as $1,000.

Tarzan, Brahma bull of invincible fame, met his master in the form of one Kid Fletcher, of Hugo, Colorado, at the 1937 Sidney, Iowa, rodeo. It was a decisive victory, a thrilling ride clear across the arena on the heretofore unconquerable animal. Fletcher drew wild applause on opening day when he hung on to the vicious skyrocket.[2]

4
TRIAL & ERROR

Secretary-Treasurer Hugh Bennett of the Cowboys Turtle Association received the following letter regarding Turtle dues: "Dear Sir, I enclose a check for $5.00 for my 1940 dues.—I rope calves and ride bulls. If you could have my card and button to me by Christmas I would appreciate it, because it is my Christmas present."[11] The Cowboys Turtle Association was adding members all the time. From the original sixty-one who signed the petition in October 1936, when they organized in Boston, the number of members had grown to 621 by April 1, 1938. There was no doubt about it, the organization was good for the cowboy, but some of the larger, more established rodeos in the country were the most difficult to convince to agree to go by Turtle "Rules."

In August 1940 fire broke out in the old grandstand during a softball game being held in the Pendleton RoundUp arena. Seventy people worked night and day to repair and replace the damaged stands. Twenty-three days later they were ready for the RoundUp. The saying "Wild and woolly and full of fleas—never been curried below the knees!" depicts the tenacity and spirit with which the dedicated people of Pendleton could handle adversity. The determination of these strong-willed people showed that anything was possible!

In 1941 the Turtle Association asked the Pendleton RoundUp to add bull riding to its program. "Too late," said the board of directors. In 1942 and 1943 there was no RoundUp due to the war situation, but it was resumed in 1944. In 1945 Brahma steer riding opened the four-day

World Champions of the Madison Square Garden Rodeo, 1940, the predecessor event to the National Finals. Left to right: Dick Griffith, steer riding; Hank Mills, bareback bronc riding; Jackie Cooper, saddle bronc riding; Bill Clemens, secretary, Cowboys Turtle Assoc.; Gene Autry, cowboy movie star and guest artist; Cherrie Lee Osborne, ranch girl sponsor contest winner; Alice Greenough, cowgirl bronc riding; Col. John Reed Kilpatrick, president, Madison Square Garden Corp.; Everett E. Colborn, managing director of rodeo; Toots Mansfield, calf roping; Howard McCrory, steer wrestling.
—*Photographer unknown. Courtesy of Jack Long.*

show. In 1946 the prize money for bull riding was $2,000, with a $30 entry fee, same as the bronc riding. Bareback riding was made an official event in 1948, but bull riding was dropped. The argument was on to put the bull riding event back in the program, but the directors denied all requests to do so: "It was too dangerous, hard to put on, and would require added purses." The event did not return until 1952, but was just held the one year, then left out again until 1955. Officials said that "it was merely an entertainment," but in 1956 it reappeared as an official event.[6]

In the early 1940s Prescott put out the word their rodeo was staged for regular range cowboys, but others were permitted to come and participate. The *Prescott Evening Courier*

Trial & Error 49

Scotty Bagnell, bullfighter, tries to lure bull away from fallen rider, Tony Benedictus, at the Omak, Washington, Stampede.—Photo by Jim Chamberlain. Courtesy of *Hoofs & Horns*.

Everett E. Colborn of Dublin, Texas, managing director of Gene Autry's World Championship Rodeo, and later the respected owner and producer. —Photographer unknown. Courtesy of Jack Long.

on June 30, 1945, had the following announcement: *"The show will feature both amateurs, who are not amateurs at all when it comes to rodeo performing, and the so-called 'turtles.' The RCA (Rodeo Cowboys Association) successor to the Turtles has not formally approved the rules of the Prescott show, which makes its own rules, but many of the Turtles here say they are not members of the national association and will compete. So, the Prescott show in 1945 is open to the world and it gives promise of being a bang up show from start to finish."* [5] An excerpt from the June 1946 *Yavapai County Messenger* said regarding the Prescott rodeo: "This is a non-professional cowboy contest and all members of the Rodeo Cowboys Association formerly known as the Cowboys Turtle Association are barred." By 1948, however, the Prescott rodeo was approved by the RCA, with a special provision that stated "Prescott Rules Will Govern."[5]

Many changes were taking place during this time. World War II had become a reality and was affecting the world. Many cowboys joined the military or were notified by the draft to report. Buttons Yonnick, bull rider, was notified to report for the army February 27, 1942. He contested at Houston, then drove to Kissimmee, Florida, to rodeo. Yonnick was bucked off the first day, February 18, and suffered a broken shoulder. After he got patched up, he journeyed back to Texas and February 27 presented himself at the Selective Service Office for camp assignment.

Some rodeos had to be canceled since there were not enough cowboys in the area to make a good competition. But the government encouraged rodeos to continue whenever they could. It was not unusual to see cowboys in uniform compete. Their presence was a good morale booster to communities, and the patriotism shown at rodeos was always at a high. In a March 1943 issue of *Hoofs & Horns,* editor Ma Hopkins wrote: "All the rodeos that have been held the last few months report the largest attendance they ever had. It is important that rodeos be held wherever possible and especially when they are located near service camps, in such a way that they will not interfere with the war effort. There are lots of cowboys in the camps, and many who are not cowboys, but who love the sport, and a rodeo is as good as a shot in the arm to them."[22]

Cowboys in the military became dependent on receiving the *Hoofs & Horns* magazine, produced by Ma Hopkins and her staff. She carried information about rodeo and rodeo people from all sections of the country, and many of the uniformed cowboys said that was the thread that kept them connected while in remote parts of the world defending their country. Harry Rowell, of Rowell Rodeo at Hayward, California, contributed many subscriptions to be sent to servicemen throughout the world during this time. In turn, many of the cowboys-turned-soldiers wrote to Ma. James A. Dalton, from somewhere in the Pacific, wrote: "We have recently had a rodeo here which was nearly an all Marine show, although the native boys teamed up with the Marines for team roping and wild cow milking, but all the bronc and bull riding was done by Marines. We could not have asked for better stock and all prizes were paid off in war bonds, and the boys were really spurring for them."[22]

Cowboys and patriotism seem to go hand in hand. Fortunately, most of the cowboys came home; a few didn't. Some suffered injury and shock, but the majority came back to the good old U.S. of A. and picked up their civilian lives just where they had left them. You can't put cowboys in a category and say they will fit a certain mold, because it is just not true. Yet most cowboys are adaptable, and in the war they seemed to handle unfamiliar responsibilities just about as well as anyone could while under attack by the enemy.

In 1941 the RAA (Rodeo Association of America) held a convention in Salinas, California, and reported on the changes to bull or steer riding. According to their organization:

> Riders, and bulls or steers will be selected by the management for all performances. All bulls or steers to be numbered. Stock will be drawn for by the judges. If rider draws a bull or steer he has once ridden at this contest, he must draw again. Head fighting bulls or steers having bad horns, must be de-horned or kept out of the drawing.
>
> Riding to be done with one hand and loose rope, with or without handhold, or rigging and one hand. No knots or

hitches to prevent rope from falling off bull or steer when rider leaves him. Rope must have bell (no bell, no marking). Eight seconds will be allowed for ride before signal is given by Timer. Time to start when bull or steer leaves chute. Riders who are knocked off at chute, or if bull or steer falls, to be entitled to a reride at discretion of judges. Rider not to use sharp spurs, or locked rowels, and not to spur bull in the chute before the gate opens.

Any of the following offenses will disqualify a rider:

- Cheating in any manner
- Being bucked off
- Not being ready to ride when called
- Touching animal with free hand or hat
- Using sharp spurs or locked rowels
- Spurring bull or steer in chute.

The judging of the bull or steer was described as such:

Cartoon by Daryl Talbot.

Bull and rider rated separately on basis of 100 per cent. Percentage of both animal and rider to be added, thus indicating final rating. Note: Rule of eight seconds applies only to the United States, in Canada it is ten seconds.[22]

The cost of putting on a rodeo was a concern for each producer. Many variables were always necessary to contend with, so it was very important that the overall cost be determined. Everett Colborn of Dublin, Texas, had the following estimation on a show in Houston from February 6 through 14, 1943:

```
Freight: Round trip, 9 cars
         4 cars bucking horses (88)
         5 cars saddle horses (80)
         1 car longhorns (12)
         Bulldogging steers (40) and roping calves (30) can be
             bought and sold in Houston
         Total of Freight (9 cars)    $ 2,000.00
         Feed (12 days)                 1,500.00
         Trucking (In & Out)              750.00
                                      $ 4,250.00
```

World Champions at Madison Square Garden Rodeo, 1945, left to right: Toots Mansfield, calf roping; Homer Pettigrew, steer wrestling; Everett E. Colborn, managing director; Bud Linderman, bareback bronc riding; Gen. John Reed Kilpatrick, president of Madison Square Garden Corp.; G. K. Lewallen, bull riding; Roy Rogers, guest star; Shoat Webster, wild cow milking; Ned Irish, executive vice president of Madison Square Garden Corp.; and Bart Clennon, bronc riding.
—Photographer unknown. Courtesy of Jack Long.

Officials:

Arena Secretary	$ 350.00
Arena Office ($7.50 a day)	67.50
Announcer	400.00
2 Judges ($350.00 each)	700.00
2 Timers ($5.00 ea. Performance)	140.00
	1,657.50

Contract Performers:

4 Trick Ropers	
McLaughlin boys	350.00
Buff Brady	200.00
Junior Eskew	200.00
4 Trick Riders	
Polly Mills	250.00
Bernice Dossey	250.00
Myrtle Goodrich	250.00
Buff Brady [Dick G. penciled in]	200.00
Quadrille 12 @ $3.00 perf.	432.00
Basketball 10 @ $3.00 perf.	420.00
5 Characters @ $3.00 perf.	210.00
Hardy Murphy & Buck	400.00
Clowns	
George Mills or Hoyt Hefner	425.00
Jasbo or Jack Knapp (barrel)	300.00
	3,887.00

Working Departments:

12 grooms $24.50 a wk (2 weeks)	588.00
10 cowboys $28.00 a wk	560.00
2 flank men $7.50 perf.	210.00
2 pick up men $10.00 perf.	280.00
6 gate & chute men $3.00 perf.	252.00
10 extra men (in & out)	150.00
2 boss stock men 50-75 (2 wks)	250.00
1 tack man (2 wks)	100.00
1 wardrobe man (2 wks)	100.00
1 light man $85 wk (2 wks)	170.00
	2,660.00
TOTAL COST (EST.)	$12,454.50

As rodeo was evolving and bull riding, rather than steer riding, was receiving more official recognition, it was evident

This photograph by Matt Culley is entitled "Ballerina Bull," taken at the Otho Kingsley Ranch Rodeo south of Tucson in 1947. An amazing shot that proves how hard and high these heavyweight bulls can buck.—Courtesy of June & Buster Ivory.

from the number of injuries riders were incurring when getting bucked off or finishing a bull ride that something must be done to protect the bull rider. Ironically, the rodeo clown—the laugh-getter, the buffoon—got the job of protecting the cowboy.

Ed McCarty and Verne Elliott, early-day stock contractors, are given credit for using the first Brahma bulls in Fort Worth in the early 1920s. However, as is often the case in rodeo, if an innovative producer or cowboy tries something different in one arena, it is probably happening in another arena elsewhere around the same time. Since the Brahma was a breed developed in the Texas (by way of India) area, it is logical that the first use was somewhere in that state. McCarty and Elliott had two very good rodeo clowns working their rodeos, Red Sublett and Homer Holcomb. Both funnymen took to the duties of cowboy protection with ease.

Sublett and Holcomb had been in the rodeo world since 1919 as rodeo clowns. In 1941 the following report was made on Holcomb:

> Three thousand times a year Homer Holcomb rushes in to protect bull riders ——. Everyone agrees the Brahma bull is the "meanest animal on earth," it is a Texas-bred cross between the comparatively gentle Brahma of India and the evil-dispositioned Mexican longhorn. Result is nearly a ton of concentrated dynamite. An animal with the strength of a Sampson, cunning of a fox, sight of an eagle, speed of an antelope, and the vile heart of a Black Widow spider.
> Homer says, "Brahmas charge with their eyes open, unlike a fighting bull and you have to watch them every second. I got a broken leg in Denver by under-rating a bull."[22]

Leo Cremer, stock contractor from Montana, was known for his good Brahmas during the thirties and forties. Although the Brahma did not have the genetics for cold winters in Montana, Cremer housed them in a big barn with a basement. Doug O'Donnell, who tended the bulls and also worked as pick-up man at rodeos for Cremer, drove a team of horses pulling a wagonload of hay to feed them. "At night I'd get 'em in there and close the doors. You get a bunch of cows or bulls in together, it gets pretty warm. You had to watch them 'Brahmers,' or they'd freeze their 'dink,'" he said. "This is bad country for them 'Brahmers.'"

Jimmy Nesbitt, another well-known rodeo clown of the day, got the bullfighting chores for Cremer rodeos. In 1940 at Salt Lake City he thrilled the crowd by fighting three mean, spoiled Brahma bulls, fresh from a winter and spring of easy living on the Cremer ranch. He sidestepped the bulls that ripped up his straw-stuffed dummy.[9] Only two bull riders rode the eight-second requirement. Nesbitt saved the lives of seven boys, with absolute disregard for his own life. Four times death missed Jimmy by an inch, and the crowds went crazy.[22]

At New Orleans, Jimmy Nesbitt came boiling in fast to challenge Spillum, one of Cremer's premier Brahmas. He wanted to attract the bull's attention. Jimmy started running and made a side step. On the next go-round, Jimmy's foot slipped. Spillum tossed the champion clown ten feet in the air. He caught Jimmy on his horns coming down, and Nesbitt went into a roll. When the clown got up, he gave that savage bull all the fight he wanted. Jimmy was mad all the way through, and he was hurt. But he slapped the bull in the face, threw his dummy, Herr Hitler, on Spillum's horns, and performed one of the greatest bullfights ever witnessed in any arena.[9]

In 1947 at Fort Worth the bull riding was reported as wild and rough for all concerned. Clowns taking care of the bullfighting business were Jasbo Fulkerson and Jack Knapp, mainly barrelmen, with John Lindsey and George Mills doing the cowboy protecting. One of the arena laugh-getters said, "Those bulls remind me of dynamite; you are only allowed one mistake in handling them."[22]

Slim Pickens was the bullfighter at Clovis, California, in 1947. A very bad Brahma bull leaped out of the arena onto the racetrack. As usual, it was crowded with people—men, women, and children. Slim leaped the fence right along with the bull, and the result was that in all that crowded mass of people, not a soul was hurt. Slim held the attention of the bull until help could arrive. It didn't take long to realize that those bullfighters weren't just out there to be funny.[22]

It has always been a game with the spectators to count whether the bulls or the cowboys are winning in the bull riding event. At the Las Vegas Helldorado Rodeo in 1940, after three days of competition, not one qualified ride on a Brahma bull had been made. Top-ranked cowboys were participating, but the Brahmas, furnished by Colborn and Sorensen of Blackfoot, Idaho, proved too much for the riders. There was nothing to do but divide the prize money in the event among the twenty-two cowboys who competed.[22] From Tucson came the report: "Double Trouble, who is reputed never to have been ridden by any contestant, did it again! The Brahmas weren't content with just turning on the riders after they were thrown, but were determined to roister among the newspapermen and news photographers, whom they either put to flight or scattered hither and yon with abandon.[22] At a Tulsa rodeo a Brahma bull hopped the arena fence, climbed the stadium steps, and circled the top deck of the spacious Tulsa fairgrounds enclosure a couple of times.[22] Those Brahmas were getting a reputation *in* the arena and *outside* as well!

In 1941 the Rodeo Association of America made the decision to bar the outlaw bull Black Devil from active competition. A part of Leo Cremer's string of Brahmas, Black Devil would be used for exhibition rides only. At the RAA convention it was determined he was too dangerous an animal to tangle with cowboys in competition.[22]

In 1944 Tim Bernard and Leo Moomaw, stock contractors from the northwest, had a rough old bull, Number 7, with a reputation for fighting the cowboys who tried to ride him. He hooked one boy in the face and cut him badly, nearly gouging out an eye. Knowing Number 7's reputation, some riders would turn out and not ride if they drew him. They decided to keep him out of the string at some of the early shows that year, but evidently the event grew dull and the big gray menace was put back into the chutes. At the Lewiston, Idaho, rodeo Fess Reynolds, the able bullfighter, came out on Number 7. Fess stayed with him for seven or eight seconds, not winning any money, but he had the crowd on their feet.[22] Finally, at the Ellensburg Rodeo in the fall of 1945, Tommy Kunktz of Wilbur, Washington, drew Number 7 and rode him to win the first day money. Until this ride he had been unridden for five years.

Bull Rider Biographies

WAG BLESSING

Wag Blessing was born in Marble Falls, Texas, in 1920. He was raised on a cattle spread and started rodeoing in

Wag Blessing, World Champion Bull Rider and Bareback Bronc Rider, wearing one of the colorful shirts for which he was known.
—Photo by Knutson-Bowers. Courtesy of *Hoofs & Horns*.

1939. His first big show was at Prescott, Arizona. Blessing weighed 160 pounds, had unusual strength in his arms and shoulders, and was known for the colorful flowered shirts he wore. He joined the Cowboys Turtle Association.

Cowboys who influenced Blessing were Fritz Truan, George Yardley, and Jackie Cooper. He watched riders like Dick Griffith, who made bull riding look easy. The greatest thrill Blessing had was riding Cremer's "brimmer" Sky High, according to Chuck Martin in a 1948 *Hoofs & Horns*. "That bull threw many a good rider. Wag won the bull riding at Madison Square Garden in 1946. At the 'Garden' rodeo he unhinged a vertebrae and every day before the Cow Palace rodeo (which was right after the New York rodeo) he'd sneak off to a 'croaker' and have it put back in place. Then he'd ride a saddle bronc and bull that night. Next day he'd be back to have this wobbly joint slapped back where it belonged—it's just plain GUTS in any language."[22]

DICK GRIFFITH

Dick Griffith was born in Canton, Oklahoma, in 1913 and lived his early years with his grandparents while his father, Curley Griffith, rodeoed. Whenever Curley was home he would teach Dick the rudiments of cowboying, including

Handsome Dick Griffith, World Champion Bull Rider from 1939 through 1942. Always dressed to the nines!—Photo by Fischer. Courtesy of Jack Long.

Roman riding and trick riding. With such expert instructions from Curley, Dick had his own act by the time he was seven years old. During summers Dick traveled the rodeo circuit with his dad and stepmother, Toots, who also rode broncs and did trick riding. He had Shetland ponies and performed trick riding and Roman riding on them. He even rode one of the Shetlands up the stairs of the Capitol and the White House in Washington, D.C., in 1923 and performed for President Warren G. Harding.

Griffith won his first trick riding contest at Omaha, Nebraska, in 1924, beating the older performers. He also won a second trick riding competition that year in Monte Vista, Colorado.

Often Dick would remember he and his father, Curley, both riding a bucking bull together. Curley would sit backwards on the neck, riding with one hand, and little Dick would ride straight. Dick said his father would keep him from getting bucked off, using his free hand to keep him upright.[48]

In 1925 Curley was kicked in the face by a horse and was injured so badly he died the next day. It was a real shock to Dick, who was only twelve. His grandparents insisted he quit the rodeo circuit and come home to live with them and complete his education. They sold his Shetlands to Will Rogers,

Dick Griffith takes to the air, over a convertible, with his fireball jumpers. He was World Champion Trick Rider many times.
—Photo by McLaughlin. Courtesy of Jack Long.

who in turn gave them to his children to ride. Griffith never stopped practicing his trick riding while at home.

When Griffith was eighteen, he returned to rodeo. Fort Worth was the first rodeo he attended, and since he had no money for entry fees, he rented his horse to Chester Byers to use in his trick roping program. Then he used the monies he received from Byers to enter the contests. Griffith won the bull riding.

He was victorious at several other rodeos, and in 1933 he won the bull riding at the Chicago World's Fair. He also rode bareback broncs that year and won nine straight rodeos in those events.

In 1934 Griffith was asked by Tex Austin to give an exhibition of his trick riding and be part of his show that was going to London, England. Griffith had natural ability, as well as the courage and willingness to put all his mental and physical strength into the perfection of his tricks. He won the competitive trick riding at various major rodeos throughout the country, including Fort Worth twice. He also won an International Trick Riding Competition, riding a borrowed horse. But he was not content with the honors that his skill in trick riding brought him. He considered trick riding work, but bull riding he thought of as fun![1] Griffith was World Champion Bull Rider four consecutive years, from 1939 to 1942.

In December 1946, Richard Merchant and Otho Kinsley sponsored a twelve-steer, matched-roping between Carl Arnold and Ike Rude, and a matched bull ride pitting Dick Griffith against Otho Kinsley's famous speckled Brahma, Old Speck, who had not been ridden up to that time. It is said that just before the bull riding match Kinsley walked up to Griffith and said, "I think I've made a mistake, Griffith." When Griffith asked him what he meant, he answered, "I hear you can ride Old Speck." All Griffith would say was, "We'll see."

Old Speck, a spinner, was ridden that day. Griffith stayed on for the eight-second ride, then stayed a little longer and jumped off and landed on his feet. The gamblers watching this important match won or lost over $10,000, and Griffith won $2,000 for his ride.

Dick Griffith was one of the most colorful performers and competitors of the day. He was a handsome man who was always dressed in snappy western clothes, often white. His convertible cars and horse trailers were painted to match, and his horses were well matched, trained, and groomed. He died August 10, 1984, in Van Nuys, California.

Well-Known Bulls of the Day

SONORA RED

A bull named Sonora Red, owned by Harry Rowell, was known for his orneriness and kept clown Homer Holcomb busy rescuing numerous fallen riders. In nineteen times out of the chute, only two cowboys managed to last on his back.[18] In 1941 it was reported: "Sonora Red has never learned the word 'quit.' Even on the rare occasions that ugly brute has been ridden to a finish, he's not been ready to call it a day. On hundreds of occasions Homer Holcomb, that funny man of the arena, has been called upon to dash to the rescue of some fallen cowboy.[22]

JASBO, THE BUCKING BULL

This old Brahma was one of Leo Cremer's stars, and had earned the respect, if not the love, of most of the top-notch bull riders of his day.

Jasbo acquired his name the first time he bucked out of the chute. He hit Jasbo Fulkerson's barrel, knocked it over, and then tried to get in the barrel with Jasbo. He seemed to have a special "mad" worked up for George Mills, for he never failed to fight him every time George was in the arena when Jasbo came out. He downed such good riders as Carl Mendes, George Mills, Buttons Yonnick, Jim Patch, Fritz Becker, Jim Whiteman, Lou Quirk, Casey Tibbs, Dogie Davidson, Howard Baker, Wart Baughman, Jimmie Hazen, Art Cook, and many others.

He was bucked in every go-round at eight shows in 1947, and Wag Blessing was the only rider to stay on.

Cremer bought Jasbo in Houston as a five-year-old, and bucked him at every show for the next six years. He had no horns and looked like a Jersey cross. Cremer said, "A better bull never stuck his head out of a chute, and the boys think he's a 'toughie.'"[22]

5
Cowboys Are Too Tough to Kill

It has been suggested that the favorite colors of bull riders are black and blue. They have been plagued with so many injuries. Reports from across the country include the following: Jim Whiteman injured his knee and shoulder at New Orleans; Carroll Johnson crushed all the ribs on one side and injured a lung at Waverly, New York; Red Daugherty had multiple lacerations at Rochester, New York; a bull stepped on Frankie Schneider's chest, crushing it and injuring a lung. Added to the list was Clayton Hill who was injured in the bull riding at Madison Square Garden, 1944, when struck in the side by the horn of a bull. As the pain increased, he had to undergo an appendix operation. Jimmy Schumacher suffered a concussion and a lacerated scalp that required twenty stitches when gored by a bull, but he procured a football helmet and stayed in the competition at the Madison Square Garden Rodeo. Schumacher was not the only reported injury at that year's Garden event: Mike Hastings needed fifteen stitches in his lower lip when ripped by a steer's horn; a kick from a bull broke Horace Hitchcock's lower jaw.

At the 1946 Madison Square Garden Rodeo it was rumored that Glenn Tyler, bull rider, had been killed. Not so—actually he won the bull riding and got third in the steer "doggin." The following year, Tyler made another mark for himself. This time it was not a rumored scare but on the innovative side—he was one of the first to begin rodeoing by airplane. He made most of the major shows in the western U.S. this way. For example, Tyler, Ross Dollarhide, Fred Barry, and Orie

Dooley flew from the Salt Lake City rodeo to the Modesto, California, rodeo and then on to Ogden, Utah.

In 1946 Dogie Davidson drew Colborn's mean bull, "88," at the final performance of the Phoenix rodeo. Upon dismounting he was caught by the enraged Brahma, gored, and trampled during terrifying seconds while rodeo clowns worked feverishly to save him. When the battered body of Dogie Davidson was carried from the arena, cowboys and spectators alike bared their heads in silent tribute to a man whose survival chances seemed slim. Twice the Phoenix newspapers carried the story of Dogie's death. Yet the valiant little Texan rallied. With the passing of days his heartbeat grew stronger, and finally, at the end of many months, he left the hospital. Definitely proof of a cowboy's will to live.[22]

Fortunately, death or injury didn't happen to all bull riders. From the plus side of the competition Dick Griffith won the bull riding at Madison Square Garden in 1944. At Houston that year Todd Whatley rode and scored highest on the bulls. In 1945 the total purse at Madison Square Garden was $145,825, with forty-eight performances in thirty-three days. In the bull riding event prize money was $23,628 and G. K. Lewallen won it.

Buster Ivory reminisced about the days at Madison Square Garden. After partying all night Buster and Bill Ward were returning to the hotel, at the same time that Gene Rambo and George and Polly Mills were arriving. Next to the Belvedere Hotel was a grocery/pharmacy on the corner. The milkman was inside delivering milk, and had put the feedbag on the horse that pulled his milk wagon. Still raring to party, Rambo picked up Polly (famous trick rider of the day) and put her on the back of the milk wagon horse. It startled the horse, and he bolted down the street. Once Polly got situated she settled the horse right down, but by this time the milkman was on the street shaking his fist and threatening to kill someone.

Cowboy standings at the end of the year in bull riding were Ken Roberts, first with 7,317 points; Dick Griffith, second with 5,345 points; Gerald Roberts, third with 4,761 points; and G. K. Lewallen, fourth with 3,652 points.

Besides the name change of the Cowboys Turtle Associa-

Illustration by Gail Gandolfi.

tion to the Rodeo Cowboy Association, which they decided was a more appropriate name for the organization, many other changes were taking place in 1945. It was a time when many organizations had been formed in the sport. Each organization had its list of priorities, but always with the intent to better the sport of rodeo. A working agreement between the Cowboy Amateur Association of America (CAA) and the RCA said that blacklist members of either association could not work shows of the other group, until they had been cleared. Any member of the CAA who had won $2,000 in 1946 must give up their amateur status and could no longer be a member of the CAA. The Rodeo Association of America and the National Rodeo Association (formerly the Southwest Rodeo Association formed by cowboys in Oklahoma, Texas, New Mexico, and other adjacent states) consolidated to form the International Rodeo Association. The Cowboy Protective Association was organized on July 13, 1944, in Canada, a comparable organization to the Turtle group in the United States.

The Northwest Cowboys Association was formed in 1947 and included cowboys from North and South Dakota, Ne-

Roy Rogers, often a celebrity guest at rodeos, center; surrounded by the Sons of the Pioneers, and cowboys. Front row, left to right: George Mills, Doff Aber, Carl Dossey, Homer Pettigrew, Everett Bowman, Hub Whiteman, Dick Griffith, with Buckshot Sorrells behind Griffith.—Photographer unknown. Courtesy of Jack Long.

braska, Colorado, Montana, Wyoming, Utah, Idaho, Washington, and Oregon. The purpose of the association was for area cowboys to be able to compete freely at rodeos within the region. An RCA member was required to live in the area of the association for at least two years to be eligible at these rodeos.[22] The IRA and RCA worked together in 1948 and agreed on one set of Rodeo Rules to be adopted by both organizations, with the final rules being known as "Official Rodeo Rules."

Also in 1948 a short article in *Hoofs & Horns* voiced the complaint that rodeo audiences wanted to know the judges' decisions on the score of each rider in the roughstock events as soon as the ride was finished. Prior to this it was not a requirement of the announcer to inform the audience. Hobart Normand, an announcer from El Paso, was one of the first to follow this suggestion and found the results very popular with the crowds at rodeos he announced. He also informed the

1946 Fort Worth Rodeo champions, left to right: James Kenney, calf roping; Jack Favor, steer wrestling; George Yardley, saddle bronc riding; Dick Griffith, Brahma bull riding; and Louis Brooks, bareback bronc riding.—Photographer unknown. Courtesy of Jack Long.

spectators how the scoring was done, and found it added a great deal to the interest and enthusiasm of the crowd.[22]

In the late 1940s Porter Loring, age nineteen, along with several other young cowboys from around the San Antonio area, decided to follow the rodeo circuit. They rode broncs and bulls. As Loring recalled, "It hurts just as much to get bucked off in Cheyenne as it does in Bandera, Texas. It's just that the entry fee is much higher at Cheyenne!"[80]

The National Intercollegiate Rodeo Association was organized in January 1949. A few colleges had been holding rodeos for several years, but there were no official rules to regulate these events prior to the formation of this organization. In November 1949 the Texas Arts & Industrial College put on a collegiate rodeo with invitations to twenty colleges to attend. The first official collegiate rodeo in San Francisco was in April of 1949. Fourteen teams from nine states came to the Cow Palace. Sul Ross, from Texas, captured the Levi Strauss Perpet-

Louis Quirk on bull at Texas State Fair Rodeo in 1948.
—Photographer unknown. Courtesy of Louis Quirk.

ual Trophy. Harley May, from Sul Ross, took All Around Cowboy honors, plus the bareback and bull riding. California Polytechnic College, sparked by Cotton Rosser, looked as if they might win early in the competition. Cotton placed second in the All Around. The first All Girl Championship Rodeo was being planned in Corpus Christi in October 1949. Brahma bull riding was one of the events in the all-girl venue.[22]

Blaine Allen Goyins, born in 1924, was a Montana cowboy during the 1940s. One winter, while rodeoing down south, he ran into a con man, a rodeo nut who would stake a cowboy to entry fees for a fourth of his winnings. Since Goyins said he was always broke, he and this con man did quite a bit of business. Goyins was a good bull rider, and if he drew a decent bull he usually won money.

The gambler convinced Goyins he could make some real

dough, without robbing a bank, and a deal was made. Goyins quit entering the bull riding. Instead he dressed in a light suit, wore a pair of oxford shoes, and mingled with the rodeo spectators. He acted as though he were drunk and made derogatory remarks about bull riders who bucked off. When a good bull bucked someone off, he would flash a roll of bills and offer to bet a bundle that "even I could ride that one." The gambler would con someone into challenging Goyins and putting up money. The bet was on.

The promoter would run the "ox" back in. Goyins would sign a release showing the promoter was not responsible if he got hurt, which was a great concern to the promoter since Goyins looked so inappropriate.

By the time Goyins got dressed in his riding clothes and had his rope and bell, the bettors began to see they had been taken, and were hoping he got thrown off.

Goyins recalled:

> About half the time I rode with a broken bone or so. If it was a knee, ankle or wrist, any place away from the face, I would get a can of ether from the drug store. They weren't suppose to sell it without a prescription, but I have used gallons of it and never been turned down anywhere. Just before the ride, I would pour a little ether on the break, and it will freeze up a leg to where you can run on a broken bone with no pain until the freeze wears off, then you better be taking on some 100 proof to deaden the pain.
>
> I found out by accident that ether was also handy with a bull. I was putting the final freeze on a busted wrist and accidentally dropped some on the old "brammer" I was ready to ride. The bull normally had a spin that was hard to weather and he was trying to tear down the chute. Once I spilled the ether on his tender nose he came out and bucked good, but slower than usual and didn't have the snap he normally did. I won the bull riding that day and gained some valuable knowledge along with it. However, I couldn't keep a good thing to myself and it wasn't long until the knowledge was a community project. An arena smelled like an operating room along about bull riding time. Once the stock contractors got the word they put a bounty on anyone around the chutes with as much as too strong a shavin' lotion on.[27]

"Hang in there!"
Cartoon by Bonnie Shields.

At the Big Spring, Texas, rodeo in 1949, a rodeo contestant shot and killed a rodeo judge and a collegiate cowboy. Dying of .38-caliber gun wounds on the night of August 4 were Henry Preston "Buck" Jones, age forty-five, and Carl C. Myers, age twenty-three. Myers was president of the Hardin-Simmons University Rodeo Association.

Sheriff Bob Wolf arrested Herb Frizzell, a bull rider from Beaumont, in connection with the fatal shootings, which occurred as 2,500 spectators were waiting to watch the grand entry. According to others, Herb Frizzell and Buck Jones had had words at an earlier rodeo, over Jones judging Frizzell's ride with a low score. Frizzell had protested. Jones had allegedly told Frizzell, "Don't mess with me or I'll kill you!"

Frizzell had been warned, just before the Big Spring rodeo, that Jones had a gun hidden under his shirt. Frizzell went to a friend's car and got a gun to protect himself. Frizzell said later he saw Jones reach in his shirt, and thinking he was going for a gun, he shot. The first shot ricocheted off the handle of Jones' gun, and hit Myers accidentally, killing him. Frizzell fired a second shot, killing Jones.

After being questioned by the law, it was determined that Herb Frizzell had shot Buck Jones in self-defense, and charges were dropped.[22]

An article by Julia Osborn in the *Hoofs & Horns* October 1948 issue, entitled "BULLS . . . AND BULLS," read, in part:

> Brahmas or otherwise, heretofore have belonged in two classes. MEAN and MEANER. And if you had asked me which Christensen bull is the champion meanie I would have promptly answered Leppy—for hasn't he bucked off the most riders, and aren't the meanest bulls the worst buckers?
>
> The announcer at the West Klicktat Horsemen's rodeo at White Salmon, August 14-15, put an end to that idea. "Watch the bull that is about to come out of chute No. 3," he told the excited crowd. "That is Leppy, the famous Christensen bull that has an almost unbroken record of throwing his riders. Notice how quietly he stands in the chute till the gate it opened. Then watch what happens."
>
> Three thousand pairs of eyes turned to chute No. 3. There, apparently bored by the delay, stood Leppy. Ferdinand, dreaming of fragrant posies, couldn't have looked more serene. What happened when the gate opened was the

"Stop clownin'! He's gainin' on us!" Cartoon by Daryl Talbot.

wildest few seconds you could imagine. The crowd was tense as the cowboy sprawled in the dirt. Would Leppy attack his victim? But clown, Bill Markley, who has been close in front of some of the bulls, ready to attract their immediate attention to prevent their turning upon luckless riders, was standing relaxed at one side. As for Leppy, he gave a couple of disdainful kicks and ran readily over to the exit gate. Finding it closed, he took a graceful turn about that end of the arena and again approached the gate. This time it swung open, and he trotted out.

Trot isn't the word for the gait those Brahmas use. Though they are hilariously awkward as they buck and cavort, their motion as they run is beautiful to watch. There is no bounce to their running. Their backs remain at a smooth level while their legs move in effortless rhythm.

Till that incident I had not noticed how much more alert the clown is while some bulls are performing than while others are. Markley knows the Christensen stock as a mother knows her children. He didn't fool around with some of those beasts. He was ready for anything. But the spectators howled with merriment over the dirt pawing, snorting and head-shaking that Bill and the bull, Muley, engaged in after the animal had thrown his rider. And when Muley finally charged, the crowd could not decide whether Bill's incredible speed was due to necessity or merely part of the act. Speaking of speed, how Bill's long legs can carry him! And he must hold the world's record for shinnying up a fence. Surely his talent for sprinting and fence vaulting were acquired from necessity. No human could learn to move that fast without inspiration.[22]

During the late 1940s, two new names were appearing in the "Win" column of the bull riding event—Jim Shoulders and Harry Tompkins. It would come to pass that these two names would dominate any event in which they competed for the next twenty years.

Cowboys of the Forties

KEN ROBERTS

Born in 1918, Ken Roberts came from the Strong City, Kansas, area. He began competing in the 1930s and became

Champion bull rider Ken Roberts at Tulsa rodeo.—Photograph by Ferrell Butler. Courtesy of Imogene Veach Beals.

World Champion Bull Rider for 1943, 1944, and 1945. He was also a good saddle bronc rider. Roberts served as a bull riding director for the Turtles in the late 1930s. He is credited with recommending in 1939 the rule that bulls be spurred out of the chute. The rule stood for one year and then was dropped.

He went into the stock contracting business with his father, E. C. Roberts, in 1947. A grandstand at Mayetta, Kansas, collapsed during a rodeo produced by Roberts' Flint Hills Rodeo Company. Few were injured seriously, but legal actions put him out of business, and he refused bankruptcy.[38]

Roberts was known for his grim determination, was a square shooter, would stand up and be counted, and his word was his bond. He never complained when he lost, and he never bragged when he won. He died in 1975.[23]

HOMER TODD

Homer Todd was born in 1900 in Muskogee, Oklahoma. Todd was known as the Bull Man in the 1940s. He created one of the meanest strings of rodeo bulls ever to be put together. He bought his bulls in Texas and Louisiana, and produced his first rodeo in 1933. From his Fort Smith location he put on rodeos throughout the Midwest. Charley Beals, bull rider of that era, said, "Todd was the only stock contractor I knew that flanked his own bulls. Whenever he put the flank on one of them he would pull the bottom of your pant leg, and say, 'You can ride now, son,' and you knew you'd be bucked off!"[23]

Charley Beals at Fort Smith, Arkansas, riding #22 in 1946.
—Photographer unknown. Courtesy of Imogene Veach Beals.

Bad Bulls of the Forties

SLEEPY

Sleepy was a famous Millerick bull. No one knows how many climbed aboard his back, but few rode him. He was originally owned by Monroe Harmon, and Jack Millerick of California purchased him as a young bull. He was branded "1," and lived up to it as he was Number One in the string.

Sleepy was a gentle, peace-loving bull most of the time, uninterested in fighting other bulls; however, he did assert his position by insisting on being the leader when getting in or out of the truck when being hauled. Otherwise he was on good terms with the world. A person could approach him on foot with safety and at a rodeo he would stand like a rock in the chute, chewing his cud like a docile old milk cow. But when the chute gate slammed open, it was another story. His style of bucking was always a spin, sometimes changing direction. While bucking he usually bawled at every jump. When the rider came off he knew his work was done and would amble off to the catch pens.

As the years rolled by, Sleepy's joints began to stiffen and his condition weakened, but he continued to buck riders off. In 1948 Jerry Fredericks drew Sleepy; the bull did his best but it was not good enough. There was a mourning in his bawl, as if to say he knew he was finished.

When the truck pulled up to the unloading chute at home, Sleepy tried to lead the way, as usual. Just as he stepped out he slipped and fell and never got up. His back was broken.

BULL NUMBER 40

Earl and Jack Sellers of Del Rio, Texas, had a nine-year-old bull in 1949 that weighed around 1,600 pounds. He was bought as a calf from the Chapman ranch at Corpus Christi. His sire was a registered Hudgins bull, and the dam was a grade Brahma cow. He was used the first time as a calf for kids at Kerrville in 1939. Every kid that thought he was a junior bull rider tried him and was bucked off. Number 40 started spinning the first time out and kept it up. He would usually spin one way but would sometimes reverse, if necessary, which didn't happen often.

Number 40 had been bucked at every show except when he was a two-year-old. He had bucked out of the chute some 240 times and had been successfully ridden once, by David Shellenberger of Marietta, Oklahoma, at the Arlington, Texas, show in 1946.

The bull had a wonderful disposition, had never tried to hurt a cowboy, but had sent several to the hospital from the high, hard falls they got.[22]

6
THE GOLDEN YEARS OF RODEO

The 1950s have been called the Golden Age of Rodeo. Many of the kinks had been worked out of the operational end of the sport. Enough organizations had formed to represent various aspects of the rodeo, and membership had grown. By this time most of the rules and judging were the same at most rodeos, whether it was a "punkin' rollin'," Cheyenne Frontier Days, or a thirty-day rodeo at Madison Square Garden in New York. Organizations were all working toward one common goal, even if they were doing it from different points of view, and that goal was for the betterment of the sport.

Arnold Jones liked to tell how he learned to ride bulls. As a teenager he worked on the Spider Ranch, northwest of Prescott, Arizona, with Fred Cook and Virgil Maxwell. He kept asking them to teach him to ride bulls. One day Cook said, "I'll teach you how to ride bulls. See those fifty-two bulls we have feeding in the corral? We are about ready to turn them out in the pasture with the cows. Before we do, you can ride each one."

Jones did just that, riding them all in a week. He joined the Rodeo Cowboys Association in 1950 and was a spokesperson for the organization for eight years.[5]

In January 1954 the International Rodeo Association reorganized. They had changed their format to keep up with the times. It was dedicated to the aid and assistance of members and the general welfare of rodeo. Specifically, the association vowed to "serve members when called upon to do so in disputes and disagreements, will foster and promote legisla-

Gene Autry, rodeo producer and famous western movie star, and bull riding champion Gerald Roberts, talk about Gerald's upcoming ride on the mean-eyed mount.—Photographer unknown. Courtesy of Jack Long.

tion favorable to rodeos, including an effort to alleviate the hardships imposed by the federal admissions tax; disseminate favorable publicity and information to members, maintain a good working relationship with RCA, encourage and assist in the formation of state and provincial organizations," etc.[22]

Although rodeo organizations were updating their directions and priorities, the basic nature of the cowboy to be independent was not disturbed. As Gene Lamb wrote in 1956: "Cowboys have an indomitable spirit of trying that can't be dampened. The Rodeo cowboy as a single unit is the most independent creature in the world. When he enters a rodeo he does so because that was the rodeo he wanted to enter. He is not booked into a town, he just arrives. When he is entered and ready to compete, he may need help, and one of his friends, also competing against him, helps him. But that is different. That's being neighborly. When somebody suggests they form a group to set up rules—the cowboy objects. He wants no interference in his personal freedom."[44]

One of the dilemmas in the sport, as it grew in numbers of competing rodeos and cowboys, was that although they needed to be consistent in rules and judging, the cowboy fought the idea of compromise and following orders. It was not his nature to be "corralled." Since the beginning, a cowboy's independence has probably been the one factor that has kept the sport from accomplishing more than it has, in the time it has been around.

Hoofs & Horns had a history of being the official publica-

At the Cow Palace Rodeo in San Francisco, 1950, Mrs. Jones presents an award to Ma Hopkins, editor of Hoofs & Horns. *The award was for seventeen years of publication and being the official publication of the Cowboys Turtle Association.*
—Photographer unknown. Courtesy of *Hoofs & Horns*.

tion of rodeo, reporting the news and developments of the Rodeo Association of America, later called the International Rodeo Association. The Cowboys Turtle Association was reorganized in 1945 to become the Rodeo Cowboys Association (RCA), and the RCA started their own publication, called *The Buckboard,* in 1945. Eventually the name was changed to *Rodeo Sports News.* By the 1950s *Hoofs & Horns* was no longer the official publication, but it still had a place in the rodeo world. In 1950 *Hoofs & Horns* had completed seventeen years of publication.[35]

The Rodeo Cowboys Association formed the Rodeo Information Commission in 1955 with the primary responsibility to provide to all RCA-approved rodeos the basic publicity services seeking to augment the rodeo. The commission also worked for better coverage of the sport on a national level through newspapers, magazines, radio, and television.[34]

Television coverage of rodeo was developed cautiously. Other sports had reported that once their event was shown on television the attendance numbers had suffered, hurting the sport.[22] In 1953 and 1954 the Fort Worth Rodeo was given national coverage.[7] In 1957 Pendleton RoundUp was seen in an hour-long program by over thirty-eight million Americans. In 1958 RCA was determined to keep television at a minimum in rodeo and limited it to two events per year.[35]

Neal Gay remembered a Fort Worth Rodeo finals that was televised in 1959 or so. He provided some of the bucking stock and took Elvis, a little black muley bull that loved to fight and would buck and fight as long as anyone would stay with him. Junior Meek was bullfighting at Fort Worth, and was familiar with Elvis. In front of a full house at Fort Worth, plus millions of watching fans on nationwide television, Meek would ease back on Elvis' head, then the bull would toss Meek in the air. Once Meek landed, on his feet, he would again sit on Elvis' head and the same thing would happen to the delight of everyone.

Major changes took place at the Pendleton RoundUp during this time. In 1951 the arena was turfed. The purpose of the grass was for athletic events connected with the Pendleton schools, which had signed a five-year lease. This change pro-

Junior Meek is bailing off Steiner's #61 at St. Louis, Missouri, 1966.—Photo by Bern Gregory. Bern Gregory Collection, National Cowboy Hall of Fame.

vided a new challenge for cowboys, as the grassy infield sometimes caused the stock or a horse to slip. Brahma bull riding returned in 1952, and by 1955 it had replaced the northwest bucking event on the program. But by 1959 the RoundUp committee was talking to RCA about eliminating the bull riding again because of the large size of the arena. Their decision resulted in reducing the purse 20% and using the money instead to build a portable bull riding area within the arena.[6]

Permit holders were allowed in RCA for the first time in 1957, in order to encourage newcomers to consider the organization. Since so many cowboys started competing early in life, with high school and college rodeo organizations, in addition to non-professional rodeos around the country, for $5.00 the permit holder could compete in RCA-approved rodeos until he placed in the money. Once he placed in the money the permit became void. Then the permit holder had to pay a $100 initiation fee, and became a full-fledged member.

In 1958 a new rule went into effect that cowboys could no longer "trade out" with other cowboys at a rodeo. Previously, once the stock was drawn and the cowboy's position in the rodeo was known, the cowboy would trade with another cowboy if the trade would allow them to make more rodeos on a given day or weekend. Allowing cowboys to trade out was bothering the spectators. A paying customer at a rodeo, expecting to see a certain cowboy, was short-changed when he did not show up after trading with someone else. Rodeo directors were working very hard to give the rodeo spectator the most for his money.[35]

Rodeo clowns had been pleasing the crowd since the early days of rodeo, when their profession originated strictly as comic relief between events or during lulls in the program. The funnymen developed acts, many using animals, and were in high demand to perform. By the fifties the rodeo clown's profession had become a paradoxical combination of buffoonery and cowboy protection during the bull riding event. The arena clowns began to recognize the actions of certain bulls they were pitted against. It was not unusual for a bull rider, prior to his ride, to ask the rodeo clown for

Two top-rated fearless funnymen, Buck LeGrand and Kajun Kidd, find a safe haven atop of the bull at the Vinita, Oklahoma, rodeo. —Photo by Ferrell Butler. Courtesy of D. J. Gaudin (Kajun Kidd).

information on the bull he had drawn. Who better than the man standing outside the chute, waiting for 2,000 pounds of muscle to run him down and stomp him, to know what patterns the bull might have? The bull-baiters would tempt the bulls into more wild antics and near-misses after the rider bailed off, and the audience went wild. Bull riders had come to depend on the man in the funny outfit, with the crazy paint on his face, to make sure they made it out of the arena safely.

Kajun Kidd, well-known bullfighter of that time, told of working the Madison Square Garden Rodeo. He and Buck LeGrand were working their first rodeo at the Garden. Frank Moore, manager of Madison Square Garden, called them into his office. He said, "I've hired you sight unseen and you don't look very damn funny to me. If you're not funny I'll fire you." Everett Colborn, stock contractor who furnished the stock, said, "I brought these clowns, Frank, and if you aren't satisfied I'll pay them, and you won't have to."

Buck LeGrand (left) and Kajun Kidd talk with late-night television talk-show host Johnny Carson while in New York during the Madison Square Garden Rodeo, 1956.—Photographer unknown. Courtesy of D. J. Gaudin.

Kajun remembered that after a few performances they were called back to Frank Moore's office. They just knew they were going to be fired. Instead Moore said to them, "You guys aren't going to make it through the rodeo, because you are going to get yourselves killed!" Needless to say, he was extremely happy with their performances.

Madison Square Garden Rodeo had some unique problems. One year as the rodeo was over and they were loading the stock onto the train to be transported to Boston Garden, a Brahma bull escaped and ran down the street as fast as he could go. Dan Taylor, who worked the rodeo and was pickup man much of the time, was horseback and headed after the wild bull. The bull was no longer in sight, but a taxicab driver pointed the way he had gone. Taylor finally found the Brahma in front of a hotel near the corner of 42nd Street and Broadway. The police were already on the scene and were ready to shoot the animal for fear he might injure someone. "I assured the officer I could handle the situation if they would allow me to rope him," Taylor told. They agreed and Taylor threw his

Illustration by Gail Gandolfi.

loop, catching him. "The bull was so strong," Taylor said, "everyone scattered! It looked like I had lit four cutting torches as the bull pulled me and my horse down the street." [The horse wore metal horseshoes and sparks were shooting from the shoes' resistance on the street.] Finally, Pat Butram and his famous jeep pulled up, and a cowboy with Pat also roped the bull. Now we had him tied to my saddle, and the jeep. Eventually we got him back to the 'Garden' with both of us pulling him," recalled Taylor.

Most of the cowboys stayed at the Belvedere Hotel in New York during the Madison Square Garden Rodeo. It was close to the Garden and the personnel of the hotel took good care of the cowboys. During the parades a cowboy might spot a good-looking girl along the street and hand her a piece of paper with his hotel room number written on it. How many of these young ladies showed up at the hotel rooms will remain a mystery. Kajun Kidd laughingly reminisced, "Since I was married,

Rodeo Cowboys Association World Champions for 1956, left to right: Ray Wharton, calf roping; Harley May, steer wrestling; Jim Shoulders, bareback, bull riding, and All-Around; Deb Copenhaver, saddle bronc; and Dale Smith, team roper.—Photo by Devere Helfrich. Courtesy of Jack Long. Devere Helfrich Collection, National Cowboy Hall of Fame.

Todd Whatley asked me if I would give his room number to the girls. I found the ugliest girl I could find, and gave it to her."

In spite of everything the bullfighter did to help the bull rider, injuries still occurred. At the Cow Palace Rodeo in 1950 Jerry Fredericks of Visalia, California, was trampled by a Brahma and suffered a badly broken leg; Duncan Brown suffered a badly injured jaw when hit by a bull; and Andy Womack, the bullfighter, got walloped when a bull charged him and hit him dead center. In 1951 Freckles Brown broke his leg when dismounting a bull, after a successful ride. At Ardmore, Oklahoma, Jim Shoulders was thrown by a bull and dislocated his jaw, but headed on to the next rodeo. Joe Brasington got hooked in the right eye by a bull at a Florida rodeo. He had already lost the sight in his other eye as a child. Although doctors tried several things to keep him from losing his sight, their efforts failed.[22] In 1955 Buck Rutherford suffered a fractured skull and concussion at Lubbock when a bull hit him head on. Usually a rider will lie still until the bullfighter has a chance to get the bull away from the fallen rider, but a dazed Rutherford stood up and the bull slammed him. He was hospitalized for the concussion. Doctors wanted him to stay so they could take tests, but he refused. Harry Nelson, owner of J-H Rodeo at Camdenton, Missouri, arranged for a specialist to see Rutherford. After hearing Nelson and the specialist talk about spinal taps, and possibly drilling a hole in his skull, Rutherford was sure he wanted no part of it.[44]

During the late 1950s Casey Tibbs, a charismatic top cowboy who was a worldwide persona for the sport of rodeo, wrote a column for the *Rodeo Sports News*. In one column he wrote about a friend, Ken Madland of Portland, Oregon, who lost his life in the arena. Tibbs wrote:

> Ken's death was a sorry pity in a place on the edge of nowhere where we had to let him go hurtin' for hours without a doctor, medicine, or even a decent chance to come out of it.
>
> It was out in the California desert, near a town called Apple Valley and cold—man, it was colder'n a witch! A December rodeo with a blue norther blowin' and sand flyin'

thick through the arena. Why, it was colder'n 30 below woulda been back in South Dakota!

Ken was ridin' high on the bulls. It was a bull that got him . . . a high and nasty bucker that had bucked off many a cowboy. Ken was ridin' good, rollin' easy on the loose hide and grippin' hard. Right on the horn that bull made a high jump, throwed his head back, whipped Ken forward and bumped heads with him . . . then fell and rolled completely over him.

When we got to him, Ken still had the rope in his hand and a back that was broken to pieces. It took him fifteen

RCA World Champions for 1957, left to right: Alvin Nelson, saddle bronc; Duane Howard, second in All-Around; Willard Combs, steer wrestling; Jim Shoulders, bareback bull riding and All-Around; Don McLaughlin, calf roper; and Dale Smith, team roper.
—Devere Helfrich, photographer. Courtesy of Jack Long, Devere Helfrich Collection, National Cowboy Hall of Fame.

days to die after we finally got him to a San Bernardino hospital and he didn't win any money that day either . . . .

Maybe I quit ridin' bulls because of Ken Madland . . . I don't know . . . I do know that every cowboy who boards a wild animal has to watch him every minute, has to outthink him and has to learn how to protect himself. And, even when he does these things, the purse he's goin' for isn't gonna rub out the chance he's takin'.[35]

Kenny Madland was twenty years old when he died from injuries suffered at the 1950 charity rodeo at Victorville, California. Forty-eight cowboy friends signed $100 notes to pay his bills, sixty-eight signed a petition promising to pay, and four cowboys paid cash. When the bills were tallied the total was $2,518.78. Two cowboys who signed notes had to withdraw due to sickness or accident. The rest were billed $48.45 each to cover the cost. No one can say cowboys don't rally when tragedy strikes.[22]

A black Brahma bull with horns curved tight against his head trampled Odis Sullivan of Kaneb, Utah, at the 1957 Prescott Frontier Days Rodeo. The bull, named Number 2 and owned by Andy Jauregui, had been ridden only twice.[35] He began spinning as the chute gate opened, threw Sullivan off right in front of the chute, and trampled him in the chest, in spite of bullfighter Zebbie Eddis' efforts to lure the bull away. Sullivan, twenty-six, died shortly after reaching the hospital. He left a wife and two small children. This was the third fatality at Prescott since its beginning in 1888.[5]

But not every bull ride ends up in injury. Many riders come out unscathed, even though they may not win. At the West of the Pecos Rodeo in 1951 Sonny Lavender was the only man to make it to the whistle on a bull. That same year at Gooding, Idaho, out of thirty-four rides by seventeen good bull riders, only one qualified—Don Maynard.

In 1953, at the Al Kadir Shrine Rodeo in Spokane, five Brahma bulls broke out of the holding pens and ran right through a group of people seated in wheelchairs. The bulls didn't injure a soul. How they managed to avoid it, no one knows.

Bob Maynard, a cocky bull rider from California, drew

Everett Colborn's big Number 31 bull. The animal had never been ridden to the whistle and was considered to be mighty rank. Maynard made a $100 bet, at 3 to 1, that he could ride the bull. He did, winning the bet and the day money as well. Later that year he rode another unridden bull to win the bull riding finals at Salinas. Jokester Casey Tibbs had hot-shotted Maynard just as he left the chute, and Tibbs claimed he helped him to make the ride.

At Fort Pierre, South Dakota, in 1954, a ten-dollar bill was tied to the tail of a mean-tempered Brahma bull. Boys willing to attempt to snatch the bill ducked and dived at the nimble-footed bull, thrilling and delighting the crowd. Someone said this was a good event for an undertaker to sponsor![22]

At Cheyenne Frontier Days Jim Shoulders rode a bull for what *seemed* like fifteen minutes. The judge could not get the gun to go off to announce the eight-second ride was over. They never did get the gun to fire, evidently because of bad shells. Possibly that is why they use a whistle or horn today.[13]

In 1958 several cowboys got together and decided to form a rodeo company in the Dallas area, and hold rodeos every Friday and Saturday nights from spring through September. They named it Mesquite Rodeo, as it was located in Mesquite, a suburb east of Dallas. The partners were Neal Gay, Jim Shoulders, Harry Tompkins, D. J. Gaudin (better known as the Kajun Kidd, bullfighter), Ira Akers, and Bob Grant. Each put in $5,000. Grant had twenty head of stock that they used, and the group paid Neal Gay $100 a week to put on the rodeo. Although all but Grant had been rodeo competitors, it was a trial and error experience. Gay borrowed stock from stock contractors Tommy Steiner, Everett Colborn, and Harry Knight to try them at the Mesquite Rodeo. If they didn't buck enough, Gay would recommend selling them. The good performers went back to their owners, after they had been bucked awhile at Mesquite.

By the end of the first year, Gaudin and Tompkins had dropped out. Later Ira Akers and Bob Grant died, but their families were still involved. For a long time it was tough going. Just keeping the bills paid was crucial. When it got too tough, they took in another partner.

A young Jim Shoulders on Steiner's Number 22 bull.—Photo by Devere Helfrich. Courtesy of Bobby Steiner. Devere Helfrich Collection, National Cowboy Hall of Fame.

Although the Dallas area was certainly not known for its western attitude, the rodeo continued to grow. Many of the top cowboys would compete at Mesquite whenever they could. Rodeo fans were as likely to see a rodeo cowboy who led in his event as they were to see local competitors. Several champions, including Donny Gay, World Champion Bull Rider from 1974 through 1981, and Monty Henson, World Champion Saddle Bronc Rider of 1975, learned their trade at Mesquite.

Often the Mesquite Rodeo is defined as being for tourists and people wanting to see their very first rodeo. Seldom does anyone who knows rodeo ever criticize the Mesquite Rodeo. The reason is because Neal Gay has a foolproof philosophy about producing rodeos: "I try to put on the best rodeo I can

George Mills, well-known rodeo clown, keeps the bull away by using the barrel.—Photo by R. R. Doubleday. Courtesy of Jack Long. R. R. Doubleday Collection National Cowboy Hall of Fame.

at every performance. A good rodeo is a good rodeo no matter who it's for. It doesn't hurt, once the draw is made, to put a potentially high scoring bull and top level rider at the end of an event so the event can end on a high note. But you can't always provide it. Animals don't always comply with our plans and hopes."

One complaint about rodeo was that there was no climax to each year—no final championship rodeo, no smashing end to the year. The figures were tallied and a presentation was made during the first rodeo of the following year—but it was too long of a delay. By that time the excitement of a finale was gone. The decision was therefore made to create a National Finals Rodeo in 1959. After much deliberation, Dallas was selected as the site. There would be two performances a day for five days, with the top fifteen contestants in each of five events competing. It was also determined the most outstand-

Bob Wegner rides Beutler Brothers Number 27 in the eighth round at the first National Finals Rodeo, held in Dallas, 1959. Wegner scored 180 points on this ride to get second in the eighth round.—Photo by Devere Helfrich. Courtesy of Imogene Veach Beals. Devere Helfrich Collection, National Cowboy Hall of Fame.

ing stock in rodeo would be brought to the Finals. Stock contractors were required to keep records on their bucking stock: how many times they were used, who rode successfully, who did not, and so on. Stock that had not been bucked at least five times during the season could not be considered. After all the information was gathered, 250 head of stock was picked to participate, 210 saddle broncs, bareback horses and bulls, with forty more in reserve.

The top fifteen bull riders in the RCA to compete at the first National Finals Rodeo in 1959 were, in order of their rank beginning with first: Jim Shoulders, Bob Wegner, Bill Rinestine, Joe Green, Ed LeTourneau, Duane Howard, Bob Shepard, Benny Reynolds, Jim Charles, Pete Crump, Wayne Lewis, Ronnie Rossen, Harry Tompkins, Freckles Brown, and Bob Cullison. Old Speck, a Beutler Brothers & Son bull, was chosen as the top bull in the National Finals that first year.

The Kajun Kidd (D. J. Gaudin) and Gene Clark were chosen as the bullfighters that year, and Buck LeGrand was the barrelman. Pete Logan and Cy Taillon announced the first Finals. Buster Ivory was superintendent of Livestock, a position he continued to hold for twenty-five years. John Van Cronkhite was the NFR general manager, and Cecil Jones was the arena secretary. Prize money at the Finals in 1959 was $50,000.

In the third go-round of the first National Finals Rodeo, Jim Shoulders tore the palm of his riding hand. He still had fifteen head to ride, counting a re-ride, and was in a position to win the All-Around title if he could make all the rides. The skin in his palm had been torn away and was so sore he could hardly grip the rope. He put a rubber glove inside his riding glove and poured ether down in the palm of it, which would freeze it during the ride, so that Shoulders couldn't feel a thing.

Before the tenth round Bob Wegner led the bull riding standings by $42. But Shoulders finished the Finals riding nine of ten bulls—the only rider to record nine qualified rides. He also placed third in the bareback riding average and placed on six bulls to win the bull riding average. Shoulders did win the All Around World Championship and the Bull Riding World Championship that year, despite his injured hand.[19, 29] Cowboys have to be tough!

Champions of the Golden Age

JIM SHOULDERS

When the author told Shoulders she was writing the history of bull riding and would like to talk to him, he said with typical Shoulders humor, "Now don't blame THAT on me!" Shoulders' good friend, Neal Gay, said Jim could always get away with saying the darndest things, and if Gay had said them, he'd probably get clobbered.

Shoulders was born in Tulsa, Oklahoma, May 13, 1928. He started riding when he was thirteen and entered his first rodeo at Oiltown, Oklahoma, winning $18. He wasn't born to ranching; his father was an automobile mechanic, living on an acreage at the edge of Tulsa. He spent much of his young life on his grandfather's farm.

A pleased Jim Shoulders shows his 1957 World Champion buckles for bareback bronc riding, bull riding, and All-Around Cowboy of the World.—Photo by Devere Helfrich. Courtesy of Jack Long. Devere Helfrich Collection, National Cowboy Hall of Fame.

A year after high school graduation he married his high school sweetheart, Sharron. They headed to Madison Square Garden Rodeo that fall, the largest rodeo in the country at that time. Shoulders was just beginning his rodeo career, but he won the bull riding and the bareback riding there. He says that was the biggest surprise and most exciting time in his rodeo career. At age twenty-one he won his first All-Around World Champion title. In all he captured five All-Around World Championships, seven World Champion Bull Riding titles, and four Bareback Riding World Championships, totaling sixteen in all.

Shoulders never wavered from his purpose in rodeo. He always treated rodeo like a business, and the goal was money. "I thought if I could get two things going at once, I could live off one, and accumulate the other." To explain his meaning he said he always tried to work the rodeo labor pool or ride in the quadrille to guarantee extra money coming in. Rodeo provided him with a ranch near Henryetta, Oklahoma, where he and Sharron raise Salorn and Texas longhorn cattle.

Shoulders has been said to have a "perfect seat" on a bull.

He believes balance, not strength, is most important. At 5'11, weighing 145 pounds, Shoulders has a right arm (which grips the rigging) that is 20% thicker than his left arm. Plus he wears a size 7½ boot on one foot, which was broken, and a size 7 on the other.[50, 52, 53]

At the age of forty-two he quit competing. He had plenty of injuries to help him make this decision, but he never quit rodeo. After retiring from competition he formed the Jim Shoulders Rodeo Company and supplied stock to rodeos throughout the country. His stock included the four-time winner of the National Finals Rodeo Bull of the Year, 1962-65, Tornado. He was also a partner in the Mesquite Rodeo Company, but sold his interest in 1980.

The first bull riding and roughstock school was held by Shoulders, starting in 1962. He has endorsed Wrangler western clothing for over fifty years, has been a representative of Miller Lite beer for ten years, and has had a relationship with Justin Boots nearly as long as his Wrangler association.

Injuries, no matter how serious, never discouraged the Oklahoma cowboy. At the Houston rodeo in 1960 Shoulders made a sensational ride on a Brahma bull that reversed his spin, tossed him forward, and hooked back with his horns, causing seventeen fractures of the face. Shoulders finished the ride, stepped off the bull, and was rushed to the hospital for X-rays. Surgery on his nose was scheduled, as his nose had been moved to the left side of his face, among other injuries. He asked the doctor if he couldn't postpone the surgery until after his ride the following day. The doctor's answer was "Good God, man, you can't ride with a nose like that!" Shoulders' response, in his typical humorous manner, was, "Hell, Doc, I don't ride with my nose!"

In another injury during a Midland, Texas, rodeo in 1953, a bull jumped high, twisted, and fell on Shoulders, fracturing his collarbone. A steel pin had to be inserted. The doctor suggested he quit rodeoing for a while and heal. Eight rodeos later, at Cheyenne Frontier Days, Shoulders rode a sun-fishing bronc and bent the steel pin, resulting in another surgery. Shoulders said none of these injuries were accidents, because he knows the bull or bronc deliberately set out to hurt him![53]

Jim Shoulders is truly a rodeo renaissance man. He has been involved in every aspect of the business—competition, stock contracting, producing, schools, endorsee for sponsors, board positions of the RCA—and in general serves as an all-around representative of the sport.

HARRY TOMPKINS

Harry Tompkins was born in Peekskill, New York, in 1927. When he was sixteen he worked at nearby Cimarron Dude Ranch doing whatever was asked of him. Mike Hastings, a well-known cowboy, was the wrangler there. Tompkins' interest leaned toward making sure the horses were broken sufficiently for dudes to ride, and during his time off he enjoyed riding the steers. They put on rodeos for the dudes with horses that were used in the Wild Horse Race at Madison Square Garden. When they stopped bucking, Hastings turned them into riding horses for the dudes.

Tompkins says he was born with good reflexes, but he also had coordination, both important abilities in riding bulls. "I ice skated from seven in the morning until ten at night as often as I could," Tompkins remembered. "I also walked pipes, cable, tight ropes, anything that would help my balance. I made a saw horse that was two feet by six inches by sixteen feet and I walked it every day." He considers eye contact to be very important when riding a bull. "If you are concen-

Harry Tompkins at Cow Palace, San Francisco, holding winning buckle for Champion Bull Riding.
—Photograph by Lucille Stewart. Courtesy of Hoofs & Horns.

This photograph by Devere Helfrich, famous rodeo photographer, of Harry Tompkins has been copied many times. Tompkins doesn't seem to be having a bit of trouble riding this bull as he waves to the crowd.—Courtesy of Harry Tompkins. Devere Helfrich Collection, National Cowboy Hall of Fame.

trating it is just as plain as can be and feels like you are riding in slow motion," he explained.

The first steer Tompkins rode was at Bridgeport, Connecticut, in 1946 at a Colonel Eskew rodeo. Red Wilmer took him there. Tompkins rode an exhibition steer and made $15. He then went to another rodeo thirty or forty miles from Bridgeport and drew the same bull. When Cimarron entered him at the 1946 Madison Square Garden Rodeo, they sponsored him in the bull riding and the bareback riding events. He remembers bucking off most of his draws, but he did win $316. In 1948 he became World Champion Bull Rider, and repeated the win four more times (1949, 1950, 1952, and 1960). He won the Bareback Bronc World Championship in 1952 and the All-Around World Championship, which he won again in 1960.

His career was cut short in 1961 in Las Vegas when a bull's horn hit his elbow and knocked it out of joint. Although doctors worked with his arm for many months, his reflexes were never the same. Later he judged many rodeos across the country.

Harry Tompkins is a man of few words, unless he is reminiscing about rodeo days. "I have had lots of fun and made many friends in rodeo. I hope I'll be remembered as being honest, fair and respected for what I did."

GERALD ROBERTS

In 1919 Gerald Roberts was born to a rodeo family. His father, E. C., became known as a respected stock contractor and produced rodeos in and around their Flint Hills area of Kansas. Older brother Ken and sister Margie were also well-known rodeo competitors.

When only thirteen years of age, Gerald jumped a train and caught up with the Clyde Miller Wild West Show in Perry, Iowa. Both Ken and Margie were working with the show, and Gerald was hired to ride bucking horses. He got knocked out shortly after he began working, and Miller, concerned about his young age, sent him home. He returned the next year with written permission from E. C., saying it was all right if he got knocked out!

Gerald Roberts entered his first rodeo when he was fifteen, but it took awhile before he ever got in the winning column. He convinced an ice-cream concessionaire to pay his entry fees until he started winning, plus all the ice cream he could eat. Some days that was all he had to eat.

Roberts won the All-Around World Champion title in 1942 and 1948 and competed in bareback bronc riding, bull riding, and saddle bronc riding. He also scored four other years in the top ten for the All-Around title. Roberts never won a bull riding championship, although he scored in one of the top five slots eight times between 1945 and 1955.

Gerald Roberts rides Number 11 at Lewiston, Idaho, in 1947.
—Photo by Devere Helfrich. Courtesy of Jack Long. Devere Helfrich Collection, National Cowboy Hall of Fame.

Bulls of the Golden Age

EARL ANDERSON'S THREE GENERATIONS:
NUMBER "3," J-5, and JET AGE

Earl Anderson, an early-day stock contractor from Grover, Colorado, started a breeding program with his bulls in the early 1940s. One of his early bulls had been a cross-bred Brahma roping calf. Anderson thought that roping calves made good bucking bulls because they generally handled better.

The Brahma calf was black and grew to weigh between

1,200 and 1,500 pounds, and Anderson named him "Number 3." Everyone in that part of the country knew of him, but few rode him. By the time Number 3 was around eleven years old, bull riders were beginning to be able to ride him. The blizzard of 1949 took its toll with Anderson's cattle, but Number 3 was not one of them. After the blizzard subsided, they went out to check their cattle and found steam coming from a huge mound of snow. When they dug into it, they found Number 3. He was just too tough to die!

Anderson got many calves out of him. One that made quite a name for himself was called J-5. He too was black with little short horns. When he was bucked he would go into a spin so fast no one could believe it.

For seven years J-5 went unridden. In 1957 at the Boulder, Colorado, rodeo Joe Green, of Sulphur, Oklahoma, drew

Pete Burns rides J5, famous black bull of the Earl Anderson string, at Laramie, Wyoming, 1958.—Photographer unknown.
Courtesy of Jack Anderson.

J-5. Green said, "I reached down and got my dally. I was really dizzy, he was spinning so fast, and everything was a blur. I'd never seen a bull spin so fast. The momentum made me rare back and by doing so my feet went into his neck just at the right place. Once that happened I rode him dead easy."

Green went on to say, "I was at Cheyenne Frontier Days that year, and Harry Knight had leased J-5 from Anderson for Cheyenne. Pete Crump drew him and he bucked Pete off. I rode bulls for twenty years and J-5 was by far the rankest bull I ever rode."

Later, according to Jack Anderson, Earl's son, J-5 got into some poison weed and became really sick. "All he could do was lay on the ground. But he eventually got better," said Anderson.

J-5's offspring, Jet Age, was just a calf when Earl Anderson died. His son Jack bought all the bulls from the estate and bred cows to Jet Age in the 1960s. "Dad would have liked his offspring, including Sunny's Velvet."

Bull named Jet Age, progeny of Anderson's J5, keeps an unknown rider alert at Casper, Wyoming, in 1965.—Photographer unknown. Courtesy of Jack Anderson.

Jet Age went to the National Finals in 1964 and bucked off both riders. He was chosen as the number three bull in the world that year, according to Jack Anderson. In 1965 at NFR he bucked his riders off again, which included Bob Wegner in the eighth round.

MIGHTY MIKE

By 1955, Mighty Mike, a Mack Barbour bull, had been around the arena for six years and only one person had ridden him. The successful ride was early in his bucking career. Jack Spurling of Portland, Oregon, rode him at Red Bluff, California. It was reported the bull stumbled coming out of the chute and didn't get fully wound up by the time the whistle blew. He had thrown the world's greatest bull riders, such as Tompkins, Shoulders, Maynard, and others.

Mighty Mike was pure Brahma and unusually powerful, fast and agile. He would buck in a tight spin, so fast that he appeared to be a blur, and kicked sky-high at every turn. Riders were thrown far and hard, but if they attempted to weather the storm they were flung down under Mike's flying heels.

Johnny Gravit, a GI cowboy from Travis Air Base, was killed at the Petaluma, California, rodeo in 1953, by refusing to let go of the rope. He was swept off and fell in direct line of both hind feet of the bull, causing chest and heart injuries, from which he died that night.

Mighty Mike did not have a history of attacking a fallen rider. Bullfighters said he showed no particular desire to fight them. He wanted to get his work done and get out of the arena, going to the gate the minute the rider was off. But if the gate was closed he would come charging with blood in his eye, demanding to know who was responsible for the closed gate.

7
SCHOOL DAZE

For the first time, rodeo "schools" started cropping up in the early 1960s. Every event was represented in these training sessions, generally taught by former champions or top-level cowboys in each event. Jim Shoulders was a front runner in this innovative, and much needed, idea. In 1962 he started a roughstock riding school, with three to four sessions a year, at his 5,000-acre ranch near Henryetta, Oklahoma. In a visit with Shoulders he explained, "Toots Mansfield had the very first rodeo school—for ropers. I had the first rodeo riding school. The first five years there weren't many schools, then about anyone who had a 'big buckle' had a school."

Shoulders' training was for bull riders, and he shared his expertise in saddle bronc and bareback riding, as well. Limiting his students to around twenty per event, he always had a full house.

Bull riding was becoming the most popular event in rodeo, and many young men were paying their entry fees and getting on bulls without any training or knowledge about how to ride a bull. Consequently, they were getting banged up and incurred many unnecessary injuries. The only experience a beginning rider could get prior to the schools was by entering "jackpot" bull ridings, which were usually held on someone's ranch on a Sunday afternoon. Beginners would ride a bronc or a bull, one after another. The advice they got was generally given only by their peers, and whether the advice was beneficial or even good advice was questionable. Shoulders knew he could help these novice bull and bronc riders be better pre-

"*Get this foot down—get your arm in—lift this knee, . . .*" Cartoon by Boots Reynolds taken from a book of cartoons entitled "Rodeo School Champion Drop-Outs" *he put together after attending Jim Shoulders' Roughstock School, 1977.*

pared when they crawled on their first competitive head of bucking stock.

Bill Roberts of Peetz, Colorado, attended Shoulders' bull riding school. He had been riding bulls for a few years but was eager to improve his skills. He drove to Henryetta, Oklahoma, from northeastern Colorado and arrived the night before the class began. He made a trial run and drove out to Shoulders' ranch that evening, just to make sure he would not get lost and be late for the 8:00 A.M. class the next morning.

It was hot and sticky that first week of June in eastern Oklahoma, when fifteen young men arrived to learn everything the sixteen-time world champion had to teach them. The first morning Shoulders checked the students' equipment—gloves, spurs, and bull ropes. He complimented some of the equipment students had chosen, and told others what he recommended they should change. He advised them to use a good thick buckskin glove, with a surgical rubber glove inside the leather glove if the rider had blisters on his riding hand. The fingers of the surgical glove were to be cut off. The inside

Young bull rider Chip Cole, son of Chili Cole of San Angelo, Texas, giving the ride his all.—Photo by Dulany. Courtesy of Jack Long.

glove would help the rider not tear up the palm of his hand. Shoulders said spurs are as different for riders as ball gloves and bats are for baseball players. The rider should not sharpen spurs, and each should pick what feels best to the rider. The angle of the rowel is strictly a personal decision. The bull rope, a loose Manila rope which has been braided by hand, needs rosin on it and it needs to be stretched. Extra rosin needs to be put on the hand-hold and the tail of the rope to help the rider's glove to stick. Shoulders said he preferred a hand-hold just high enough for him to be able to put three fingers on the base and have them touch the top of the hand-hold, about twelve inches along the base. Every man needed to experiment and find the methods that fit him best.[54]

He also advised students to only ride two or three bulls

that first day of school. They could ride as many as they wanted, but he advised that some students who rode too many at the beginning of the course were too sore to get out of bed by the third day.

In an interview, Shoulders said he felt the success of any roughstock riding school was to provide stock the novice riders could ride and be able to think about their free hand, where their feet were, how their body was held. "If the stock is so rough all they have time to do is run to the fence, then they don't have time to learn anything else." Shoulders bought old "blooper" broncs from other stock contractors, and Hereford and Holstein bulls that didn't have quite the zest for bucking that the class would encounter later on.

When the students began getting on the bulls, Shoulders was in the arena on horseback. He would give suggestions as they prepared for their ride. "Ooze down on the bull's back

"Now remember, kid, she's just an ol' practice cow—." Cartoon by Boots Reynolds taken from "Rodeo School Champion Drop-Outs."

quietly and slowly so as not to startle him. Getting astride the bull a rider wants to have his feet out ahead of his body. If the animal becomes unruly in the chute they generally put their heads down and kick; with feet ahead of the body a rider can get up and away much easier. Be sure toes are pointed in toward the animal so the rider has no chance of 'accidentally' spurring him in the chute. Be down close to the animal and have your feet on the lowest boards, don't lean over."

When the ride was over, Shoulders would critique each ride. Roberts said that prior to the school he had received so much advice *and* bad information that he had become confused on how he should ride. It was Roberts' hope that the school would eliminate all the misinformation he had received earlier. "I remember Jim telling us to spit on the Brahma's hump, then watch it. That was to get a rider to watch the hump, instead of the bull's head," said Roberts, who also remembered the advice given when getting ready in the chute. For the rider's safety a helper should put his arm in front of the rider, instead of grabbing the rider in back, by the belt of their pants, which some helpers would do to help the rider in the event the bull acted up in the chute. Lifting the rider from the back automatically made the rider lean forward, causing him to come face to head with the back of the bull's head—a bad combination that always caused injury.

Shoulders advised that before slack is pulled in the bull rope, the hand-hold should be placed as close to the bull's backbone as possible without being on top of it. Right-handed riders would put it a little to the right side of the backbone, left-handed riders just to the left. The slack should be pulled tight so there is no way the rope can slip after the action starts. "I bring the tail of the rope across my palm," said Shoulders, "take a loose wrap around behind my hand, leaving a little slack, then lay the rope in my hand. I ride with a split finger dally . . . bringing the rope between my little finger and forefinger; but I don't tell my students to do this because it can cause them to hang up." This is called the "suicide wrap," and Jim Shoulders was the first bull rider known to use it.

Finally students were told not to turn and nod to the gate

"... and there is, as Willie so thoughtlessly demonstrated, one more good reason why you don't lean too far over your stock." Cartoon by Boots Reynolds taken from "Rodeo School Champion Drop-Outs."

man, but keep their eyes on the bull's hump, and settle down toward the bull as much as possible. The rider was directed to pull the stomach down close to the back of the bull and put the back pockets on his back. The rider should hold his legs right to the rope or a little in front of it, get the feet ready to squeeze, and pull while nodding for the gate.[54]

The only way a rider can find his natural position is through practice and experience, according to Shoulders. Riding a bull properly is an art. Balance is being able to freely move the body. In getting off, the rider should roll off on the same side on which he rides (right-handed to the right, and left-handed to the left). Getting off of a bull standing still is dangerous because he will immediately turn and try to hurt you. As the rider rolls, he lifts the opposite leg from the side the rider is getting off on, and this will swing the rider free of the animal.

Shoulders tells each class that not every one will be a champion, but at the school they could decide if they had the talent to ride and win, or if they should be looking for another way to participate in the sport of rodeo.

Roberts, who took the training over thirty years ago, has vivid memories of the school and said it definitely improved his riding ability. Unfortunately, a pulled groin muscle kept him from making bull riding a full-time profession.

The Beutler Brothers of Elk City, Oklahoma, were well-known stock contractors during the 1950s and 1960s. They provided stock for rodeos all across the country and often were covering several rodeos at the same time. "Slim" Whaley, by the age of sixty, had been with the Beutlers for many years, and knew everything there was to know about horses and cattle. He was part vet/part cowboy, and the Beutlers trusted him with their animals.

When the animals arrived at a rodeo destination, Whaley watched each animal come off the truck, checking for injuries, which seldom happened. They generally had a slight gauntness from lack of feed, water, and relaxation. But Whaley would have each head watered and fed immediately so that they were all settled and rested by the next day.

In an article written in *Argosy Magazine* in 1957 about

Duke Clark rides Jim Shoulders' Number 40 Coonrad at Ponca City, Oklahoma, in 1963.—Photo by Ferrell Butler. Courtesy of Imogene Veach Beals.

this colorful but all-business rodeo hand, Willard H. Porter wrote: "A kind of perennial baby sitter for the Beutler's bucking stock, Slim Whaley's feelings toward his charges runs the gamut from affection to disgust: he travels with them, feeds them, doctors them, curses them, pleads with them, and occasionally takes a rope after them with all the fervor of an outraged headmaster chasing a back-country school delinquent. And Whaley's a cowboy who claims he was weaned on a catch rope."

At a Wichita, Kansas, rodeo a big pinto bull named "Spot" broke out of the pens and headed to town. It happened often; Spot loved to jump fences and head to town.

The townsfolk were milling about in utter bewilderment. Traffic was jammed bumper to bumper. One man was out of his car, examining a long, paint-ripped gash down the side. Shaking his fist, he threatened suit as Whaley loped past.

The bull appeared three blocks ahead, still scattering pedestrians and vehicles as if he were a tank heading for battle with all turret guns blazing.

Whaley overtook him and ran him four more blocks before he had a chance to use his rope. Then, right in front of the Broadview Hotel and much to the amazement of horrified on-lookers, he whipped a loop around both horns, waved a trip behind the broad rump, rode hard away, and flopped 1,800 pounds of stubborn Brahma onto the slick pavement. He dismounted and tied Spot down. And he sat on him, smoking a cigar and looking for a dog to kick.

"That son-of-a-buck sure made me mad," Whaley recalls.

"He made his ride just fine, but his hat was jammed on so tight, he passed out at the whistle!" Cartoon by Bonnie Shields.

"Hell, he mighta killed somebody! We shoved him into a double horse trailer on his head like a big pile of meat. When we got him back to the pens, we left him tied up all night just to think it over a spell."[55]

The article also told of another bull:

A huge black bull, with a tremendous hump and high, curving horns, dynamited a cowboy and spun on him, its great head butting and jabbing. The clowns rushed in to lure the bull away, but the beast lunged at them, on the hook, and drove them off. Then it charged back at the fallen rider, who had just unscrambled his brains enough to make a run for the fence. As he started his sprint, he fell sprawling, with a ton of bellowing Brahma right at his back.

Always alert and ready for any emergency, Whaley hastened to the rescue. A perfect loop settled over the bull's head. Slack tore from the rope and the taut line sung like a banjo string as Whaley's stout bull horse, Blue, every muscle straining, took the full impact of the charging Brahma on the end of it.

The bull was brought to a thumping halt inches from the grounded cowboy. The fight was taken out of him and Whaley led him through a double gate, Blue going on one side of a stout partition, while the bull, snuffling and jumping with rage, entered the holding pens on the other side.

"Brimmers are funny customers," says Whaley. "Some are might dangerous . . . like the fightin' bulls we haul to please the crowd. Them kind is on the prod all the time. But some of the others are plumb gentle.

"One time at Oklahoma City, old No. 30, a kinda reddish bull without horns, jumped outta the pens at night. We didn't know nothin' about it until the police called Lynn (Beutler) up. That bull had wandered around town for a spell and then bedded down in some lady's backyard. She said there was a lion in her flower bed—and for the police to come shoot it!"[55]

In spite of the added training for bull riders, like Shoulders' school and other bull riding schools across the country, injuries and worse still occurred from the "ton of bad attitude lookin' for a person to hurt." Vern Neal, of Deer Park, Washington, was killed opening night of the Diamond Spur Rodeo in Spokane, Washington, in 1960, when he bucked off bull

Having a drink at the Grand National Rodeo, San Francisco Cow Palace, are Buster Ivory, "Big" John Williams, Cecil Jones, and Dan Taylor.—Photo by Caxt. Courtesy of John Williams.

Number 6 of the Joe Kelsey string. The bull stepped on him, crushing his chest and killing him instantly. Gordon Casey Sampson, age twenty-six, of White Swan, Washington, bucked off Kelsey's Number 53 bull in 1968. Going over the bull's head, he was struck by its horns. He died after surgery. In June 1969 Fred Scotia, age twenty-five, who joined RCA a year earlier as a permit holder, was killed at a Woodlake, California, rodeo when he was whipped down under the mount. The bull stepped on his head, causing compound fractures of the skull. He died instantly.[35]

In 1964 Buster Ivory kept bull rider Alvin Cooke from death with his quick thinking. It was at the Lake Isabella, California, rodeo, and Cooke had drawn the Flying U's bull named Snowdrift. He was bucked off and hit in the jaw by the bull's head, then Cooke fell inside the spin and was stepped on. The bull's foot cut in two the muscle that runs from the ear to the shoulder, and almost severed the jugular vein. Cooke was bleeding to death. Ivory quickly reacted and

Ronny Webb rides Harley Tucker's Number 29 Chief Joseph bull at Pendleton RoundUp in 1960.—Photo by Devere Helfrich. Courtesy of Ronny Webb. Devere Helfrich Collection, National Cowboy Hall of Fame.

pinched off the flow of blood with his thumb and forefinger until the ambulance arrived.

Snowball wasn't satisfied with this bit of destruction but made his mark again when he injured Ed LeTourneau at the Angels Camp rodeo. When LeTourneau bucked off, he landed on his neck and shoulders, then Snowball hit him in the back, overflexing the spine, crushing one vertebra, and chipping another. Surgery on the damaged back, a body cast, followed by a leather brace for a year helped the injury.[35] LeTourneau continued to ride bulls for the next thirty years, including the Senior ProRodeo Association.

Jim Shoulders commented on injury: "You can't stop some-

1962 National Finals bull riders. Left to right, front row: Bob Wegner, Bernis Johnson, Don Adams, Pete Crump, Bob Robinson. Second row: Ronnie Rossen, Billy Hand, Rocky Rockabar, Jim Shoulders, Joe Green. Third row: Jim Charles, Bill Rinestine, Roy Wallace, Leo Brown, and Larry Condon.—Photo by Devere Helfrich. Courtesy of Imogene Veach Beals. Devere Helfrich Collection, National Cowboy Hall of Fame.

thing like this from hurtin' but you can damn well not let it bother you." To acquire that attitude and to abide by it are what professional rodeo is all about.[11]

Improvements continued to be made in the rodeo world, both at rodeos and with the associations that worked diligently toward the betterment of the sport. At Pendleton RoundUp in 1964 the committee replaced the wooden arena fence with sections of lightweight plastic pipe. The fence was tested often; pieces flew and were put right back together with no injury or damage to man or beast.[6]

Trading out at rodeos was optional as of 1961. The four previous years there was no trading allowed. But at a fall membership meeting a vote was very equal pro and con. The stock contractors were generally not in favor of it, but it was passed. The rule stated that both rodeo committee and stock contractor must advise RCA that they will allow it six weeks prior to the event, so rodeos could have more top cowboys participating. Another rule posted in 1961 was that no bull could be put in the rodeo draw until his horns had been cut back to a reasonable distance. Also, no bull could be hot shot from the time a rider got on the bull until the bull was turned out.[35]

A new judging system was used at the Denver rodeo in 1964, with the rider being scored 1 to 25, and the bull scored 1 to 25, with 100 points as a perfect score. This judging system is still in effect today.

RCA also installed field men in 1967. Eleven men were chosen to provide information to prospective and existing rodeo committees in their area regarding the association. Also that year a judging manual was instituted by the Rodeo Foundation, and edited by Gene Pruett.[35]

The National Finals was still making progressive changes as well. In 1960 bull riders voted for the bullfighters which would protect the riders at the National Finals Rodeo. Fourteen rodeo clowns applied for the two positions and seven barrelmen applied. In 1962 judges wanting to be considered for the Finals were asked to apply by October 15. Judges would not be voted on by the contestants but determined by the association and Finals directors.[35]

Harry Tompkins won the All-Around World Championship in 1960. He also won the bull riding championship, which makes him one of the few to ever win world championships in three decades in the same event (1948-1950, 1952, 1960). Freckles Brown won the world champion bull riding title in 1962 without even getting in the arena at the National Finals that year. In October of that year he suffered a broken neck

118   COWBOY UP!

and was in a body cast during the Finals, but in spite of it, his lead kept him ahead of the pack. He won $18,675 that year to thrust him into the championship.[29]

In 1965 Larry Mahan won his first bull riding world championship, at the age of twenty-two, winning just a little over $1,000 more than Ronnie Rossen. In 1967 Freckles Brown rode the formerly unridden bull owned by Jim Shoulders, Tornado, in the first round of the National Finals Rodeo. Just shy of his forty-seventh birthday, Brown could have been elected as governor of Oklahoma that night, commented

1963 National Finals bull riders: Left to right, front row: Jim Charles, Kenny Stanton, Ed Conway, Howard Carroll, Lawrence Hutchison. Second row: Mac Griffith, Pete Crump, Bill Kornell, Carl Nafzger, Joe Green. Back row: Delbert Hataway, Bob Wegner, Leo Brown, Dickey Cox, and Dallas Chartier.—Photo by Devere Helfrich. Courtesy of Imogene Veach Beals. Devere Helfrich Collection, National Cowboy Hall of Fame.

Everett Shaw. The audience came to their feet with a standing ovation at the end of the ride as Brown stood in the spotlight, hat in hand, and thanked his fans. Brown won the National Finals bull riding average that year, and Larry Mahan won the world championship.

The following year, George Paul of Del Rio, Texas, won the bull riding world championship. Paul, only twenty-one, was knocked out in the first round by a blow to the jaw three jumps out of the chutes. He covered the next eight bulls to win $27,822—over $10,000 more than his closest opponent, Gary Leffew.[29]

In 1961 San Angelo rodeo elected one-time bull rider C. A. "Chili" Cole as president of the Rodeo and Stock Show.

1964 National Finals bull riders: Left to right, front row: Hank Abbie, Kenny Stanton, Bill Kornell, Eddie Conway, Lowell James, Joe Green, Delbert Hataway, Joel Sublette. Second row: Jim Steen, Bob Wegner, Myrtis Dightman, Bob Robinson, Dickey Cox, Dave Glover, and Ronnie Rossen.—Photo by Devere Helfrich. Courtesy of Imogene Veach Beals. Devere Helfrich Collection, National Cowboy Hall of Fame.

On receiving the honor Cole said, "It's been a long time since I first hit San Angelo in 1938 dragging a bull rope. I never thought a bull rider would ever get up to this end of the table."[20]

Anti-rodeo bills were brought to court in Connecticut and West Virginia in 1967. Ohio already had a bill in effect. Gene Pruett, editor of the *Rodeo Sports News,* RCA's newspaper, wrote in an article about the bill outlawing rodeo: "Apathy, and the old idea 'they can't do that,' will let those misguided souls who want to abolish the sport have their way if steps are not taken to provide some strong opposition when, and if, such bills are put before the state legislatures."[68] But that same year the Ohio law was found unconstitutional, and although it had been in effect for two years, it was in violation of the 14th Amendment of the United States Constitution.[35] In an article entitled "Is Rodeo a Cruel Sport" in the February 1966 issue of *The Western Horseman,* Robert M. Miller, D.V.M. reports: "the definition of 'cruelty' in the Oxford University Dictionary is 'the disposition to inflict suffering—delight in another's pain—mercilessness.'" He goes on to cite Spanish bullfighting as a cruel sport, much like dog fighting and cock fighting, because injury is deliberate. Boxing is a cruel sport because a knockout is the *object* of the game, he said. "Rodeo by contrast is not cruel. It can be a dangerous sport. Injuries to both contestants and animals occur. But such injuries are unintentional, accidental and regrettable."[67]

Bob Wegner of Auburn, Washington, became World Champion Bull Rider for 1964, winning $20,757. Bill Kornell was second, with a little over $1,700 behind Wegner. Nine other years Wegner finished in the top five, beginning with 1956 until 1965. He finished second four times, beaten by Ronnie Rossen two of those years and Jim Shoulders the other two.

In the state of Washington, Wegner incorporated an organization entitled American Cowboys Association. The organization called for twenty-man teams in rodeo that would compete as home teams in a new rodeo league. In May 1967 the *Rodeo Sports News* reported that Wegner had been suspended from the Rodeo Cowboys Association "due to actions detrimental to the best interests of RCA." In an October issue of the magazine it was reported Wegner filed suit against the Rodeo Cowboys Association and George Williams, of *Rodeo Sports News,* for damage to his reputation in controversy over team rodeo competition. Wegner was asking for $300,500.[35] According to Wegner, the case was settled out of court and he received $25,000 and a promise that his name would be removed from the RCA blacklist. Wegner said his name was removed for one issue of the *Rodeo Sports News,* then in the following issue it was back on the blacklist, despite the out-of-court decision. He then filed a second suit against the Rodeo Cowboys Association for $1 million. In 1969 another out-of-court decision was made, and Wegner received $7,500. His name was removed from the blacklist once more. This incident helped set the standard toward allowing athletes in all sports to be free agents.[35] Thirty-some years later, Wegner is still promoting the team rodeo program.

The sixties were well known as the hippie era. A hippie was generally perceived as a long-haired young person dressed in tie-dyed clothes, who had a tendency to refrain from

Dickey Cox rides Beutler Brothers Number 22 at Sidney, Iowa, in 1967.—Photo by Ferrell Butler. Courtesy of Imogene Veach Beals.

bathing, and often smoked "pot." They often lived in communes and thought they were going to "save the world" and "find" themselves. They spent much time planning protests and sit-ins, to express their feelings on many subjects. Needless to say, most cowboys and rural dwellers were not in favor of the type of life chosen by the hippie. Although cowboys were definitely not viewed as hippies, some wore their hair a little longer and the dress was a little more colorful for some in this era. Dan Taylor told, "At Fort Worth Buster Ivory asked me and Harley May to be pick up men at the rodeo. May came by and said, 'Hey, let's go to the office and suit out in those pretty shirts!'" It was evident the new age was infiltrating the cowboy world, in subtle ways.

Taylor continued, "Later we were sitting in the alley waiting for the rodeo to begin and Jim Shoulders had been kidding Mahan about his long hair. I asked Shoulders about his new son-in-law and his answer was, 'He's just like all young people, his hair is down to his ass, and his pants are up to his knees.' And I replied, 'Hey, that sounds like Mahan.'

"Shoulders went and got big James Bynum and another big bulldogger to hold Mahan," recalled Taylor. "Shoulders kidded Mahan and told him he was going to cut his hair, but instead he cut Mahan's pants off at the knees with the sharp knife he always carried. Mahan did not have time to change pants before he was up for his next ride, so he put on his chaps and rode with those knee-length pants."

Gail Gandolfi illustration.

Larry Mahan scored 92 points in the bull riding at Denver's National Western Stock Show and Rodeo in the late 1960s. At that time 92 was the highest score ever given in bull riding.[35]

It's evident the rodeo cowboy thrives on humor. He likes to tell a good story and enjoys pulling a good joke on another cowboy, especially if it's a good friend. D. J. Gaudin, better known as bullfighter Kajun Kidd, recalled, "It was in Las Vegas and there were outhouses behind the chutes for everyone to use. Just before the bronc riding Casey Tibbs went in one. Harry Tompkins and Jim Shoulders saw Tibbs go in. They waited a minute, then began to shake the outhouse, Casey was yelling, and they finally turned it completely over. Casey came out real mad!"

Harry Tompkins recalled one time he had a new car and he, Jim Shoulders, Dan Taylor, and Harley May were traveling a long distance from one rodeo to the next. Harry drove a long way, then Taylor and May drove some. They were about forty miles from their destination when Shoulders offered to drive. Everyone gave Shoulders a bad time for not offering sooner. His response was, "Well, someone has to drive, and someone has to think."

Bullriding Cowboys of the '60s

FRECKLES BROWN

Warren Granger "Freckles" Brown was born January 18, 1921, in Wheatland, Wyoming, the youngest son of a farmer's ten children. He started rodeoing in the 1930s and rode his first bull at Willcox, Arizona, in 1937. He went to Madison Square Garden in 1949 and won second in the bull riding. The $3,000 he won allowed him to go home to Soper, Oklahoma, and modernize the "shack" on his 160-acre spread.

He didn't hit his stride until 1959, when he finished fourteenth in the standings. The following year he was sixth, and in 1961 he ended the year in the number-three spot. The next year, 1962, he became World Champion Bull Rider, at age

Freckles Brown rides Steiner's Number 67 at the Waco Fair & Rodeo in 1961.—Photo by Ferrell Butler. Courtesy of Bobby Steiner.

forty-one. For a few years he didn't make the top fifteen, but by 1966 he was third at year's end, in 1967 he was fifth, in 1968 third again, and 1969 he finished seventh, at forty-eight years of age. Jackson Sundown, who cowboyed and rode roughstock twenty years before Freckles, was compared to Brown for durability in the rodeo arena.

In his years of rodeoing Brown had nine broken legs, four broken ribs, two broken collar bones, and two broken necks.[58] Pretty typical for a long-time bull rider. On October 28, 1962, at Portland, Oregon, Brown rode Christensen Brothers' bull, Black Smoke. The whistle blew, and as he was getting off, with his hand still in the rope, he got hit twice. He sustained a broken neck and was "sidelined" for some time. Although he never mounted a bull during the National Finals Rodeo, he did win the title of World Champion that year, since he was so far ahead in monies at the time he was injured.

The following July in Coleman, Texas, Brown was ready to

ride his first bull after the devastating injury he incurred the past October. Clem McSpadden, the announcer, reviewed Brown's career for the crowd. As he mounted the bull, preparing for the ride, the crowd was silent. Brown nodded for the gate to open. The bull bucked, Freckles was a bit slow and missed him, and landed on the ground. But his neck felt good. Two nights later he had to ride his second bull, and it went well. So well, in fact, he wired Cheyenne to cancel his judging job there and instead enter him in the bull riding and the saddle bronc riding.

Once-in-a-lifetime events happen rarely, and if a person is fortunate enough to experience one they will never forget it. Freckles Brown's ride on Tornado, the previously unridden bull, owned by Jim Shoulders, at the first go-round of the 1967 National Finals, was truly one of those events. Everyone who witnessed it remembers it like it was yesterday—especially Brown. "The amount of try you have," Freckles Brown once said, "determines if you really have the desire and courage it takes to be a winning cowboy."[59]

At age fifty-one he won the average in the bull riding at the New Mexico State Fair Rodeo (1972). It can be safely stated that Brown had plenty of TRY.

LEO BROWN

Leo Brown of The Czar, Alberta, Canada, was the first National Finals bull rider to ride all his bulls at the National Finals Rodeo (in 1963, at the fifth annual Finals). He was also the first Canadian to qualify for the National Finals in bull riding. The ten-time Canadian champion never won a world title in the PRCA, but finished the 1963 season in seventh place in the world by placing in the money in five rounds of the National Finals.

Brown got blood poisoning in his leg when stepped on in the third round by a bull. "It was from the needles they used on my knee, so they had to freeze my knee before I rode. The last three rounds I couldn't feel my leg at all."[36]

RONNIE ROSSEN

Ronnie Rossen was born July 7, 1937 in Ogallala, Nebraska.

Ronnie Rossen rides Ole Speck at Burwell, Nebraska.
—Photographer unknown. Courtesy of Imogene Veach Beals.

The second born in a family of five rambunctious boys, Rossen began his love of being a cowboy early. The family moved to Crook, Colorado, and the Rossen boys were considered "off limits" to neighborhood youngsters. It seems that when they played cowboys and Indians, they used BB guns! Area parents were afraid for the safety of their little ones.

Rossen's father was a truck driver and the family moved frequently. Young Ronnie spent the third grade at Merino,

Colorado, remembered his first cousin, Kay Rossen Gentry, who was also in the Merino third grade. "It was not unusual for us to beg our teacher to let Ronnie sing and yodel for us. He had a great voice," she recalled.

Although the family continued moving from place to place, Ronnie went back to Merino and lived with his Uncle Wayne and Aunt Ruby Rossen, so he could attend the high school there and play football. His uncle also trained and raced quarter horses, and Ronnie loved to be around them. Since Ronnie and cousin Kay were the same age, there was much competition between them. They rode everything on the place—horses, goats, milk cows. Kay's memory is, "Ronnie wanted everything to buck! I dreaded having him behind me on a horse because I knew he had his heels in the horse's flank the entire time."

Rossen never borrowed anything, he just helped himself. "If he were wearing a coat when we were ready to go to school I'd make him take his coat off, because more than likely he'd have my western shirt on, too. When he left our place, my spurs went with him," Kay Gentry lamented.

The 5'9, 165-pound Rossen joined RCA in 1956. At the first National Finals Rodeo he won money the last night on a bull named Black Smoke, with his jaw wired shut. He had broken it that afternoon riding a bull.[49] But his strength and ability to ignore pain or injury was well known by those who went down the road with Rossen.

Rossen's ability to ride bulls and his love of riding earned him a World Champion Bull Riding title in 1961 and again in 1966. The 1961 title was won in spite of spending three days in the hospital during the National Finals that year. Stock contractor Harry Knight's bull, No Doze, a one-eyed Brahma and Hereford cross, broke four ribs and ruptured Rossen's liver. The "wreck" would have been much worse if Wick Peth, the bullfighter, hadn't been there to help. No Doze caught him on one horn and Rossen on the other.[49] Rossen made $616 at the National Finals and beat runner-up Bob Wegner by $300 for the year to win the title.[29]

Gentry remembered him as a tough cowboy. He lost a finger when a bull he was riding hit the fence at a rodeo in

Sterling, Colorado, but he carried on. At a Nebraska rodeo a bull riding injury required he be carried out of the arena on a stretcher. Spectators said he raised up from the stretcher, waved to the crowd, and lay back down. In a *Hoofs & Horns* article entitled "Best Bull Riders Today," Jim Shoulders wrote of Rossen: "He pulls a tight rope, gets a good hold and tries to 'out-stout' a bull . . . ride with brute strength. When he gets a good hold on that rope, it would just about take dynamite to pry him loose."[22]

Bob Pope, another northeastern Colorado cowboy, and Rossen traveled the rodeo circuit in the early days of his career. Later in life Rossen would occasionally visit Pope "for a few days." Pope's wife, Norma, remembered vividly those "few days" often turned into "a few weeks."

"You couldn't hurt his feelings or embarrass him," Gentry laughed. "When he left someone's home his duffel bag was usually full of extra socks and underwear!"

The colorful bullbuster with no front teeth lived by the motto, "Chicken today, feathers tomorrow." He loved to ride bulls, and he died riding a bull. He was competing at an Old-Timers Rodeo in Rocky Ford, Colorado, when he was stepped on and killed, at the age of fifty-five.

LARRY MAHAN

Larry Mahan rode and excelled in all three roughstock events. Saddle bronc riding was his favorite event, but he is quick to say, "Bull riding was certainly the most mentally challenging, and I got the greatest gratification from my bull riding wins." He won the All-Around World Championship six times, 1966 through 1970 and again in 1973, and the Bull Riding Champion title twice, 1965 and 1967.

Born in Oregon, on a farm near Salem, November 21, 1943, Mahan made his first rodeo when he was twelve years old and won $6.00 in the boys' calf riding. From then on his rodeo career shot upward. He was considered a "new" kind of cowboy because he worked out in YMCA gymnasiums to prepare for his competitions. He also promoted having the right mental attitude to ride to win. Mahan does not feel he was much different from some of the other aspiring cowboys of his

Larry Mahan, many times All-Around, Bull Riding, and Bareback Champion, waits for his next head of stock. Mahan rode in all three roughstock events.— Photo by Ferrell Butler. Courtesy of Imogene Veach Beals.

day, like Shawn Davis. Many cowboys were coming from a collegiate background where they had gained important rodeo experience. He also feels that in this era more emphasis was being placed on the athletic ability of the competitors in rodeo than it had ever done in the past. The Oregon cowboy flew his own plane and found aviation very challenging as well.

Any time he was at a rodeo where Pete Logan, rodeo announcer, was working, he and Logan, also a pilot, would sneak off to a nearby airport and hang around. Mahan said flying would put him in another world, and when he arrived at the next rodeo he would truly be refreshed. By the time he quit competing Mahan had investments in various endeavors.

Today Larry Mahan can be seen supporting many rodeo venues; however, most of his time is spent on his ranch near Guffey, Colorado. The champion made a concerted effort to study horses and learn as much as he could about them. He finds an inner peace working with horses and a real opportunity to get away from the rest of the world and stress-related issues. He is very excited about the program he and Diana McNab, a sports psychologist and former Canadian ski team member, are presenting at his ranch. Through the University of Denver, McNab has created a course for people which includes coming to stay at the ranch, and learning stress management, tai chi, and how to benefit from nature. Mahan works with the students through horses. "Everything from the horse comes from the inside. With people they are inside their heads too much," stated Mahan. Always striving for a happy horse, he hopes students can learn through the horse how to take stress out of their own lives.

GEORGE PAUL

George Paul of Del Rio, Texas, was born March 5, 1947. He entered the bull riding and bareback events in his rookie year of RCA, 1967, and ended up fourth in the world. He also placed second in the NFR average in bull riding and thirteenth in the All-Around. Prior to his professional career he had won American Junior Rodeo Association bull riding and bareback titles in the sixteen- to nineteen-year-old group.

George Paul and James Bynum kibbitz at St. Louis, Missouri, in 1967.—Photo by Bern Gregory. Bern Gregory Collection, National Cowboy Hall of Fame.

George Paul, 1968 RCA World Champion Bull Rider on Knight's Number 11 at Fort Madison, Iowa, that year.—Photo by Bern Gregory. Courtesy of Imogene Veach Beals. Bern Gregory Collection, National Cowboy Hall of Fame.

In 1968 Paul won the World Championship in Bull Riding and the average. He rode seventy-nine bulls in a row during the season—a fantastic record. As a pilot, Paul traveled most of his rodeo miles in the air and ferried himself to 150 rodeos that year.

When not involved in rodeo Paul was involved in family ranching in Mexico with 5,000 horses, 1,000 Herefords, and 40,000 sheep and goats. In 1969 this operation took much of his time, but 1970 saw him back on the rodeo road. The last of July 1970, Paul fatally crashed his own light plane near Kemmerer, Wyoming. He had ridden and won the bull riding and bareback events at Monte Vista, Colorado, on July 30; flew to Casper, Wyoming, to compete in that night's performance; and was on his way to Mexico in his plane.[35]

Preparing for the parade are June Ivory, "Big John" Williams, Berva Don Taylor, Dan Taylor, and Caroline Ramsey Rose, 1964.
—Photographer unknown. Courtesy of John Williams.

"BIG JOHN" WILLIAMS

Born and raised in Springfield, Missouri, John Williams rode a few broncs and bulls as a young man. He joined the service during World War II and was stationed at a prisoner of war camp at Garwood, Texas, after serving in the South Pacific. In Garwood he met a local girl, Charlene Frnka, lost his heart, and never left.

Williams produced a few rodeos for the Southwestern Rodeo Association. He built a rodeo arena in Garwood and held "shows" for amateur "rope pullers." In the early 1950s Slim Pickens, whom Williams had met on the West Coast when he was rodeoing, came to the San Antonio Livestock Show & Rodeo with Rex Allen and spent some time with Williams. They talked a lot about rodeo. Williams realized there was a big demand for good bucking bulls in the world of rodeo, and not long after began buying and selling bulls.

In the following years he sold bulls to many of the major stock contractors, including Korkow, Sutton, Harry Knight, Steiner, Claude Robinson, Gay, Shoulders, and Rosser, just to name a few. He also provided bull dogging steers and roping calves to rodeo producers as far away as San Francisco.

In the early 1950s Williams developed a way of bucking bulls without having to have cowboys to ride them. He made a near life-size dummy that would sit on the back of a bull, with a mechanism that, after a few seconds, would release the rigging and the dummy. The dummy would fall to the ground and the bull would then be free. This method would not break the bull's bucking spirit, but would give Williams, or a stock contractor, an opportunity to see what kind of a bucker each bull would make.

A good friend of Williams, B. J. Whitley, vice president of the Pipeline and Land Department of Tennessee Gas & Transmission Company in Houston, and his son, an electrical engineer for the company, were fascinated with the idea Williams had. They spent over $2,000 inventing a mechanism that would work. The device was a hydraulic plunger, used to close a screen door. By hand the timer would be set for two to four seconds. Once the apparatus and dummy were in place the bull was released and he would buck out. When the timer went off, a nail through a ring would release and the entire apparatus fell to the ground. It was innovative and allowed Williams to "dummy his bulls" and determine their capabilities quicker and with less cost. Williams' reputation and his invention spread quickly, and he became "the bull man" stock contractors came to when buying bulls. In the year 2000 Williams was selling a new, updated device, which will be discussed later in the book.

One year at National Finals there were thirteen bulls, sent by various stock contractors, that wore the Williams brand, "Rafter J." John Williams was made an "Honorary Texan" by

Governor Preston Smith. He is a lifetime member of the Houston and San Antonio Livestock Show & Rodeos, has been chairman of the Calf Scramble for many, many years at San Antonio's rodeo, and is a lifetime director emeritus.

Famous Bucking Bulls of the '60s

TORNADO

Tornado was the most famous bull in rodeo for many years. He was bucked 220 times without being ridden before Freckles Brown rode him to the whistle.

Born and raised on the Clive Reynolds end of the Pierce Estate Ranch in Wharton County, Texas, Tornado was sold at

Wick Peth, great bullfighter, tries to outmaneuver the famous Tornado at the Los Angeles National Finals. Tornado was out of the chutes 220 times before he was ridden.—Photographer unknown. Courtesy of John Williams.

a Bay City auction ring in the spring of 1961. John Williams bought him for $147, along with some other bulls. When Williams got him back to Garwood, the bull was in poor shape. He was thin and the hair was off his neck. In fact, Brown Todd, a stock contractor from Louisiana, was at Williams' place to buy bulls, and passed over the red bull, later named Tornado, buying another red bull instead.

Williams discovered the bull was full of liver flukes, and after a couple of doses of medicine, the bull began to blossom. Williams named him "Number Four" and tried his "dummy" on him. Williams discovered the bull could really buck, plus he didn't like people. Shortly thereafter Neal Gay came to pick up three bulls from Williams for the Mesquite Rodeo. Gay paid Williams $247 for Number Four, which was eventually named Tornado.

When Jim Shoulders, a partner with Gay in the Mesquite Rodeo company, decided to go into the stock contracting business, his transaction with Mesquite included the bull Tornado. The bull became a tremendous asset to the new stock contractor.

Two hundred and twenty times Tornado bucked out of a rodeo chute and kept his rider from getting a score. He was a tremendous draw, and since he didn't care for humans he always went to the barrel and gave the audience their money's worth.

The very first year, 1961, Tornado went to the National Finals Rodeo, and continued going for the next seven years, through 1968. In nineteen draws at National Finals he was never ridden until Freckles Brown made a score in 1967, and the crowd went wild! Only one other man rode him, in 1967. In the ninth round Jim Charles rode him for a score of 68. Charles had drawn Tornado three times at earlier National Finals performances (1961, 1962, and 1966) before he finally rode to the whistle on him. John Quintana was the only other rider to make a score on Tornado during his entire rodeo career.

Shoulders retired Tornado, and when he died in 1972 he was buried on Persimmon Hill, at the National Cowboy Hall of Fame in Oklahoma City.

SPEEDY GONZALES

Speedy Gonzales was a black Brangus bull that weighed in at 1,350 pounds and was owned by Bill McKee of Savery, Wyoming. In 1965 his record that year was fourteen times out and fourteen buck offs. He was known as one of the "waspiest" bucking bulls of the time. He went to the National Finals that year, bucking off Gid Garstad, reigning Champion Bull Rider of Canada, in the first go-round; Phil Heinen in the fourth go-round; and Bill Kornell, 1963 World's Champion Bull Rider, in the final, eighth round.

He was unstoppable, with a total of 242 buck-outs and no qualified rides. Speedy Gonzales died at the age of nine, of dust pneumonia, in a pasture near Greeley, Colorado.

8
THE MIGHTY SPONSORS AND THE '70s ERA

Rodeo sponsors have been around since the beginning of rodeo in some form or other. Homer Holcomb, one of the first rodeo clowns to bullfight, used a cape with big letters spelling "C–A–L–V–E–R–T" on it. When Holcomb waved it at the bull, it clearly advertised the popular whiskey of that era.

By the 1970s many sponsors were being introduced to the sport of rodeo, and finding it a lucrative way to promote their products. In turn they were giving the contestants, stock contractors, and other rodeo people extra funds or merchandise for jobs well done.

One of the longest running sponsorships in American sports is the association Wrangler has had with rodeo. In October 1947, Blue Bell, Inc. (Wrangler's earlier name) arrived at Madison Square Garden Rodeo, which in those days was considered the grand finale to the rodeo season, much like the National Finals Rodeo of today. They brought a truckload of Wrangler jeans, western shirts, and denim jackets and presented them to each contestant. They also signed Gerald Roberts and Bill Linderman, both rodeo champions, as endorsees of their product.

Previously Blue Bell, Inc. had not only sold clothing to the Armed Forces during World War II but also made work clothes and play clothes, which were sold through J. C. Penney and Sears & Roebuck. Rodeo and cowboys were a new direction for this company, and they decided to "enter the ring" and compete with jeans-makers like Levi Strauss and Lee Rider, whose presence was already known in rodeo circles.

Bob Mayo keeps going on Barnes' Number 7 at Bolivar, Missouri, in 1970.—Photo by Bern Gregory. Bern Gregory Collection, National Cowboy Hall of Fame.

Wrangler hired well-known tailor Rodeo Ben of Hollywood fame, and with the recommendations from cowboys such as Jim Shoulders, Freckles Brown, Bill Linderman, Todd Whatley, Harry Tompkins, and Gerald Roberts a jeans design was created to fit cowboys.

Shoulders recalled, "I had won the bareback riding and the bull riding at Madison Square Garden in the fall. The next spring, 1948, at Denver I was asked by Norm Considine, who represented Wrangler, to sign a contract to endorse Wrangler jeans. Wranglers were $3.00 a pair and shirts were almost as much. I got $150 a year, and all the 'rags' I could wear." Shoulders said Wrangler dressed all his kids as they grew up. They never wore anything but that brand. In fact, the company provided the Shoulders family its first color television set, which was given as a bonus. He still has a contract with Wrangler today.

Shoulders said at one time Wrangler did a survey and dis-

Clyde Kimbro bucks off Steiner's "YD" at St. Louis, 1968. At the next jump "YD" kicked the bell off the rope and it hit a man on the head sitting in a box seat.—Photo by Bern Gregory. Bern Gregory Collection, National Cowboy Hall of Fame.

covered his association with Wrangler was the longest running endorsement of any person with a particular product. His career as a spokesperson for Justin Boots has been almost as long.

Justin Boots began their sponsorship with the first National Finals Rodeo in 1959. Since that time they have sponsored rodeo activities at all levels. Their Justin Sports Medicine Program, which has had a twenty-year reign, is one of their best known programs, along with the Justin Cowboy Crisis Fund, which helps cowboys who have been injured in rodeo to continue to pay non-medical bills.

Resistol Hats also began their sponsorship with the National Finals Rodeo in 1959. Their Rookie of the Year Program is a bonus program which honors the overall Rookie of the Year based on the most money won, plus rookies from each of the seven major PRCA events and Women's Professional Rodeo Association barrel racing. They also honor rookies in each of the twelve circuits in the United States.

Numerous other companies have been major sponsors in rodeo. Copenhagen-Skoal of U.S. Tobacco, which began their activities in rodeo in 1974 at the Intercollegiate rodeos sponsoring the Copenhagen-Skoal Scholarship Award Program, is also responsible for the official scoreboard provided at many rodeos across the country. Crown Royal supplied the PRCA's World Standings at more than 750 PRCA rodeos and provided $7,500 to the winners for the year, in each event, plus a buckle.

Coors is known as the official beer of the PRCA, and that company has provided bonus monies at various levels since 1979. They also have had the Coors Chute Out Rodeo Series, the Coors Man in a Can, and Coors Favorite Cowboy honors. Dodge Trucks provides a new truck to be used by each event winner for a year, and they have sponsored the Dodge National Circuit Final Rodeo in Pocatello, Idaho, since its inception, plus many other programs.

As the years roll by other sponsors have been added; some that were very active in earlier years have dropped their affiliation. The sponsors have added a tremendous amount of additional products and money to the top cowboys' accounts,

Bobby (left) and Gene Clark, bullfighting brothers, have the Steiner bull #214's attention, after LeRoy Burden bucked off and scrambles for safety. St. Louis, Missouri, 1971.—Photo by Bern Gregory. Bern Gregory Collection, National Cowboy Hall of Fame.

in all events. Relying on monies won alone would never have allowed these outstanding athletes the opportunities they have achieved, thanks to interested sponsors. And in turn there is no one better to serve a sponsor than an athlete who is constantly moving from one location to another and is highly visible to the public.

In an article in the *ProRodeo Sports News,* September 1978, Bull Riding Coordinator Bryan McDonald wrote that in less than ten weeks the PRCA Permit Bull Riding Program proved to be an overwhelming success.

The new program gave the permit holders opportunities to compete at permit holder events held by various members across the country because few rodeos would allow permit holding bull riders to enter. Additionally, the objective of the program was to teach novice bull riders the ins and outs of professional rodeo, how to handle themselves with the bulls,

Casey Tibbs' Old Time Cowboy's Reunion was held May 28, 1972, at Pueblo, Colorado. Front row, left to right: Jim Like, Turk Greenough, Gene Pruett, Harry Tompkins, Burel Mulkey. Back row: Eddie Woods, Casey Tibbs, Freckles Brown, Johnie Schneider, Hugh Bennett, Larry Finley, Harley May, Ken Roberts, Hub Whiteman, Gene Rambo, Charley Beals, Red Dougherty, and Gerald Roberts.
—Photographer unknown. Courtesy of Jack Long.

142 COWBOY UP!

and the business it takes to get the job done. Rodeo secretaries and PROCOM operators (the people who handle the PRCA rodeo-entering system at PRCA headquarters) were impressed with the abilities of novice bull riders to handle business.

Bryan McDonald, twenty-three-year bull riding representative with PRCA, said the purpose of the permit events was to keep a novice bull rider from having to drive so far to fulfill his permit. Bryan gave an example: "Randy Major held events in Comanche, Texas, Gary Leffew in California, and Pete Burns in Laramie, Wyoming, but they only lasted for five or six years." They quit holding them because more and more rodeos began allowing permit holders to enter, and of course, a rider would rather compete in a rodeo. McDonald said, "Ted Nuce was a champion who came out of this program."

The new program also introduced novice bulls—giving them an opportunity to get more comfortable in the chutes,

Starting to rodeo young, thirteen-year-old junior bull rider Tate Stratton from Stanley, New Mexico. Tate was the 1998 American Junior Bull Riding Association Senior Steer Riding Champion and Junior Bull Riding Champion.—Photo by © Gene Peach.

with the riders, to say nothing about the "pecking order" they would meet when they started going to regular PRCA-sanctioned rodeos. The older, wiser, more experienced bulls made sure new kids on the block got short rations, with many bumps and bruises, until they established themselves. Also the bulls had to get used to extensive travel, different climates than they were accustomed to, and having top-ranked bull riders test their mettle. Only the top athletes in the bull world make it to professional rodeo arenas.

Lyle Sankey and brother Ike began a roughstock riding school in the mid-1970s. Lyle rode all three events, was tenth

At the Cow Palace Rodeo Carl Nafzger is caught on film in the air as he flips off an Andy Jauregui bull. Wick Peth comes from behind to capture the bull's attention.—Photo by Devere Helfrich. Courtesy of June & Buster Ivory. Devere Helfrich Collection, National Cowboy Hall of Fame.

144   COWBOY UP!

in the All-Around race in 1976, in 1978 placed third in the bull riding standings, and won the bull riding average at the 1978 National Finals Rodeo. He not only taught the school for adult bull riders but also trained Little Britches Rodeo Association contestants, as he was a competitor at this level when he was a youngster.

The school that Sankey taught was covered in a series of

Sandy Kirby draws and rides Barnes' "Walco" during the seventh round of the 1975 National Finals Rodeo. Kirby scored 66 on this ride, and ended up third in the average by Finals end.—Photo by Bern Gregory. Courtesy of Imogene Veach Beals. Bern Gregory Collection, National Cowboy Hall of Fame.

articles in the 1978 *ProRodeo Sports News* by Jane Pattie. The subject included bull riding technique, equipment, and safety. Sankey covered the bull rope, how to resin and clean it up, the rider's glove, spurs, bull rope pads, bells, and boot straps. He discussed accidents (especially "freak accidents," in the bucking chute), where to place the feet and the hands. Step-by-step instructions were given as to how to get a bull rope ready and how to ride. If a beginner could absorb all the instructions and advice and *remember* it, he could come out a winner.

In the year 2000 Sankey was still offering rodeo schools across the country. Some advertised were held at Branson, Missouri; Summerville, Georgia; Spokane, Washington; Carthage, Texas; Valley City, North Dakota; and Rio Linda, California. And that was just for the first three months of the year.

Funny stories never run out of supply in the rodeo circuit. When Mike Bandy, Monty Taylor, and Ricky Bolin were competing in a rodeo in California, they needed to get back to Texas, as the next rodeo was near Dallas. They knew there was a flight that left Los Angeles International Airport for Dallas at 1:00 A.M., having taken it many times.

They arrived at the airport around 7:00 that evening. Since they had time on their hands, they proceeded to the bar. As will happen with cowboys on occasion, they all had too much to drink, and were finally escorted out of the bar. Now they were loose in the airport.

They went to their gate, although it was much too early, and checked to see if they could get their boarding passes. Mike Bandy had an argument with the ticket agent, and walked away with anger mounting. He proceeded out through the swinging glass doors, down a corridor, and spotted a mechanized kiosk, from which vendors sold pretzels and other snacks. Since no one was in attendance, Mike got the kiosk's motor started and drove it through the glass doors as far as he could, before he bailed out.

Meanwhile, Ricky Bolin was standing near the ticket counter, holding up the wall, not saying a word. Monty Taylor, on the other hand, had found at a nearby, unattended ticket counter the public announcing system to all of LAX (Los Angeles International Airport). Crouched down behind the

Ricky Bolin is sliding off Steiner's Number 11, also known as Red Lightning, at Houston, 1978.
—Photo by Hoffman. Courtesy of Bobby Steiner.

ticket counter, where he could not be seen, Monty announced over the loudspeaker, "All you sober son-of-a-bitches get off the plane headed to Dallas, and all you drunk son-of-a-bitches, go get on."

The announcement was heard by one and all from one end of the terminal to the other. Here came the security guards looking for the culprit, but they were unable to find where it was coming from, as Monty was still crouched behind the unattended counter. His cohorts, Bandy and Bolin, were hysterical with laughter.

Taylor attempted to peek out from behind the counter, and the security guards got a glimpse of his Resistol. In no time they had all three cowboys handcuffed and taken to the Los Angeles Police Station. Each cowboy was given one phone call. Ricky Bolin, the only married one, was not about to call his wife and let her know what a scrape they were in this time.

Taylor tried to reach someone, but got no answer. After much discussion it was determined that friend Bobby Brown would be the last attempted telephone call. Brown was dating Tanya Tucker, the famous singer, at that time and surely he could get them some help, they decided.

When they reached him and asked if Brown could get Tanya's attorney to get them released, his response was, "Hey, don't you guys know how expensive he is Monday through Friday? How much do you think he charges to be called on during a weekend?" In spite of Brown's concern, they were released early Sunday morning.

Bobby Steiner remembered a time he, Gary Leffew, and Ronnie "Punch" Rossen were driving from Helena, Montana, to Cheyenne, Wyoming. Leffew had been driving, and Rossen offered to drive, provided someone had "a driving pill" he could take. In those days many a cowboy relied on certain prescription drugs to get from one place to another. Steiner told

Vanas Hedden riding Steiner's Black 6, one of their best, at Sikestown, Missouri.—Photo by Bern Gregory. Courtesy of Bobby Steiner. Bern Gregory Collection, National Cowboy Hall of Fame.

Punch they didn't have any "driving pills" but Leffew took a Contac capsule, a popular over-the-counter aid for nasal decongestion, dumped the contents, and put some plain baby powder in it.

Leffew told Rossen he had a pill, but it was a *bad* one, and he really didn't want to give it to him. "Give it to me," begged Rossen excitedly. "No," said Leffew, "you might be up for two days." Rossen begged and begged, and finally Leffew gave in. They stopped, Rossen downed the pill, and took over the driving chores.

About thirty minutes later Rossen said, "Hey, Stinky [nickname for Leffew], I don't think this damn pill is working."

"Give it some more time, it'll kick in," Leffew responded as he winked at Steiner.

In another thirty minutes Rossen reported, "Hey, I think the goddamn pill is working," and with that he drove the rest of the way to Cheyenne, arriving around daybreak. Steiner said Rossen began drinking when they got to Cheyenne, and the following night he was still at it, had ridden his stock, partied day and night, had never been to bed, and was giving that little pill all the credit. Mind over matter.

Bobby Steiner, World Champion Bull Rider in 1973, admitted that he got pretty full of himself during the early days of his rodeo career. He remembered that in 1971 he grew his hair longer, like Mahan, colored his hair blond, and wore a goatee. He just *knew* everyone was aware of him. Bobby Steiner received a letter from his dad, Tommy Steiner, and the letter said, "You aren't nearly as great as you think you are. Everyone is *not* looking at you, and your #@&% stinks just like everyone else's." Steiner admitted the letter was a shock, but it brought him back to reality, which he admitted he needed a good dose of.

Bull Riders of the '70s

MYRTIS DIGHTMAN

Myrtis Dightman was the first black cowboy to go to the National Finals Rodeo in Bull Riding. He was considered the

"Jackie Robinson of Rodeo," as he paved the way for other black cowboys to compete in professional rodeo and successfully win.

Dightman was born in Crockett, Texas, in 1936. When he was twenty-two years of age he became a rodeo clown, but eventually took up bronc riding, steer wrestling, and bull riding. Although racial discrimination had made some progress by that time, there was still much to be resolved on that issue. The black cowboy was not recognized as an equal in most rodeos.

Some rodeos that Dightman entered made him compete after the regular rodeo performance, because he was black. Once, in Alice, Texas, he rode bull after bull. The town was outraged that he had to ride after the rodeo performance and they did not get to see the "best" rider.

At a Little Rock, Arkansas, rodeo he got there late and the gatekeeper wouldn't let him into the grounds. The gateman did not believe, because he was black, that he was entered, and Dightman had no proof he had paid his entry fee. He heard the announcer call his name. Fortunately someone who recognized him came to the gate and insisted the gateman let Dightman in. They apologized to him for the inconvenience, and put his bull, which had already been turned out, back in the chutes. He rode, scored, and walked away with second place.

Jim Shoulders has said, "No one will ever know how good Myrtis Dightman really was as a bull rider and rodeo contestant because of the numerous times judges gave him a gooseegg, just because he was black, when he should have received a score."

At a Steiner-produced rodeo, Tommy Steiner asked the judge why he had scored Dightman with a zero. Steiner was sure Dightman should have received a score. The judge told Steiner, "That is a great bull and I am not about to let a Negro take this bull's reputation!" Steiner just looked at the judge and said, "You will never judge another rodeo for me."

Dightman and Freckles Brown, a top-flight bull rider, were good friends. Once Dightman asked Brown why he (Dightman) couldn't win the world championship in bull riding. Freckles Brown responded, "Myrtis, we're good friends

Jerome Robinson sliding off Del Hall's Number 105 at Sikeston, Missouri, 1981. The bull tied for Bull of the Year in 1981 and won it again in 1984.—Photo by Bern Gregory. Bern Gregory Collection, National Cowboy Hall of Fame.

and I want to be real honest with you. Number one, you just have to keep riding these bulls the way you are now. And number two, you have to turn white."

At the National Finals Rodeo, Dightman finished seventeenth in 1964, but Bernis Johnson, number eight, and Carl Nafzger, tenth, could not compete, so he and Dave Glover, in sixteenth place, went in their places. He qualified in 1966 and ended up the year in eighth place. He also qualified in 1967 and ended up in third place; in 1968 he was fourth; and he qualified for the NFR in 1969, 1970, and 1972.

Dightman was inducted into the National Cowboy Hall of Fame in 1997. Having been called "the invisible cowboy" by

The Mighty Sponsors and the '70s Era 151

a journalist in a November 1975 issue of *Real West* magazine, because of all the scores and honors he was *not* allowed to win, this NCHF honor will give this history-making, courageous front-runner the visibility he truly deserves.

DON GAY

Don Gay was raised in rodeo. His mother died shortly after he was born and Don and older brother Pete were raised by their dad, Neal Gay, with input from friends like Jim Shoulders and Harry Tompkins. At nine years of age Don Gay was telling veteran bull riders how various bulls bucked, and what they could expect when they attempted to ride those bulls.[90]

Don Gay riding Steiner's #11+ at Kansas City, Missouri, 1976. Gay has won more Bull Riding World Championships than any other cowboy—eight in all.—Photo by Bern Gregory. Courtesy of Imogene Veach Beals. Bern Gregory Collection, National Cowboy Hall of Fame.

The first annual Old-Timers Rodeo, January 1976, at Temple, Texas.
—Photographer unknown. Courtesy of Jack Long.

It was not a surprise that when he graduated from high school, in 1972, Gay immediately went on the rodeo road. He qualified for the National Finals that first year, and so did brother Pete. Don finished eighth in the world. It took him only two more years to win his first World Champion Bull Riding title, and then he followed it with seven more! He was champ in 1974, 1975, 1976, and 1978, then in 1979, 1980, 1981, and 1984. Gay qualified for the National Finals Rodeo thirteen times. Neal Gay is not a bit hesitant to tell anyone his son Don is the best bull rider ever. "He won eight bull riding titles, no one else has done it," he reported.

Gay says he worked harder at bull riding than some because he didn't have natural ability. If that was the case he didn't let it bother him. "My dad and Jim [Shoulders] taught me that when all else fails, don't let go. A 7-second ride doesn't pay a cent."[89]

After retiring from bull riding in 1986, Gay went into the field of sports commentating plus several other rodeo-related businesses. He always does a superb job in announcing, because he is willing to share his knowledge of bull riding, which is a tremendous plus for fans watching his broadcasts.

BOBBY STEINER

Bobby Steiner was another who grew up in the rodeo world. His parents, Tommy and Beverly Steiner, were rodeo

Bobby Steiner, World Champion Bull Rider in 1973, on unknown bull.—Photographer unknown. Courtesy of Bobby Steiner.

producers during his childhood. They were premier stock contractors and producers and put on as many as thirty-three rodeos each year. For four years the three Steiner boys went to school on the rodeo road. "I really enjoyed it," reported Bobby Steiner. "I remember being in Havana, Cuba, with my folks, putting on a rodeo when I was five. There was always something happening, and I was a hyper kid. I had to be doing something."

At five years old Steiner began riding calves. He rode steers at seven, then started competing at Junior Rodeos when he was eight. When he was eleven he rode his first young bull. He also excelled at baseball and football, but bull riding was his first love. At sixteen, after football season, Steiner looked around at school and said, "What am I doing here?" and left to follow the rodeo, leaving a note for his parents (who were elsewhere producing a rodeo).

In 1969 he won only $300 all year, but the following year he qualified for the National Finals. "I'll never forget the Grand Entry that year," reminisced Steiner. "We rode in with the Texas flag. I thought that was the greatest moment of my life! I had goosebumps, and tears in my eyes. It was great! I'll never forget it." Steiner finished eighth in the world and fifth in the average that year. In 1971 he finished third in the world. The barrel racer Joleen Hurst of Oklahoma, who would become Mrs. Bobby Steiner, also went to the National Finals and won third in the world, in her event, that same year. In 1972 Steiner did not qualify for the National Finals, but as he watched it on television at home he made a commitment to go for the championship the following year.

Bobby Steiner did win the world title at bull riding in 1973. He had just turned twenty-two years old, was married, and his first child was a little over a month old. He went into the Finals just $162 ahead of Donnie Gay. When it was over he was $1,210 ahead of Gay, and had won $28,099 for the year.

He announced his retirement from bull riding shortly after winning the championship and began taking over the reins of the stock contracting business from his dad, who was ready to slow down. He continued producing rodeos for the next eleven years. Steiner is now in charge of the family ranch at Bastrop, Texas, where they raise premier Black Brangus cattle. Although Bobby Steiner was a top-rate champion, he says it is more important to him to be remembered for being a good husband and dad.

DENNY FLYNN

The name Denny Flynn comes up often when bull riders talk about the best bull riders they ever saw. Denny Flynn was born in Paris, Arkansas, in 1951. The family lived on a farm. Older brother Mike and Denny participated in high school rodeos. Mike won the high school All-Around for Arkansas in 1967, and with the win came a saddle. That was all the motivation Denny needed to do the same. He won the Arkansas High School All-Around in 1969.

Flynn continued to compete in amateur rodeos for a time. He signed up for a Larry Mahan Bull Riding School to be held at the Steiner ranch near Austin. When Flynn arrived he was raring to ride but was dismayed when they ran in some little black bulls that didn't impress him one bit. One of the guys helping Mahan heard the Arkansas-native complaining and told the champion. In a short time they brought out an old National Finals bull that had been crippled, and told Flynn to get on him and see what he could do. "I'm sure they thought that would quiet me down," laughed Flynn. But much to their amazement Flynn rode him. Next came out an old longhorn bull, and Flynn rode him—even spurred him. As the school progressed over the four days, Mahan got to know Flynn. In fact, when the school was over and Mahan found out Flynn had a permit from RCA, he took him to a rodeo in Beaumont and entered him in the bull riding. Flynn won fourth. Mahan introduced him to Myrtis Dightman and everyone else whom Flynn had admired in the bull riding circle.

"I came home," Flynn relayed, "and told everyone how I had gotten to be friends with Mahan, and how he had taken me to Beaumont, entered me in the bull riding, and I won fourth, and introduced me to everyone he saw. All my friends listened. Then the next twenty bulls I rode I couldn't even make the whistle! Boy, did I get razzed."

"Awright Buford, quit showing off. You can have tougher stock next out." Cartoon by Boots Reynolds.

Flynn said riding bulls came naturally to him. "I could just feel it," said the former bull rider. "I never had much strength, but I did have balance, and just knew how to hold on with my legs and feet."

Once during his early rodeo years Flynn was at San

Denny Flynn on Steiner's "O" at St. Louis, Missouri, 1979. This was the first time the bull was ridden in PRCA.—Photo by Bern Gregory. Courtesy of Imogene Veach Beals. Bern Gregory Collection, National Cowboy Hall of Fame.

Angelo and was broke. He drew Mr. Bubbles, a Billy Minick bull that hadn't been ridden. He was determined he would *not* buck off. "I made a good ride on him," recalled Flynn, "but one of the judges, Barney Brahmer, marked me so low I didn't even place. Years later, when Barney and I got to be friends I reminded him of that time and told him that he *almost* convinced me to go home and forget bull riding."

But things got better for the Arkansas bull rider. He qualified for the National Finals from 1974 through 1982, and again in 1985. He never won a world championship but was first in the average at the National Finals in 1975, 1981, and 1982.

Although he rode Steiner's bull Red Lightning and scored 98 points in 1979, he thinks his best bull ride ever was made at Ada, Oklahoma, in 1977. "I rode a bull called 'O-Bar' that

Denny Flynn on Steiner's Number 11 "Red Lightning" at the tenth performance of the 1980 National Finals scores a 90. He finished second in the world.—Photo by Bern Gregory. Courtesy of Imogene Veach Beals. Bern Gregory Collection, National Cowboy Hall of Fame.

Del Hall had just bought from an amateur stock contractor. He had bucked off some of the best bull riders the week before but that is about all anyone knew about him," remembered Flynn. "That bull was so muscled up he looked like he had just gotten out of the Marines! He bucked just great and I had a good ride and scored 94 points."

When discussing his career Flynn says he was too conservative to win the World. "I just didn't go to as many rodeos as the other bull riders. I always admired Donny Gay's motivation because he'd make all the rodeos—and it paid off for him."

Today Flynn, his wife Lynn and two children live on a farm in Charleston, Arkansas, where he takes care of his cattle and rides a few horses. He and a friend own the rights to BullMania, and he has been putting on the U.S. Team Roping Championship for Arkansas for the last eight or nine years. He hasn't given up rodeo yet.

Famous Bulls of the '70s

RED LIGHTNING

Leon Coffee, longtime rodeo clown, said of Red Lightning, "He was the gentleman of bucking bulls. He'd let you do whatever you wanted to him, until you opened the gate, then he did his job."

Red Lightning, sometimes called Number 11, was owned by the Steiner Rodeo Company. Steiner bought him from Cecil Hill of Oak Hill, just outside of Austin. Denny Flynn drew him four times during his career. Flynn said, "He wasn't unrideable, and someone would ride him two or three times a year, but he was a rank bull. He was a good honest bull, would spin both ways. My first experience on him was in Saint Louis and he bucked me off! The second time I drew him was at the George Paul Memorial Bull Riding in Del Rio and I rode him and won it. The third time I rode him was at Palestine, Illinois. The judges were Butch Kirby and Joe Bonner, both bull riders. Red Lightning had a good day, and so did I—we scored 98

Steiner's Number 11 "Red Lightning" was Bull of the Year in 1978. In 1980 at St. Louis, Missouri, Butch Kirby rode him for a score of 91.—Photo by Bern Gregory. Bern Gregory Collection, National Cowboy Hall of Fame.

points. I always felt good about the score because the judges were bull riders.

"I quit riding bulls in March of 1986," told Flynn. "In 1987 I got a call from Palestine, Illinois, and they wanted me to come back and ride Red Lightning again because they were

Cody Snyder doesn't bite the dust in this photo, but falls in a quagmire of mud at Cheyenne Frontier Days in 1982.—Photo courtesy of Cheyenne Frontier Days, by Randall A. Wagner.

going to retire him after that ride. I hadn't been on a bull in eighteen months, but they offered me a good amount of money to come so I decided to go. He still bucked real good and I had to hustle to stay with him. Someone said I probably could have won the rodeo on that ride, if it hadn't been an exhibition."

And with that last hurrah, Red Lightning and Denny Flynn went out to pasture.

V61

V61 was bought by Rudy Vela, a Rio Grande Valley rancher from Edinburg, Texas, for twenty-two cents a pound in 1965. He was unregistered and unacceptable for breeding, and he tested higher at bucking than he would for baloney. Vela sold him to the Harry Knight Rodeo Company.

V61 was a gray Brahma with upturned horns, weighing in at 1,800 pounds. He was bucked 956 times and only ridden five times. Billy Minick owned him during most of his bucking career, and admitted, "I had a lot of good horses and bulls in my rodeo company, but everywhere I went, they promoted V61. He was the best thing going for me."[36]

On June 9, 1971, at Gladewater, Texas, John Quintana of Creswell, Oregon, drew the gray menace. He had studied the bucking history of this unridden bull and prepared himself and his gear with all the attention he could. V61 had a reputation for anticipating the opening of the gate, and would burst out with tremendous force. This time was no exception, and the gateman had to steady himself against the gate's force, as the bull charged into the arena. V61 gave the ride his best, twisting and turning, changing directions, but Quintana held on.

The 5,000-plus crowd knew this four-legged athlete had not been ridden, and as the seconds ticked by they realized they were witnessing something special. Because of the crowd noise Quintana did not hear the whistle, but when he finally left the bull he landed in a crouch. George Doak, bullfighter, was prepared to protect the rider, but the bull trotted to the gate and left the arena; he knew his job was done.

Judges Dickie Cox and Ed Galemba scored Quintana 94 points, the highest recorded score in bucking stock history at that time. Cox, a former bull rider, had drawn V61 in the sixth go-round of the 1970 National Finals and had smashed his face against the bull's skull, causing Cox to spend nine days in the Oklahoma City hospital getting his face repaired.[26]

V61 was credited with allowing only five riders to complete eight-second rides in his career. Minick retired him during the Fort Worth Stock Show in 1974. Quintana lives in Australia today and raises cattle.[36]

OSCAR

Oscar was born on the Bob Barmby ranch near Sacramento, California. Barmby was an early-day stock contractor who produced his first rodeo in 1922. He sold his stock contract business in 1958 but continued to breed and raise stock, primarily bulls. Oscar was a result of his carefully cross-bred and interbreeding program.

Barmby sold Oscar to Bob Cook, owner of Rodeo Stock Contractors, Inc. (RSC), and in his first five years as a bucking bull Oscar came out of the chutes over 100 times and was never ridden.

Oscar was a small bull, weighing about 1,350 pounds. His bucking style was a violent spin to the left. He went to the National Finals Rodeo for RSC seven years, 1972 through 1978. He dumped his riders eight times, and was ridden three times, all receiving scores in the 80s.

Don Gay rode Oscar at the Grand National Rodeo, San Francisco, in 1977 for a world record 97 points. In 1978 Allan Jordan scored 96 on Oscar. Oscar retired at the Pro-Rodeo Hall of Fame, where he resided until his death in 1983.

John Growney bought Rodeo Stock Contractors, Inc., in 1979, and developed Growney Brothers Rodeo Company. John Growney and Don Kish got the bloodlines in their stock of Oscar, which included his son, Fonzie. Growney's combination of breeding with Oscar and Red Rock resulted in numerous top buckers.[36, 23, 29]

9
THE FEMININE TOUCH

From the beginning of rodeo, where cowboys gathered there have always been cowgirls. Cowgirls involved in rodeo haven't equaled the cowboy in numbers but were as tough as the boots they wore—and had to be. Although cowgirls participated in Wild West shows and rodeo since the 1880s, there were very few steer or bull riders among them.

The gals who chose rodeo in the first part of the twentieth century were generally running away from home or performing their rodeo talents without the knowledge of their families. Rodeo was not a choice parents would have made for their daughters. But not all women wanted the femininity, frilly clothes, corseted figure, and shy demeanor expected of women of the era. Some girls were "tomboys," and chose to be more rough and tumble in their nature and attitude. Yet many kept their femininity in tact, despite the Wild West or rodeo lifestyle. It was possible to ride and rope and maintain their femininity, as indicated by many photographs of early-day cowgirls. Those who were determined to rodeo said in later life they wouldn't have changed their rodeo years in any way.

Vera McGinnis joined Doc Pardee's Wild West show in Tulsa, Oklahoma, in 1914. McGinnis was an early-day bronc and trick rider. Doc had a bull named Napoleon, and without notice Doc swooped McGinnis up and placed her on the bull's broad back. The snubbers stepped away from the bull's head and the exhibition began!

McGinnis recalled, "The animal was so wide I felt as if I

What a stylish group! Early-day cowgirls show off their finery, from jodphers to woolly chaps. Left to right: Fox Hastings, Dona Cowan, Marie Gibson, Florence Hughes, Tad Lucas, Grace Runyan, Ruth Roach, Rose Smith, Bonnie McCarroll, Vera McGinnis, and Mabel Strickland.
—Photographer unknown. Courtesy of Jack Long.

were straddling the dining room table, and to top everything else, his hide was loose, and I rolled around like butter on a hot plate. Once free from the handlers, the bull snorted and tossed his huge head in the air, throwing slobbers in my face. Then he began doing his stuff. It reminded me of hopscotch. Two feet here and two feet there, hitting the ground, with almost a ton of belligerence at every bounce."[10]

Tad Barnes Lucas rode a calf on the main street of Gordon, Nebraska, in 1917. The hat was passed to the spectators and the monies collected were given to charity. A few years later she entered the steer riding at Gordon, and won all the money. At Miami, Oklahoma, in 1921 Barnes came to ride steers. She was not well known at the time, but it was evident to the spectators she was an excellent rider. She was bitten badly by the rodeo bug and began entering steer riding contests and horse races at all the fairs near her home in Nebraska. She moved to Fort Worth with her brother and entered small rodeos to improve her riding skills until she felt

Tad Lucas, a cowgirl who was best known for her trick riding abilities, but could also ride broncs and steers. She won the Metro-Goldwyn-Mayer trophy, which is now housed at the National Cowboy Hall of Fame, Oklahoma City.
—Photographer unknown. Courtesy of Jack Long.

she was qualified to enter the larger, more competitive rodeos. In 1922 she became a professional cowgirl, best known for her outstanding trick riding skills, but was able to ride broncs, steers, or do whatever she was asked to do in the rodeo arena. In 1923 at Fort Worth she rode Brahma stags, which she remembered as having lots of buck and showing plenty of fight.[66] Tad Lucas was a multi-talented cowgirl who spent more than forty years in the rodeo arena.

Vera McGinnis was a very capable cowgirl in the early days. By 1924 she was riding bucking steers at a rodeo in Dublin, Ireland. "I'd had my fill of bucking horses," she said after getting hurt so seriously it required a hospital stay.[10]

Nan Gable wanted to try steer riding at Cape Girardeau, New Jersey, in 1921. The steers were Brahmas and plenty tough. But Nan had lots of nerve and was game. She did attempt it, but only stayed three jumps before being thrown violently and getting badly bruised.

Mabel Strickland at San Antonio in 1923 tying her steer. Mabel was a versatile cowgirl who could do it all. She began her rodeo career in 1914.—Photographer unknown. Courtesy of Jack Long.

Mabel DeLong Strickland began her rodeo career in 1913, at age sixteen. Neighbor and friend of the family George Drumheller encouraged her, but Mabel's dad insisted a chaperone be hired to accompany her on the rodeo road. She was a versatile cowgirl and competed in roping, trick riding, bronc riding, steer riding, and relay and Roman racing. Her first roughstock ride was on a steer at Tucumcari, New Mexico, in 1918. She continued to ride steers, capturing first place in steer riding at St. Petersburg, Florida, in 1925.

Strickland was the first woman inducted into the Pendleton RoundUp Hall of Fame, and was also inducted into the National Cowboy Hall of Fame, ProRodeo Hall of Fame, and the National Cowgirl Hall of Fame. She died in 1976, at the age of seventy-nine.[81]

In Australia, in the world of roughriders and rodeos, women competitors or those who rode exhibition were always crowd-pleasers. In the recently published book *Australian Cowboys, Roughriders and Rodeos,* by Jenny Hicks, she writes, "From the beginning there were women roughriders." She names several women who rode bullocks (young steers) in the early days. "Miss Kemp was adopted into the circus community before riding bullocks and horses in all the buckjumping shows from around 1905 on and off to the mid-1920s. Ettie Edwards was roughriding and trick riding in the tent shows pre-World War I, and Violet Skuthorpe rode bucking bullocks in her husband's show from 1911. No one stole the show like a woman on a buckjumper or a bullock, especially in the practically womanless west (of Australia)."[92]

At Pendleton RoundUp in 1930 something new was attempted: cowgirls riding zebus. The animal was similar to a Brahma, but it proved awkward in the arena and was not tried again.[6]

In the thirties two sisters named Brander came from southwest Montana to Butte to ride at a rodeo where Leo Cremer furnished the stock. On a $25 bet from Cremer the girls both rode his big black steer "Texaco," together. After the whistle blew, Cremer's pickup man, Doug O'Donnell, picked both women up at once.[9]

Some of the best cowgirls rode bulls. Margie Greenough remembered, "I never had any fear of broncs, but I tried to ride bulls for awhile, and I

Marge and Alice Greenough came from a rodeo family and could ride broncs and bulls with the best. Photo taken at Madison Square Garden, 1943, by R. R. Doubleday.
—Courtesy of Jack Long, R. R. Doubleday Collection, National Cowboy Hall of Fame.

know what fear feels like. We had to ride Brahmas in six weeks of contests down south. My heart would just be thumpin' 'til I'd finish and climb up on the chute, and then I'd forget about it. I'm scared to death of those things!"[9] Marge's sister, Alice, also rode broncs and bulls. She worked one season in Spain's largest bull rings. "Every bull I rode the matadors killed," she reported.[9]

Dorothy Gaskill was born and reared on a ranch near Shannon, Texas. At fifteen she won a wager by riding a ranch steer. That incident inspired her to ride steers at a number of rodeos. She also had learned to trick ride, spending much time with experienced trick rider Marion Green of Casa Grande, Arizona.

At the Phoenix rodeo in February 1940, Gaskill made an exhibition ride on a wild Brahma bull. After the whistle blew the bull threw his head back just as she was jerked forward. One horn stuck her with full force on the side of the head, and she was knocked unconscious. She died a few hours later without regaining consciousness. Such tragedy comes to the rodeo arena occasionally, without warning.[22]

Dixie Lee Reger was born to a rodeo family and at age one began touring with the family. They had a trained longhorn named Bobby Twister. At age five she made her trick riding debut on a Shetland pony and began learning to trick rope from Junior Eskew. In 1940 her dad, Monty Reger, organized a Wild West show, as well as announcing rodeos where his children Dixie, Buddy, and Virginia trick roped, trick rode, and jumped automobiles. Reger became the first juvenile professional rodeo clown at Fay Kirkwood's Wichita Falls all-girl rodeo in 1941. She continued her rodeo clowning and bullfighting through the Girls Rodeo Association until 1953. She was the only woman to spend that long a period as a professional rodeo clown and bullfighter.(17)

Not only did Reger save cowgirls from the bulls, in her bullfighting chores she also entered many events in the rodeo as well. An October 5, 1948, rodeo program from an early girls' rodeo in Amarillo listed Dixie Lee Reger competing in Calf Roping, Bareback Bronc Riding, Cowgirls Sponsor Contest, Ribbon Roping Contest, Cutting Contest, and Brahma

Dixie Reger, in her rodeo clown costume, hangs on to a bull at Amarillo, 1948. Vivian White, 1985 honoree in the National Cowgirl Hall of Fame, standing behind the bull, judging the ride, at an all-girl rodeo.—Photographer unknown. Courtesy of Dixie Reger Mosley.

Bull Riding Contest. She and Jackie Worthington decided to enter every competition for that rodeo. Each "morning after" they would compare notes on how many aches and pains they had incurred.

Reger drew two bulls at Amarillo. When riding the first one she hit her lip, which caused it to turn blue in cold weather for years after. On the second bull her spur hung in the rope. At that point in her career she decided, "there has got to be a better way to make a living than trying to ride bulls!" So she chose to continue to bullfight and rodeo clown until 1953. She remembers one RCA rodeo, at Mead, Kansas, where she was a bullfighter and clown. When she married Bill Mosley she retired from rodeo.

Jeanette "Jackie" Worthington, only 4'8 tall and less than 100 pounds, won the Girls Rodeo Association All-Around World Champion title six times, Bareback Bronc World Cham-

Tiny Jackie Worthington (4'8), many times All-Around Champion of the Girls Rodeo Association, rides a bronc. She was one of the original group to form the Girls Rodeo Association.
—Photographer unknown. Courtesy of *Hoofs & Horns*.

pion title three times, Bull Riding Champion titles seven times, six Cutting Horse World Championships, and one Ribbon Roping world title.

On February 28, 1948, Jackie Worthington and thirty-seven women met at the San Angelus Hotel in San Angelo, Texas, and formed the Girls Rodeo Association. The original organization has developed into the Professional Women's Rodeo Association and the Women's Professional Rodeo Association. The original board of directors included Dixie Reger, Jackie Worthington, Blanche Altizer, and Vivian White.[17]

After her rodeo career, Worthington, one of three daughters, stayed on the family ranch, West Fork Ranch, at Jacksboro, Texas, and continued to run it until her death, September 26, 1987, at the age of sixty-three. At one time, when her dad could not get help on the ranch, Jackie rounded up her cowgirl friends to do the ranch work. This worked so well, she continued to use women for some time.[79]

The Girls Rodeo Association formed rules by which members would comply. The criteria of the organization was to allow women to compete in all-girl rodeo events, and in RCA-sanctioned rodeos. It was the first time in rodeo women had been so driven. The organization has continued through the years, but the purse money to be won at all-girl rodeos does not come close to the amounts their male counterparts have been able to provide.

Jonnie Jonckowski was an athlete in high school and was ready to head to the state level in track and field events when she was determined ineligible. In 1976 she qualified for the Pentathlon at the U.S. Olympic Trials. While practicing the hurdles she fell and hurt her back, and her replacement went in her place. Twice her dream of winning had been dashed, but she still had the desire.

She saw an advertisement for an all-girl rodeo at Red Lodge, Montana, just a short distance from her home in Billings. She decided to enter and tried the roughstock. She chose bull riding as her event.

Jonckowski attended a bronc and bull riding school put on by Bruce Ford and Bobby Berger in 1977. There were 106 students at the school, all men except for Jonckowski. When the school was over only thirty students finished, but she was one of the finishers. The last bull she rode kicked her in the face, requiring 160 stitches and plastic surgery.

She won the PWRA World Championship Bull Riding in 1986. Again she almost lost her opportunity, when the first bull she rode, at the finals, kicked her in the calf after the ride was over. Her leg began to swell immediately and doctors recommended that she not attempt more bull riding because a clot could cause a heart attack and life-threatening damage. She ignored the doctor's diagnosis and had four friends help her onto her bull the following night. She rode the required six seconds and secured the title. She repeated her win again in 1988.[74]

Jonckowski also competed against men in bull riding. In 1989 she lured major television networks to Cheyenne Frontier Days by telling them a woman was going to make rodeo history by riding in the bull riding event. The television program, *48 Hours,* won an Emmy for their coverage. Also in 1992 she was one of 160 bull riders to compete at the Justin World Bull Riding Championships in Scottsdale, Arizona. She

In 1919 cowgirls gather for a photo shoot. Note that skirts seemed to be the preferred dress in that era. Left to right: Fox Hastings, sitting is Rose Smith, Prairie Lilly Allen, Bonnie McCarroll, Ollie Osborn, sitting is Ruth Roach, and Bertha Kaepernik Blancett. Taken at Weiser, Idaho.—Photo by R. R. Doubleday. Courtesy of Jack Long. R. R. Doubleday Collection, National Cowboy Hall of Fame.

was the only woman competing along with Tuff Hedeman, Ty Murray, and other champions.[77]

Jonckowski said, "What I learned about success in my quest for gold is this: Success comes to those who are willing to risk more than other people feel is safe. I guess I did that, and I'm a winner."[78]

Polly Reich began riding bulls, after being trained by International Professional Rodeo Association world champion bull rider Larry Mosley. Reich was the only female bull rider in the IPRA in 1994.

Tammy Kelly, of Queen Creek, Arizona, won three PWRA bull riding championships in the 1990s. She admits to being a daredevil and thrill seeker and says you can't replace the thrill of riding a bull.[63] She has incurred various injuries including one in 1997 when a bull stepped on her calf and peeled the muscle off the bone. Eight days later, after two reconstructive surgeries, she was again riding a bull for the six seconds PWRA requires to qualify for a successful bull ride. "You can only be a bull rider if you have a high pain threshold," Kelly confirms. "You wouldn't last out there if you couldn't take some pain and keep going."[62]

Sue Pirtle was a 1981 inductee into the National Cowgirl Hall of Fame and was called the most versatile cowgirl in the history of the Girls Rodeo Association (now WPRA). She won eleven championships in twelve years of competition including the World Champion Bull Rider in 1977 and All Around in 1974 and 1976, and six World Champion Bareback Bronc Riding titles. She competed in all seven events.

In 1980 Pirtle was a technical advisor on a television film inspired by her rodeo competition on the women's rodeo circuit. The film starred Katherine Ross and was called *Rodeo Girl*. She also served as rodeo director for three terms with the Women's Professional Rodeo Association.[74]

In discussing with a reporter in 1980 the differences between the PRCA and the WPRA, she said, "We have 20 rodeos a year; the men have 600. We don't compete against the men and don't want to. There are physical limitations. We have smaller stock, but we have good rodeos. But the men make more money. We want to get $1,000 an event at each of our

Eight-year-old working ranch cowgirl, Jordan Muncy, keeps the tradition alive on her family's Ox Bar ranch in Torrance County, New Mexico.—Photo by © Gene Peach.

rodeos. The men make $2,000 to $3,000 and we make $200 to $300."[75]

Why do the women do it? It certainly isn't the money, but in that regard both men and women have one thing in common: it is the thrill of riding that beast which outweighs them twenty-fold.

Jan Youren competed in women's rodeo for four decades, riding broncs and bulls. She planned to quit riding when she reached age fifty, but it came too soon (1994), said the mother of eight and grandmother of many. Youren, from Bruneau, Idaho, reported, "I've had a collapsed lung, bruised heart, broken back. I've only got one rib that hasn't been broken. I've broken my nose eleven times, and have eight different breaks in my cheekbones. I've broken my arms and my legs, too."[63]

Youren still rides roughstock with two World Champion

Bareback Riding titles to her credit. She has given up riding bulls, but rode them for over thirty-one years. "It got to where they were on top of me more than I was on top of them," said the determined competitor. Three of her daughters have also gone on to compete in women's rodeo. The oldest, Tanya Tucker Stevenson, won the world champion title in bull riding twice and the bareback riding title four times.

Youren was born October 2, 1943, in the Payette Valley of Idaho. Her dad, Sterling B. Alley, farmed, ran a hunting pack string, and produced rodeos. Her toughness came from him, reports her daughter. He taught his family to give their best in everything—work and play. A firm believer in "getting up and out of the arena—there'd be plenty of time to die behind the chutes' attitude." Youren admits her dad is her best inspiration.[76]

These women are some of the women who have challenged 2,000 pounds of mean, cantankerous bull, and won, either with a championship to their credit or maybe just the satisfaction of knowing they could do it. The desire for the adrenaline rush and the lure of the challenge is not limited to the male of the species. The female is just as determined. She just can't rely on making a living only by wins on the women's rodeo circuit.

Most of the cowgirls who rode bulls will go nameless, and most didn't stay with it very long. But there has always been that exception, the one who has a passion for the challenge, and is determined to make it happen.

10

Doctor! Doctor!

Even as late as the 1970s, rodeo had no medical support. Although it is one of the roughest sports, and no other sport causes more injury, there was no medical aspect of the rodeo program, except for an EMS ambulance and attendants, or First Aid Room on the rodeo grounds, or an occasional doctor sitting in the grandstand as a fan.

Walt Garrison, a Dallas Cowboy football player, approached Dr. J. Pat Evans, the sports medicine doctor who treated Dallas football players. His request was that Dr. Evans see what he could do to help rodeo cowboys with their injuries. Garrison was a fan of rodeo and sponsored some events in the Dallas area.

Dr. Evans, who as a young man had done a little bareback bronc riding while working on a ranch in Colorado, also had an interest in rodeo. After observing for a time, Dr. Evans and Don Andrews, also a knowledgeable sports medicine guru, got together and formed a workable program. Previously rodeo cowboys had no professional medical personnel to help them determine how to treat an injury or what to do to keep physically fit and keep their career in rodeo going. Donnie Gay and John Davis were the first two cowboys Dr. Evans treated. Both had groin injuries.

After talking with Garrison and Donnie Gay about a workable medical program in rodeo, Dr. Evans went to the PRCA Board of Directors. Everyone was in favor of the program. Early in 1980, John Justin of Justin Boots heard about the program and volunteered to sponsor it at the National Finals Rodeo in 1980.

Jack Long, cowboy & rodeo historian, and Walt Garrison, who requested that Dr. J. Pat Evans, sports medicine doctor for the Dallas Cowboys football team, consider treating cowboys for injuries. Through this effort the Justin Heeler Program was begun.
—Photographer unknown. Courtesy of Jack Long.

At the beginning of the Finals there was very little activity in the Justin Heeler room, Dr. Evans recalled. When needed Donnie Gay brought various contestants who had incurred injuries to the Justin Heeler room. The toughest job, said Evans, was convincing the cowboys they were not going to be compromising their ability of being "tough cowboys" by getting help from the medical men. Plus, the cowboys didn't know Dr. Evans and Don Andrews. By the end of the week, however, the medical facility had become a very busy place.

The humor and ability of a cowboy to razz his peers will never be replaced. Jim Shoulders said, "Whenever I go to see Dr. Evans, I always ask 'Who's in the SISSY room?'" He also

Doctor! Doctor! 179

gives the doctors a hard time by kidding, "This is the damnedest clown room I ever saw. I'll bet you don't even have any whiskey!" The clown room was always a place a cowboy could expect to find a drink, if he was so inclined, back "in the good old days."

At first the Justin Heeler Program was outfitted with all kinds of medical machinery to treat injury. There were whirlpool baths, a defibrillator, and much more. But after treating injuries for some time it was realized that some of the equipment didn't get used enough to merit having it there. The medical supplies were honed down to what was important for most rodeo injuries.

In time the respect for Dr. Evans and his team came from the cowboys, and their credibility spread with each rodeo. Ricky Bolen, bull rider, was injured when a bull stepped on his foot, which moved all his toes over one position. Bolen was having a good year and could not afford to be out of competition. He came to Dr. J. Pat Evans for medical treatment. The doctor put some pins in his toes, to put them back in place. Fiberglass was just beginning to be

Gail Gandolfi illustration.

used in medical casts, and the doctor put a fiberglass cast on Bolen, allowing the pins to stick out in front of his toes. They took a spur, bent it, and attached it to the cast. Bolen continued to be in the business of bull riding despite the cast, and did qualify for the National Finals that year.

Sandy Kirby, a bull rider who won the average at the 1974 National Finals Rodeo, said he thought he was a "sample case" for Dr. Evans to learn how to treat cowboys. He was treated the first time by Dr. Evans in 1978, and again in 1980. At an Albuquerque, New Mexico, rodeo Kirby accidentally had a bull rope wrap around his leg during the bull ride, and he incurred a broken thigh bone. He was taken to a hospital in Albuquerque, all the while requesting they get him back to Dallas to Dr. Evans. Kirby said, "I know they put a pin in my leg WITHOUT deadening it! Then they put weights on my leg, which pulled me down to the bottom of the bed. I couldn't get to a call button to ring for a nurse or the telephone to call for help. I was suffering! I finally got a big old guy, a nurse, to bring me some ice to put on it." Friends of Kirby took up a collection, chartered a private plane, and got him back to Dallas and to Dr. Evans. They gave him a bottle of pain pills when he left the hospital in Albuquerque and he didn't hesitate to use them. When he woke up, he was looking at Dr. Evans.

Dr. Evans had to put a rod in Kirby's leg. About two months later, Kirby was healing well. He was in his corral working with some bulls, when one kicked him in his other leg, spun him around, and re-broke the leg. Dr. Evans advised, "Sandy, I think you'd better stay away from those bulls."

The *ProRodeo Sports News* printed a series of articles in the 1980s about preventative methods to keep from having muscle pulls, neck and back problems, and other medical problems that seem to haunt cowboys. Evans said they found that although this was good information that could help a cowboy prevent some common medical problems, the cowboys did not read the articles. By the time they had a need for particular advice, the *Sports News* had disappeared, and they didn't know what to do. Eventually, Dr. Evans and his Justin Sports Medicine crew had a printout on hand for each specific injury

Beutler & Sons Number 40 bull crushing Sandy Kirby at the National Finals Rodeo at Oklahoma City, 1975. Sandy Kirby said Dr. J. Pat Evans kept him competing, in spite of his injuries.
—Photo by Bern Gregory, Bern Gregory Collection, National Cowboy Hall of Fame.

and how to treat it, and these were given to cowboys when they were treated for that particular problem. This idea worked more successfully.

By the end of the 1970s, the bullfighter had been noticed, by more than just the bull rider. The rider knew he would have been in a dilemma if the courageous, funny-faced, silly-dressed clown hadn't been in front of the one-ton raging bull to distract him long enough to get to safety. The audience had found they enjoyed watching the bullfighters taunt the bulls and use their expertise to confuse and irritate the animal to the delight of the crowd. Their clever footwork and daring movements opened up a new event called the "Wrangler Bullfights." The first ever held was in Rapid City, South Dakota, and bull-

Beaver Jernigan stays aboard this speckled-face bucker, while bullfighters Bob Romer and Rick Chatman prepare to assist when necessary. Barrelman Quail Dobbs is seen behind the bull.—Photo by Randall A. Wagner, courtesy of Cheyenne Frontier Days.

baiters Miles Hare, Wick Peth, Larry Clayman, Kelly LaCoste, Bob Donaldson, and Skipper Voss fought the bulls.

In 1981 the Wrangler Jeans Bullfight Tour was started. By 1987 the event offered $420,000 in prize money, and thirty-two events were held throughout the year at various rodeos. This venue was also an opportunity for bulls of the fighting variety to become known and have a place in rodeo. Not all bulls had the ability to buck and become the athlete that would challenge a good bull rider, but they had the disposition and the desire to challenge a bullfighter in the arena. Some bulls used were Mexican fighting bulls, some cross-breds, and some pure Brahma. "Bulls are like fighters," said Rob Smets, well-known bullfighter, "the more they fight the smarter they get."[88] It makes for quite a crowd-pleasing show!

In 1987 the Dodge National Circuit Finals Rodeo (DNCFR) was created. It takes two cowboys from each of the twelve circuits in the United States, for all seven events. One competitor is the season circuit champion; the other is the winner of the circuit finals. The DNCFR is operated on a tournament-style system, with competition in two preliminary rounds for all 168 competitors. The top eight in each event compete in a semi-final round. At the completion of the semi-finals the top four contestants in each event move on to the final round, known as the Wrangler Round, where national titles are decided.[82]

This competition is held in March following the end of the season, at Pocatello, Idaho, since several of the circuit finals are not held until after the first of the year. In March of 2000 the prize money for the 1999 DNCFR was approximately $425,000.

Jeff Crockett of Twin Falls, Idaho, died of massive head injuries and a skull fracture August 28, 1988, after being thrown from a bull at the Yerington, Nevada, Lyon County Fair Rodeo. The bull kicked him in the head then stepped on him.

Don Andrews, one of the Justin Heeler originators, did a study on the cowboy's pain tolerance. Previously, Andrews and his peers had been amazed at the ability a cowboy had to endure physical pain. In spite of significant injuries a cowboy would find a way to continue competing, and there was no question that the pain was there.

The test for pain tolerance included placing a cowboy's hand in a bucket of ice water, for as long as three minutes. He rated their tolerance from 1 to 10, with 10 being most painful. He would ask them every 10 seconds to rate their feeling. A cowboy would report a "1" or "0" or "1." Athletes from other sports were tested as well, with hockey players coming closer to a cowboy's tolerance than any other athlete. But cowboys were off the scale!

Dr. Evans remembered when Tuff Hedeman got hung up on Harry Vold's Copenhagen Stinger at the National Finals

184   COWBOY UP!

Tuff Hedeman, PRCA World Champion Bull Rider in 1986, 1989, and 1991, masters a bull at Cheyenne Frontier Days, 1988.—Photo by Randall A. Wagner, courtesy of Cheyenne Frontier Days.

Rodeo, December 6, 1990. It took Rob Smets and Miles Hare, the bullfighters, plus every other cowboy within twenty feet of the chutes to finally subdue the bull to get Hedeman's securely placed hand out of the bull rope. "Of course this was after he had been drug around the arena, stepped on, hit, kicked, you name it," said Evans. "When he got to the training room I asked him, 'Tuff, what is the worst part of the ordeal?' Tuff answered, 'Doc, I'm just tired!'"

Evans said he should have had shoulder dislocations, elbow breaks, and injuries too numerous to mention, but the sports medicine team packed him in a whirlpool bath in ice, and he stayed there for 30 MINUTES. "It was incredible that he could endure that cold for so long," said Evans, "but the next day he was not nearly as sore as he would have been had he not endured the ice pack."

What is the reason cowboys can tolerate and endure pain, more than other athletes can? That reason has not been determined. The professionals are not sure if it is cultural, physiological, or something else.

Of course, there are incidents when a cowboy's judgment isn't sound. Dr. Evans had treated a cowboy with a broken collarbone. About three weeks after the injury the cowboy felt he was healing nicely. He came back to see the doctor. "Doctor Pat, I want to ride," he reported. The good doctor took his finger and squeezed the collarbone, and the cowboy turned pale from the pain. That little gesture by the doctor proved to the cowboy just how much more healing had to be done before he would actually be ready to compete. The cowboy's next statement was, "I'm not competing yet, but you had better give me a doctor's release for this next rodeo."

Bull Riders of the '80s and '90s

TUFF HEDEMAN

Richard Neale Hedeman was born March 2, 1963, in El Paso, Texas, the youngest of seven children to Clarice and Red Hedeman. Between his grandparents' ranch in northeastern New Mexico and race tracks at El Paso and Raton, where his dad worked, Hedeman enjoyed his childhood.

One day at the track his hand accidentally got caught in the door of Tater Decker's truck when it was slammed shut. When Hedeman didn't utter a sound, Decker, a well-known rodeo cowboy of the time, said, "You're a tough nut, aren't you?" The "tough" became "Tuff" and the determined youngster proved, time after time, he could live up to his name.

Hedeman lost the 1981 National High School Rodeo Association bull riding championship to Lane Frost, as well as the 1982 American Junior Rodeo Association bull riding.

Tuff Hedeman winning the bull riding at Cheyenne Frontier Days, 1995.
—Photo by and courtesy of Dan Hubbell.

Hedeman came in second. While attending Sul Ross State University in 1983, he won the bull riding title at the College National Finals on a bull that had not been ridden at the professional level, the National Finals Rodeo. He got his PRCA permit that year.

Hedeman, Lane Frost, Cody Lambert, and Jim Sharp traveled the PRCA "rodeo road" together, and one of the four won the bull riding championship from 1986 through 1991. Hedeman won it in 1986, 1989 and 1991, and came in first in the National Finals average in 1987 and tied with Sharp for 1989.

Although every bull rider gets hurt to some degree, two major injuries happened to "Tuff" that are well known in rodeo. In the eighth round of the 1993 National Finals Rodeo

Hedeman took a terrific and forceful fall from Western Rodeo Inc.'s bull Dodge Magnum Power. He could not move. For more than ten minutes he was completely paralyzed and was carried by stretcher from the arena. A few days later he had surgery at Las Vegas. A herniated disk was removed from his neck, and a bone from his hip was grafted in place of the disk. Although doctors advised him to never ride again, Tuff said he'd probably be out of action six to eight months.

On October 15, 1995, at the Professional Bull Riders Finals in Las Vegas, Hedeman drew one of Sammy Andrews' notorious bulls, Dodge Bodacious, an animal known for his ability to buck a rider's face into his skull and cause terrible injury. He accomplished the deed on Hedeman, who suffered two fractures in his upper jaw, had a fractured left cheekbone, and required reconstructive surgery that lasted almost eight hours.

Two months later, at the seventh round of the PRCA National Finals, Hedeman drew Bodacious again. Every fan in Thomas & Mack Stadium held their breath as Hedeman prepared to mount the beast. To be eligible to continue in the Finals and ride his next bull, he threw his leg over the bull, but he never left the chute. The judgment call brought the audience to its feet, and Hedeman enjoyed the standing ovation. Choosing not to ride Bodacious was not an easy decision for Hedeman, never one to walk away from a challenge. Considering the future and what was best for him, his wife and two boys, the decision was made. It was not easy for the "Tuff" competitor.

When asked if he had ever made any bad decisions in his career, Hedeman was quick to say, "I have no regrets. I don't listen, or do I worry about what other people think. I know I gave it all I had while I rode bulls. I never wanted to be someone who said, 'I wish I had done something different.' And I don't believe I am."

Today Hedeman is president of the Professional Bull Riders and a very active participant in all phases of the organization, *except* riding bulls. "I was able to turn a passion into a career," said the former champion, "and I think through PBR we are able to bring the sport to another level. PBR isn't competing with rodeo. I love rodeo and still team rope as often as I can. But I do know competition makes everyone work harder."

When asked how he felt about his two boys, if they were to choose to ride bulls, his answer was, "The oldest one has not shown much interest. The five-year-old hasn't said. But like my folks, they allowed me to make up my own mind, then they supported me all the way. I'd probably do the same . . . but I hope they won't want to ride."

CHARLES SAMPSON

As a kid growing up in the Watts District of Los Angeles, Charles Sampson would have laughed had someone said he would be a bull riding champion. When as a cub scout, his troop visited a stable, he got hooked on horses and spent as

Charles Sampson, who grew up in the Watts District of Los Angeles, rides Vold's C85 at Tulsa, Oklahoma, 1982.—Photo by Bern Gregory. Courtesy of Imogene Veach Beals. Bern Gregory Collection, National Cowboy Hall of Fame.

much time around them as possible. He also learned to rope, and eventually (because he carries a small frame; 5'4, 130 pounds), he began to ride race horses.

As a jockey he traveled to Oklahoma and entered the bull riding in a local rodeo. The bug bit him, and he took out a PRCA permit while still in high school. He was awarded a rodeo scholarship to Central Arizona College. In 1978 he got his PRCA card.

Sampson went to his first National Finals Rodeo in 1981, only the second black cowboy to compete in the Finals (the first being Myrtis Dightman). In 1982 he became the World Champion Bull Rider, the first African-American to achieve this title. Other bull riding wins for Sampson included: the Turquoise Circuit champion in 1985-86 and 1993; Sierra

1982 World Champion Bull Rider Charles Sampson, taking his last competition ride, Pocatello, Idaho, 1994.
—Photo by and courtesy of Dan Hubbell.

Circuit winner, 1984. He was also the Calgary Stampede $50,000 bonus-round champ; two-time champion at Pendleton RoundUp, as well as Grand National Rodeo in San Francisco, and the California Rodeo in Salinas, just to name a few of his accomplishments.

In 1983 at Yakima, Washington, Sampson broke his leg for the fifth time. A bull stepped on it and broke it in five places. Seventeen pins and two plates were placed in his leg and he never did wear a cast. And to top it off, he went to the National Finals a few months later, in spite of doctors telling him to keep the leg elevated and relax. He won more than $20,000 during the Finals that year.

At a Presidential Rodeo held in Washington, D.C. in 1986 for President Ronald Reagan, Sampson shattered his face in a mishap with a Silver Spurs Rodeo bull called Kiss Me. Sampson's sinus cavities were crushed, and his forehead, cheekbones, eye sockets, and jawbone received multiple fractures,

Prior to the performance of a special Presidential Rodeo, held in Washington D.C. in 1986, President Ronald Reagan entertains his listeners. Left to right: Jim Shoulders, Malcolm Baldridge, and Casey Tibbs.—Photographer unknown. Courtesy of John Williams.

requiring a six-hour surgery. President Reagan called Sampson in the hospital, and when he was released Sampson went to visit the president. Sampson, being a spokesperson for the Timex watch, is a living example of their slogan "take a licking and keep on ticking."[36]

LANE FROST

During the short go at Cheyenne Frontier Days, July 30, 1989, bull rider Lane Frost drew Bad Company Rodeo's bull Takin' Care of Business. He was excited to ride him. Frost knew if he had a successful ride he could win. He did ride and scored 85 points, but he would never know the results.

As Frost dismounted, he fell to his knees and hands.

These photos were used on Lane Frost's headstone at his grave in Hugo, Oklahoma. Although Frost's rodeo career was cut short, this 1987 World Champion Bull Rider was one of the most popular cowboys of his day.—Action photo by Linda Rosser, headshot of Frost by Vern Howell. Courtesy of Elsie and Clyde Frost.

Lane Frost's last bull ride, on "Takin' Care of Business," owned by Bad Company Rodeo during the short go at Cheyenne Frontier Days, July 30, 1989. This photo, taken by Dan Hubbell, was the third jump. Little did anyone realize Frost would not live to hear his score of 85 points.

When he stood up, he happened to be in the path of the bull and was hit in the back with a horn, knocking him to the ground. The bull then ran over Frost.

It didn't look serious to the cowboys who witnessed the incident. They'd seen Frost in tougher scrapes. But he had at least two broken ribs, and one punctured a vital artery. He stood up, walked three steps, motioned for someone to help him, and collapsed. The twenty-five-year-old bull rider was dead before he left the arena.[70]

The next morning the Cheyenne Frontier Days committee chartered a plane to fly Frost's body home to his family in Oklahoma. Tuff Hedeman and Cody Lambert accompanied their friend home.

Born in La Junta, Colorado, on October 12, 1963, Lane Clyde Frost began watching bull ridings at five months of age, according to his mother. At age seven, he practiced riding calves on the family dairy. By fourteen he was said to "ride with rhythm." At the 1981 High School Rodeo Finals, Frost won the bull riding. He joined PRCA in 1982, soon after graduating from high school. In 1984 he went to the National Finals and won the World Champion Bull Riding title in 1987.

In 1988 John Growney and Don Kish's bull Red Rock was voted PRCA Bucking Bull of the Year. They pitted the bull against Champion Bull Rider Lane Frost and called it the Challenge of the Champions, which was a seven-ride match. Seven rodeos were picked throughout the West during that season to hold these matches. The first was held April 17 at Red Bluff, California, and Frost bucked off Red Rock. April 24 at Clovis, California, he bucked off the big red bull again. May 20 at Redding, California, Lane rode Red Rock, the first time the bull had been ridden in 311 attempts out of the chutes. June 10 at Livermore, California, and June 12 at Sisters, Oregon, Frost rode the famous bucker. July 4 at St. Paul, Oregon, Red Rock got revenge and bucked Frost off. The final ride at Spanish Fork, Utah, Frost came up the winner. Final score was 4 for Frost and 3 for Red Rock. It was truly champion pitted against champion.[36]

Frost was buried in Hugo, Oklahoma, next to his friend and bull riding mentor, Freckles Brown. Frost was recognized for his outstanding bull riding career: a movie, *Eight Seconds,* was made about his life; State of Oklahoma Representative Tommy Thomas made a motion that was passed to give an Oklahoma Citation to Lane Frost[71]; the governor of Oklahoma, Henry Bellmon, declared Thursday, July 16, 1990, as Lane Frost Memorial Day in Oklahoma[72]; and the Texas House of Representatives adopted House Resolution No. 118, praising Frost and his accomplishments on December 1, 1989.[73]

It has been over ten years since his death and Frost is still remembered by his many, many fans. He had a charismatic personality, always smiling, and never hesitated to stop and visit with people. When he died the rodeo world lost a true western hero from the rodeo arena, but not from the hearts of his many admirers.

Well-Known Bulls of the '80s and '90s

RED ROCK

Red Rock was born on the Burnt River Ranch in Burns, Oregon, and orphaned as a young calf. He was raised by a milk cow in a family backyard. This red brindle was purchased as a young bull by Mert Hunking, a non-sanctioned stock contractor from Sisters, Oregon. Don Kish drew Red Rock at a rodeo in Silver Lake, Oregon, and knew he was a special bull. Kish and partner John Growney purchased him in 1984.

Red Rock had spent four years in PRCA rodeo and had bucked off 309 riders when he was retired following the 1987 National Finals Rodeo. He was runner-up Bucking Bull of National Finals Rodeos in 1984, 1985 and 1986, and was picked PRCA Bucking Bull of the Year in 1987.

In 1988 the stock contractor, Growney, matched Red Rock to Lane Frost, World Champion Bull Rider, 1987. They had seven matches, and Frost rode four times and was bucked off three. Kish said, "Most bulls have a pattern of bucking but Red Rock does what it takes to get rid of his rider." He did, however, buck away from his rider's hand, whichever hand they used. Red Rock could vary his degree of bucking with the rider's ability. Bob Feist, announcer, said, "Normally after Red Rock bucks a guy off he makes a proud little lap around the arena with his head up in the air."

Lane Frost had much respect for this twelve-year-old bull and commented, "He is so smart. I know he'll switch things up. He can change things around just like I can—it'll come down to who can outsmart who."

Red Rock was a gentle bull to handle and wouldn't fight in the chute. He retired to John Growney's ranch in Red Bluff, California. Some of his descendants have turned out to be good buckers as well. Wolfman Skoal, a grandson, was ridden in 1991 by Wade Leslie for 100 points, the only perfect score in the history of bull riding.

Red Rock died June 8, 1994, of old age (eighteen years).

Pete Burns' black and white Mr. T Copenhagen, PRCA Bull of the Year in 1986 and NFR top bull in 1986 and 1989, dumps Butch Kuhn, Jr. He had dumped everyone when he came out of the chute up to that time. Cheyenne Frontier Days, 1989.—Photo by Randall A. Wagner, courtesy of Cheyenne Frontier Days.

MR. T COPENHAGEN

Mr. T Copenhagen, a black and white bull born in 1978, was raised on Bill Mundorf's ranch in eastern Nebraska, until he was sold to an amateur stock contractor. Sutton Rodeos, Inc. acquired him as a fighting bull, and then sold him to Hal Burns with six other bulls. Mr. T was the only bull that lasted the summer with the Burns outfit, out of Laramie, Wyoming.

It took Mr. T a few years to learn how to buck, but once he learned, there was no stopping him. In 1984 he began bucking well, and by 1985 he was great. He had approximately 180 buck offs before Marty Staneart rode him for 93

In the Cheyenne Frontier Days Finals, 1989, Marty Staneart made the first successful ride on Mr. T. "A packed house of over 17,000 fans gave them both an ovation like I have never heard at CFD as he scored an arena record in the 90s. Lane Frost came out of the chutes just one bull after this and was killed. Thus, the emotional high and low in my thirty plus years experience at CFD came within minutes of each other," stated photographer Randall A. Wagner.
—Photo by Wagner. Courtesy of Cheyenne Frontier Days.

points on July 30, 1989, at Cheyenne Frontier Days. It was a bull rider's dream—to draw the best bull on the last day of the rodeo. After the successful ride, Staneart tipped his hat to Mr. T, then to the wildly cheering crowd.[12] Ty Murray and Raymond Wessel also rode him before he retired.

Burns did not want Mr. T to retire in Wyoming because of the harsh winters, so John Growney, of Growney Bros. Rodeo Company, offered to let him spend his retirement years on his southern California ranch, with Red Rock. Mr. T was fourteen and Red Rock was fifteen. After an initial confrontation, the bulls became fast friends and shared the same pasture. "I feel like I'm running a rest home," laughed Growney.[36]

SKOAL'S PACIFIC BELL

Skoal's Pacific Bell was owned by Dan Russell of Western Rodeos. In his first outing at a PRCA rodeo, in 1987, he delivered a winning ride to Ted Nuce. He had no set pattern of bucking; he just bucked hard and threw cowboys down hard. But outside of the arena he was always calm, behaving in the chute and after the whistle. "In fact, he psyches many of the riders out," said Linda Russell, Dan's wife. The brindle bull, weighing 1,750 pounds, got his name from his character. Dan said, "He likes to reach out and touch someone!" He won many awards in the late 1980s. In 1989, in thirty-five trips out of the chute, no one had gotten a score off Skoal's Pacific Bell.

SUNNY'S VELVET / A-14

Mike Cervi bought from Jack Anderson, of Grover, Colorado, a little Hereford bull with a pushed-up nose, an offspring of Jet Age. Sunny Backstom, rodeo secretary for the Cervi Championship Rodeo Company, said, "He looked like he had run in to a door." Cervi had given this bull to Sunny as a Valentine gift, and changed his name to Sunny's Velvet.

Jerry Dorenkamp, who has worked with the Cervi stock for fifteen years, said he thought he was the best bull Cervi had. Sunny's Velvet bucked well for ten years, and for nine years at the National Finals he bucked everyone off, until his last ride, according to Dorenkamp. He was bucked at National

Finals under several different names, including A-14 and Sunny or Sunni's Velvet. He was never ridden at National Finals during the 1980s until his last time out, when he injured his back. Some of the disappointed cowboys who bucked off were Ted Nuce, Glenn McIllvain, Don Gay, Wacey Cathey (twice), and Charles Sampson.

11

ATHLETES:
THE FOUR-LEGGED VARIETY

The sport of bull riding has come a long way since the early days of rodeo when a cow or steer was hauled in and ridden by a cowboy to entertain the audience. The animal offered little to the challenge, but creative thinking introduced the Brahma bull to the event. Since that historic time the event has been one that has thrilled spectators and truly challenged man against beast. It has made champions of some riders, injured others, and even been the death of a few. The bull has also become a champion. He knows what his job is, and when the chute gate opens he performs to the best of his ability.

Mike Mason, of Hollister, California, was killed from injuries sustained from a bull ride at the Original Coors Folsom Championship Rodeo in Folsom, California, July 13, 1994. The bull, owned by Flying U Rodeo Company, called Moon Walker, flipped Mason up over the top and raised his head, slamming into the bull rider's chest and shattering his sternum. The local coroner determined a laceration of the heart was the cause of death.[36]

Brent Thurman, age twenty-five, of Dripping Springs, Texas, died from injuries incurred while riding a Growney bull, Red Wolf, during the tenth round of the 1994 National Finals in Las Vegas. He suffered cranial and facial fractures from being stepped on.[36]

The national public was aware of the injury having happened at the grand finale of rodeo, and many people stepped in to help the family. Thurman was kept alive for several days after he was injured, before it was determined to take him off life support. This was the first fatality at the National Finals Rodeo in its thirty-six-year history.[36]

A permit holder, Willy Gene Larson, age twenty, of Red Rock, Texas, died of injuries sustained while riding a bull at Billy Bob's Texas in Fort Worth. It was a freak accident in that, although he was wearing a protective vest, he was kicked in the head while airborne.[36]

In 1998 Lari Sluggett, age twenty-four, of Roy, Montana, was killed when a bull owned by Wayne Vold, called Tremors, stepped on the rider's stomach after bucking him off. The rider was wearing a protective vest. Hospital records indicated he died of "blunt abdominal trauma."

Like many young men, and a few women, in the American West, Charles "Trey" Schader, of Cedar Creek, Texas, fell in love with bull riding. In 1991, at age sixteen, Trey and his friends began showing up at the Diamond W Ranch near Elroy,

Arena action in the Cheyenne Frontier Days rodeo performance each day includes three rounds of bull riding.
—Photo by and courtesy of Arthur Frank.

Texas, on Sunday afternoons. There up-and-coming cowboys would ride up-and-coming bulls. Nothing was organized and no money was won, but it was a chance for a beginner, who might have an inkling that he would like to learn more about bull riding, to make that decision.

Some guys rode only one bull, and that was enough to satisfy their curiosity and realize that sport wasn't for them. Others considered it only a "teaser" and craved to ride the next one. Many young riders described the craving they had to get on the backs of those 1,000- to 1,500-pound young bulls. The bulls had just as much of a craving to get those guys off their backs.

As years passed Schader continued to spend Sundays at the Diamond W buck-outs, but he also attended rodeos across the state. He won a little prize money, and it was evident he was passionate about the sport. He even helped Kim Harley, a slightly built girl he knew, try to ride when she was only sixteen. He loaned her his bull rope, showed her how to wear her spurs and how to rosin the rope, and he pulled her rope for her. Her first ride was short, but she was hooked on it too. "It was such a high," said Harley. "I pawned my stereo, CDs, anything I owned and didn't need, just to get money to be able to ride the next bull."

Schader's mother, Linda McCarty, said, "I knew I was wasting my breath in trying to stop Trey from riding, but I told him I would not watch him ride. When he was a little tike, the first rodeo I took him to, he said, 'Momma, someday I'm going to do that.'"

On April 3, 1999, Trey and a group of friends drove to Stockdale, a small community near San Antonio, and entered the bull riding. It was a regular rodeo and his friends were there—Adam Olivo, Andy Voss, Cheryl Mitchell. Schader settled on top of his bull and nodded for the man to open the gate. The bull bucked out, and just a second or two into the ride Schader began to lose his balance. Just as he regained his seat and began to get control, the bull came up with great force, thrusting Schader's body toward the front. His face met the bull's skull with tremendous power. The sound was crunching, and his body fell limply to the ground.

Distracting the bull when rider Ellis O'Driscoll attempts to get off is an important responsibility of bullfighters Dwayne Hargo and Rick Chatman at Cheyenne Frontier Days, 1993.—Photo by Randall A. Wagner. Courtesy of Cheyenne Frontier Days.

Schader was unconscious, and it was evident he was badly hurt. THERE WAS NO AMBULANCE OR EMS ON HAND! In time the Stockdale ambulance arrived, but it was determined Star Flight, a helicopter ambulance, should transport the injured rider to Brooke Army Medical Center in nearby San Antonio. He died six days later, never regaining consciousness.

His friends were in shock. In their minds they kept asking the same questions: "He was such a great guy, good friend, a character, always laughing, always making everyone else feel good. Why did this have to happen to him? He loved bull riding so much, why did this have to happen?"

A few weeks later, when the shock of it all subsided, Schader's friends got together and held a benefit in Austin to help with expenses for the young bull rider's family, including the purchase of a headstone for Schader's grave, and the establishment of a trust fund for his eighteen-month-old son, Brandon, who would never know his father.

These accounts show that the sport of bull riding is a dangerous one. It pits a man weighing 150 pounds against a bull weighing between 1,200 to 2,000 pounds. The challenge is to stay aboard for eight seconds with good form, and then dismount and get to safety. The bull, on the other hand, has another agenda, which is to rid himself of the rider, at all costs. He bucks, and twists, and spins, and kicks, with

Aaron Semas is being assisted by Rick Chatman and Dwayne Hargo to get out of being hung up in the handhold of the bull rope at Cheyenne Frontier Days, 1998.—Photo by Randall A. Wagner. Courtesy of Cheyenne Frontier Days.

tremendous force and speed, often making the rider lose his balance—and the bull scores! Many deaths are pure accidents, with no intent by the animal. Fortunately, considering the number of bull riders and events being held today, the statistics for death by bull are very low. Traffic accidents are still the main killers of cowboys.

Cheyenne Frontier Days is the third largest rodeo in the world, to be surpassed only by Houston Livestock Show & Rodeo and the National Finals Rodeo in Las Vegas. In 1999, in a three-and-a-half-hour period, they crammed sixteen rodeo events and various special activities being held on the race track into an action-filled afternoon performance for nine consecutive days. Included in these rodeo events were three sections of bull riding, with twelve to fifteen riders in each section.

The bullfighters in 1999, Rick Chatman and Dwayne Hargo, were no strangers to Frontier Days. Chatman has been there for fourteen years and Hargo for five years. They make an excellent team. Seldom does a bull rider get injured, thanks to their abilities. When asked why the Cheyenne Frontier Days rodeo committee keep them coming back, both bull-baiters had the same answer: "We do our job and do it right, we know we are part of a team. It works for the bull riders and fans, as well."

When asked if bull riding has changed since he began his career, Chatman said there has been a great change, both in the caliber and the depth of the bulls and the bull riders. When asked what was the most difficult part of the bullfighting job, he quickly answered, "Trying to unhang a cowboy, you have to throw caution to the wind and work through the situation in your mind as you do it. You are completely vulnerable." But on the upside of the same situation, when asked what is the best part of the profession, Chatman said it was being able to help a cowboy. He added quickly that the audience was also one of the best things about his job.

Chatman said what "chaps" him the most about bull riders is when they are not giving an honest effort—when they don't give 100%. Hargo agreed, and both admitted a rider's attitude can put everyone involved at more risk than necessary. When Chatman, a twenty-year veteran of bullfighting,

Josh O'Byrne makes a successful ride at National Western Stock Show in Denver, 2000. Protective vests are being worn by all bull riders at this time.—Courtesy of and photo by Dan Hubbell.

Tate Stratton, Junior Bull Rider, uses helmet and vest for protection, which is being encouraged by medical professionals, especially for young riders.—Photo by © Gene Peach.

was asked if he thought it was fair for a novice bull rider to be able to compete against the top-ranked bull riders, he grinned and said, "Sure! It's the American way!" He also said if he could recommend any changes to the event he felt more safety gear should be required. As examples he named vests, helmets, and quick-release bull ropes.

It is evident these two professionals take their bullfighting and cowboy protecting chores very seriously. Additionally, however, they are both personable and spend much time visiting with their fans, whenever the bull riding events aren't in session.

Protective gear was slow in coming to the rodeo arena. It is not a big surprise, however, since one of the things that cowboys are noted for is their way of dressing; the big hat, creased to their individual liking; the western cut shirt; and colorful chaps. Protective gear would get in the way of the image, plus cowboys do not want to be accused of having one iota of fear. They have the reputation of being tough, in control, and unafraid of man or beast.

But the reality of the sport is that injury does happen. And when serious injury happens to a cowboy, and he cannot compete, the income stops. In bull riding the possibility of injury is increased. The old saying, "It isn't a matter of when a cowboy gets hurt, it's how BAD he gets hurt," certainly applies to bull riding.

Cody Lambert introduced the protective vest to rodeo. The vest is designed to protect the wearer from a blow or impact to the area covered by the vest. Lambert's mother was actually the one who brought the idea to him because she learned that jockeys are required to use similar vests in some states and some other countries. She wrote a letter to the company who manufactured the vest, told them about the need for one in rodeo, and asked them if they would be interested in working together to create a vest that would be appropriate for roughstock riders. They were interested. Mrs. Lambert then turned the project over to Cody. At first Lambert thought he'd get one designed for himself, maybe a few friends, and that would be it. But the more involved he got with the manufacturing company and with the design of the vest, it became a bigger issue. Lambert did not want the vest to be restrictive in any way. It could not interfere with the movement of the rider. Being a saddle bronc and bull rider, he knew exactly what was required, and he also knew the mindset of the cowboy. The vest also had to be easy to get on and off. The vest was marketed in 1994.

In 1993 Lambert was the only one who wore a protective vest to the National Finals Rodeo. In 1994 fourteen of the fifteen bull riders competing at the National Finals wore them. According to Lambert, all bull riders wear them in professional rodeo today. Just a little less than half the bareback bronc riders and saddle bronc riders do so.

By 1995 Lambert said if the bull rider wasn't wearing his

Bull-riding veteran Cody Custer wears a protective vest during his 1999 ride at Cheyenne Frontier Days. He knows the importance of the vest.—Photo by Dan Hubbell.

protective vest, it was almost as bad as forgetting his cowboy hat. The protective vest Lambert markets is called the Lambert Master Pro, made of closed cell foam, and is covered with a fabric called "spectrashield," which is made to spread out the force of the blow, and is lightweight and flexible.

There are many different kinds of protective vests being marketed today. Some have an open cell foam, or a honeycomb foam or different variety, but "No matter what you put on, bull riding is not safe," said Lambert. "If you do not want to get hurt, or if you do not want your kids to get hurt, do not let them get on a bull. I have a thirteen-year-old son, and I am so thankful he doesn't want to ride bulls. If he did, I would have to help him, and it would be tough," admitted Lambert.

"The vest is not to give a false sense of security to a rider, but when I wore a vest I felt I was doing a better job of making a living for my family. If I didn't have to ride sore, my scores would be better, and the vest helps considerably," explained the serious-minded, totally committed cowboy.

Bull riders have been killed while wearing protective vests, but in most instances they have been injured in areas the vest could not protect. A protective vest is designed to protect against impact. "There are some blows that are too much for any vest," said Lambert.

Dr. Tandy Freeman, who began his orthopedic practice in 1992 and was introduced to Justin Sports Medicine in 1993, treats cowboys about 80% of the time. He said, "The protective vest is a lifesaver. It absorbs a lot of the energy. Too many guys would be sent to the hospital with rib fractures, punctured lungs and cracked ribs, if it were not for the vest. There are several cowboys that wouldn't be with us if they hadn't had on a vest."

The idea of riding with a helmet is very controversial. At the present time some in the medical field are of the opinion that much more research and development must be done before a helmet can be recommended for regular use. Dr. J. Pat Evans, sports medicine guru and developer of the Justin Heeler Program, said, "The head weighs about ten pounds. If you add the weight of a helmet, which would be two and a half to three pounds, what it would do to the neck might add spinal cord

Fred Boettcher rides his bull at Cheyenne Frontier Days, 1998, while the bull keeps Dwayne Hargo's whereabouts in the corner of his eye.
—Photo by Randall A. Wagner. Courtesy of Cheyenne Frontier Days.

injury. We might be saving a cowboy from a concussion, but giving him spinal cord damage." He went on to explain, "Until a material is developed that is lightweight, but can withstand the forces of the bull, it is best to be without a helmet."

Lambert said that if Tuff Hedeman, who rode Bodacious at the Professional Bull Riders (PBR) event, October 15, 1995, had been wearing a helmet, the force with which Bodacious hit Hedeman, would more than likely have broken his neck. This injury caused Hedeman to require thirteen hours of reconstructive surgery on his face.

Dr. Freeman has a different opinion. He said helmets can prevent concussions, which is the most common injury in bull riding. "I would encourage using a helmet. I don't agree with making helmets mandatory in competition that involves adults. But it should be required for younger competitors; that way they can grow up getting used to it."

Freeman also said that in other sports, where the introduction of the helmet led to an increased number of neck injuries, the reason was not because of the weight of the helmet but because of the face mask, which was used for a battering ram, and the helmet-wearers sustained injuries much like whiplash.

One of the bull riders Freeman took care of cannot ride anymore. He has had too many concussions and is suffering from post-concussion syndrome. "A helmet could have prevented this," said Dr. Freeman. "I also wish I could talk a certain PBR competitor I treat into wearing a helmet. He has had several concussions over the last four or five years, and the last one was quite serious."

When asked what injuries Dr. Freeman sees most often, he said a groin injury is very common and can come from a variety of causes. The other injury, which requires surgery, is a shoulder dislocation. The third most common is knee injury, and concussions are always a problem. A cowboy can do some things to keep from getting an injury, such as warming up, or stretching, prior to a ride, but it will not guarantee that an injury won't happen, said the doctor.

Dr. Freeman is more than a sports medicine doctor and advisor to cowboys. He enjoys interaction with cowboys socially, not just when medical treatment is called for. His respect for the cowboy is evident, as is the cowboy's respect for the doctor. Over the seven years he has been doctoring cowboys he has learned that cowboys are different from athletes in other sports.

When asked how cowboys differ, his response was, "Let me count the ways . . . ! They have a different culture, a different mindset. Cowboys have a different approach to their sport." He went on to say the cowboy is a lot more appreciative of what is done for him than other competitors. "Cowboys who get medical assistance through Justin Sports Medicine say 'Thank you' 100% of the time," the doctor said with appreciation.

Nick Dunton was a bull rider during his high school and college years. Admittedly not one of the best, he did compete enough to know what a bull rider experiences. After his schooling, he went to work on several California cattle ranches.

While watching a rodeo on television, he observed Ty Murray get hung up. His thoughts immediately went to ways to create a device that would keep riders from this dilemma that plagues many and sometimes causes injury or death. With much persistence Dunton finally came up with a prototype that he felt would not require a rider to change his riding style at all.

The device is a stainless steel bull pin with a safety release (an inch-wide nylon strap seventeen inches long) that the rider (or bullfighter) can pull. This will release the bull rope from the bull, if the rider gets hung up. The device must be braided into any bull rope to be secured.

Dunton's next move was to contact Don Gay and explain to him over the telephone what he had developed. Gay's response was, "If it's not 100% rodeo, you are wasting your time." Dunton assured him it was, and they had a meeting at Gay's Mesquite office. Gay liked what he saw and contacted Cody Lambert, vice president of the Professional Bull Riders, and explained the safety release. Lambert chose several bull riders in the organization to use the device on their bull rope.

Dunton received approval on the patent in late 2000, after working with it for several years. Neal Barstow ProRodeo

Athletes: The Four-Legged Variety 213

Ty Murray and his speckled mount head right for the photographer, Randall A. Wagner, during Cheyenne Frontier Days, 1992.
—Courtesy of Cheyenne Frontier Days.

Equipment of Corsicana, Texas, braids the device into his bull ropes. Currently, Dunton sends Barstow over 100 units every other month. Several other suppliers around the country are doing the same.

The High School Rodeo Association holds an annual meeting in January each year. According to Kent Sturman, general manager of the association, the Safety Committee discussed safety devices at their 2001 conference. It is the hope of Dunton, president, and Steve Claassen, vice president of Bull Pin Safety Release, that eventually younger riders will be required to use the safety device.

Change for rodeo cowboys is not easy. Nevertheless, several top bull riders are using extra safety gear, among them, Leslie Doyle, Ronnie Kitchens, Raymond Wessell, Judd and Brock Mortensen, Wade Leslie, and Curt Lyons. It takes time for cowboys to accept new ways. Leslie Doyle admitted, "I have been riding for twenty-four years and at first it bothered me mentally. Finally I just forgot about it being there, and I'm glad to have it." Doyle has been using it for about three years, and he has had to use it twice when he got hung up. As Don Gay said, "If we can save one broken arm, one broken leg, or even one life, we have done our job well."

Cowboys of the Day

TY MURRAY

In the Ty Murray Fan Club letter of Winter 1999, Ty announced to his fans he was not planning on entering any rodeos in 2000, only Professional Bull Riding events. Having won the PBR Finals in October 1999, Murray garnered a record $265,912 at the PBR Finals. This made a total of $395,725 PBR winnings for Murray in 1999. His winnings in professional rodeos that same year totaled $138,963.[64]

Ty Murray has always been a cowboy. Straddling his mother's portable sewing machine case when barely able to walk, as if he were riding a horse or a bull, gave his parents, Joy and Butch, an idea of where this tot was headed. As a youngster he earned money at a racetrack, where Butch worked, and spent it to buy a bucking machine. He would ride the machine until his legs were raw. In high school he took gymnastics, to learn balance. Murray competes in all three roughstock events. "He has an uncanny ability to control his body. He possesses a kind of equilibrium on an animal, that you don't often see," said Dr. Tandy Freeman.[65]

In 1989, at twenty years of age, Murray became the PRCA All-Around Cowboy of the World—the youngest cowboy to win the prestigious honor. Winner of eleven Little Britches, High School and College world titles, his rodeo honors just go on and on. Seven All-Around World Champion Cowboy titles, 1989 through 1994 and again in 1998; two Bull Riding Championship titles, 1993 and 1998; 1988 Resistol Rookie of the Year, and the Bareback Bronc Riding Resistol Rookie title; NFR Average Champion in 1993 in the Bareback event, and 1998 in the Bull Riding event.

In the Professional Bull Riders 1999 Bud Light Cup season, Murray finished second in points and first in monies won, $395,724. He won over $263,283 at the Bud Light Cup finals. He qualified for the Bud Light Cup Championship in 1994, 1995, and again in 1998 and 1999. He has undergone reconstructive surgery on both knees and both shoulders.

Ty Murray was inducted into the ProRodeo Hall of Fame in 2000. When all the record-breaking is over, Murray wants to be remembered as a good cowboy.

JEROME DAVIS

Although his home is not called cowboy country, Davis has been a cowboy and interested in all things western his entire life. His dad, Carson Davis, operated a feed store at Archdale, North Carolina, and occasionally announced area rodeos. Today Jerome and his wife, Tiffany, live on a ranch in North Carolina, where they raise bulls, produce bull riding events, and work as stock contractors. Jerome also works as a PBR commentator. He was elected to the PBR Board of Directors in 1998 and continues as board member.

Jerome Davis wanted to ride bulls, and in the doing got a full scholarship to Odessa College, well known for its rodeo program. As a freshman, in 1992, he won the Intercollegiate National Bull Riding title. He also joined the PRCA that year and was winning the Rookie of the Year title until a bull at a Reno pro-rodeo event punctured his lung and broke his collarbone. His first trip to the National Finals was 1993, and the young man from North Carolina finished fifth in the world. The following year he finished third, but in 1995 he won the World Champion Bull Riding title—the only world champion bull rider from east of the Mississippi. It wasn't a fluke; Davis ended the 1996 season in third place in the world standings and in 1997 he was runner-up to the title. Davis rode well and knew he had at least ten years of a bull riding career ahead of him. At least that was the game plan.

March 14, 1998, his plans were dashed. At a PBR Tuff Hedeman Challenge Bull Riding in Fort Worth, Davis mounted a Jerry Nelson bull, Knock 'Em Out John. He wanted to ride this bull; he had drawn him before and had been thrown off. Six seconds into the ride, the bull jumped forward out of a spin, throwing Davis forward, whacking his chin against the bull's head and knocking him out cold. "I didn't have anything to brace myself, so when I landed, I landed right on my neck," recalled Davis. The impact broke his neck between the sixth and seventh vertebrae. Although Davis had surgery, followed by treatment and rehabilitation, he remains in a wheelchair. He does have use of his hands, but very little strength yet. He continues to work daily at improving his abilities. It is not coming as quickly as Davis would like, but he has the right attitude about it: "It'll be God's speed when it gets better. But I don't think I'll be in this wheelchair the rest of my life.

"Improving my abilities is kind of like riding bulls," said Davis. "You either win something or learn something. You're always striving to get better. But I tell you what, it's a lot harder than riding bulls ever was."[91]

Riding bulls was the only thing Davis ever wanted to do. Since it is a dangerous sport, he was not totally surprised when his injury happened. His wife has been the backbone and support Davis requires, and without her he would not be able to do the things he presently does, with the heavy travel required in the business.

Terry Don West, 1996 PRCA World Champion Bull Rider, masters Playboy at Las Vegas, Nevada, rodeo.—Photo by Dan Hubbell.

BRENT THURMAN

Leon Coffee, well-known bullfighter, put Brent Thurman on his first steer. Thurman was eight years old. Unknown to Thurman, Coffee held the belt of his jeans, in the back, and because of it Thurman never bucked off or fell off. After he had ridden about twelve steers, Thurman's mom finally told Coffee he was going to have to let Brent go and learn that he could fall or get bucked off. Reluctantly, Coffee let go. The first time Thurman got bucked off he *retired!*

A year later Thurman came out of "retirement" and was riding steers again. Mom, Kay Thurman, took Brent and older brother Brock to Junior Rodeos in their area. Brent filled his PRCA permit the summer between his junior and senior year

Andrews Rodeo Company's famous Bodacious (ProRodeo Hall of Fame honoree, PRCA Bull of the Year in 1994 and 1995, and PBR Bull of the Year in 1995), shows his stuff at the 1994 National Finals. He bucked Raymond Wessell off in the fourth round and Aaron Semas was unseated in the tenth round. He was picked NFR Top Bull in 1992, 1994, and 1995.—Photo by Dan Hubbell.

Athletes: The Four-Legged Variety 219

Hadley Barrett, rodeo announcer and ProRodeo Hall of Fame honoree, smiles for the photographer during Cheyenne Frontier Days action, 1998.

of high school. He started his rookie year in PRCA in 1988 as soon as he graduated.

Thurman traveled the rodeo road for the first two years with Wacey Cathey. Later he also traveled with Randy Thornton, Brian Herman, Michael Gaffney, and Cody Lambert.

When Thurman was stepped on by Red Wolf, in the final round of the 1994 National Finals Rodeo, the entire rodeo world knew of his accident. He was in a coma, lying in a Las Vegas hospital. His family was by his side, vigilantly hoping for some glimmer of consciousness from Brent as the days ticked by. Six days after the accident, Thurman's heart stopped. He died December 17, at age twenty-five.

Thurman was a happy young man with lots of friends. No one expected this to happen, but they knew he was doing what he loved —riding bulls. Kay Thurman, his mother, said, "If my experience in losing Brent could keep someone else who loses a child from experiencing the pain, I would truly do what I could. But the truth is you can't help someone else."

Brent's friend Wacey Cathey lost his teenage son, Sloan,

in a trampoline accident six months after Thurman was killed. "Wacey and I grieved together," said Kay.

Annually, Kay Thurman holds a Brent Thurman Memorial Bull Riding in Austin, Texas. The event, which features 100 bulls, is open to anyone, because "Brent would have wanted it that way," said Kay. The proceeds go to help a Vocational Education Horticultural Program for exceptional children at Covington Middle School in Austin. "These are children that can't read, but they can grow things," explained Kay, "and Brent would have liked that."

Bulls of the Day

BODACIOUS

Bodacious had a reputation that would have been envied by any four-legged athlete or any stock contractor who might have owned him. He was a superstar—one of a kind—and yet, because he did his job so well, he was retired early. The reason for his retirement was that too many good bull riders had been seriously injured while attempting to ride him.

"Bo," as he was affectionately called by Sammy Andrews of Andrews Rodeo, Inc., owner since January of 1992, "never intentionally hurt anyone." It was his bucking style that caused so many riders to be injured by his forceful upward thrust, resulting in upper body injury, especially head injuries.

Andrews traded bull man Phil Sumner of Oklahoma for the three-year-old Charbray. Sumner, who bucked him under the name J31, knew he'd be a good bucker. When he was retired in 1995 his career record was 135 times out of the chutes, with 127 unsuccessful bull riders. The riders who were successful with him were Bubba Dunn, Terry Don West, Clint Branger, Tuff Hedeman, Legs Stevenson, and Canadian Greg Schlosser.

Hedeman drew him five times during his career and admits "Bo" gave him his best ride and his worst. At the Bull Riders Only finals in Long Beach, California, Hedeman rode him for a score of 95. "There was nothing either of us could have done to make it better." He considers this ride to be the most perfect ride of his career. Then at the PBR Finals, October 15, 1995, Hedeman drew "Bo" again. No one wanted to draw him, as his reputation had spread far and wide. But Hedeman was still not convinced. "In all honesty," he said, "I thought I could kick his butt." Two surgeries and thirteen hours of reconstructive work were necessary to put Hedeman's face back together. "I knew then I'd never get on him again," said the fierce competitor who always lived up to his name—Tuff.[85]

At the National Finals in 1995, when Hedeman drew him again, the cowboy got on his back. However, when they opened the gate, Hedeman held on to the back of the chute, and let the rank bucker leave alone. Two nights later Scott Breding drew Bodacious and was knocked unconscious. The face mask he was wearing was splintered when his upper body was thrust forward by the yellow, 1,900-pound terminator.

Hadley Barrett, rodeo announcer, who saw this bull buck many times, said, "Bodacious is not a vicious bull. It's his performance, the way he bucks and the terrible drop force with which the rider is thrown forward." He bucked so hard and fast, especially for a bull as large as he was, that the impact was incredible when a rider slammed into his hulking frame. Andrews retired Bodacious at the 1995 National Finals. It seemed premature, since the bull was only eight years old, but Andrews' conscience dictated the decision.[85]

The larger-than-life bull that had as many fans as any star, and had T-shirts, belt buckles, and even a commemorative Winchester Rifle bearing his name, died May 16, 2000. The cause of death for the twelve-year-old was kidney failure.

The positive ending to this account is that Bodacious was inducted into the ProRodeo Hall of Fame in 1999, and through semen sales and breeding "his calves are everywhere," says Andrews.[85]

WADE LESLIE & WOLFMAN:
THE ONLY HUNDRED-POINT RIDE

Central Point, Oregon, and the Wild Rogue ProRodeo in October 1991 was the setting for the first and only time a perfect ride was scored. Wade Leslie of Moses Lake, Washington, had drawn Wolfman Skoal, a Growney Brothers Rodeo Company five-year-old bull, whose father was Fonzie, son of Oscar. His mother was one of Red Rock's daughters.

Wolfman blew out of the chute and reared so hard the second jump out, he nearly butted heads with Leslie. He started spinning to the left, into Leslie's riding hand, then began traveling ahead, which got Leslie to the end of his arm, and Leslie just tried to stay with him. Leslie never heard the whistle.

Russell Davis and Raymond Lewis were judging, and gave their decision to announcer Phil Gardenhire, who shouted: "ONE HUNDRED POINTS!" The standing crowd was ecstatic. They had just witnessed the first bull ride to be awarded a perfect score.

Cody Custer also rode this bull in the tenth round of the National Finals Rodeo, for a score of 94 points. Wolfman is a difficult bull to ride because he spins to the right or the left.

12
THE TWENTY-FIRST CENTURY

On December 11, 1999, during the National Finals Rodeo in Las Vegas, an announcement was made by PRCA Commissioner Steve Hatchell. A Wrangler ProRodeo Tour would begin in January 2000 at the Denver National Western Stock Show and Rodeo. The premise of the venue was announced as (1) increasing television coverage dramatically for PRCA and appealing to a broader audience and (2) creating heroes and stars at every level.

Eight rodeos were picked beginning with Denver and progressing through June 4. At each rodeo the winners of each event would get 12 points, second place 11 points, and so on down to twelfth place, getting 1 point. Points would be added through all eight rodeos. A championship event, called the Copenhagen Cup Tour Finale, was held at the MGM Grand in Las Vegas on June 8 through June 10. The ten top-scoring cowboys in each event competed in a sudden death format. Prize money totaling $430,000 was up for grabs.

In the first Finale, winners of the roughstock events were: Kagan Sirett in Bull Riding; Mark Garrett, Bareback Riding; and Red Lemmel, Saddle Bronc Riding. Many of the familiar names in bull riding were absent. In the third round, the next to last round, the numbers diminished from eight competitors to the top four. Their previous scores were wiped out and they began with a clean slate. In the third round, no one rode a bull. The decision on which four would be chosen was determined by their average scores prior to that round. The venue was covered by TNN television.

This new concept is truly an exciting addition to PRCA and allows the successful competing cowboys the opportunity to make more money in their field. PRCA also announced that the Wrangler ProRodeo Tour would be increased in monies for 2001 and 2002. The Wrangler ProRodeo Summer Tour, a second go-round for the year, got started before the riders from the Finale had a chance to dust off their Wranglers and leave the MGM Grand. The second go-round of the Wrangler ProRodeo Tour ended with the Copenhagen Cup Finale held at Mesquite October 19-21. The roughstock winners for this event were Bobby Mote in Bareback Riding; Dan Mortensen in Saddle Bronc Riding; and Lee Akin, of Weatherford, Oklahoma,

Josh O'Byrne scores an 81 on Three Hill Rodeo's Dry Ice in the first go-round of the 1998 National Finals.—Photo by Dan Hubbell.

Close-up of Jeff Wahlert of Grover, Colorado, making it all count at Cheyenne Frontier Days, 1992.—Photo by Randall A. Wagner. Courtesy of Cheyenne Frontier Days.

in Bull Riding. The Copenhagen top bulls of the Finale were: Number one to Rafter G Rodeo's Dodge Durango; Rafter H Rodeo's Skoal's King Kong as second; and third was Andrews Rodeo Company's Sand Man.

These "tours," which made their debut in 2000, are bonuses to those who choose to enter, and certainly can put more money in their pockets. Lee Akin, a full-time student, won $22,375 and a Copenhagen Cup, plus he was sitting in ninth place for the upcoming 2000 National Finals Rodeo with $59,358 won up to that point. Professional rodeo takes another step in the right direction.

The decision of the governing body of the Rodeo Cowboy Association back in the 1950s that television coverage needed to be held to a minimum, because it could cause some negative results in rodeo, had disappeared. The opportunity to have television exposure was considered a big plus by the PRCA the last thirty or more years of the twentieth century.

In giving rodeo as much television exposure as possible, PRCA, ESPN, and ESPN2 closed a deal to show eighty-six hours of PRCA rodeo between May and December of 2000. Considering the sixteen hours of event coverage by TNN between January and June, total television coverage of PRCA events for the year 2000 added up to 102 network broadcast hours—the most ever for professional rodeo.[36]

As the new millennium rolled in, it was time to reflect on the past. Hadley Barrett, rodeo announcer for over thirty-five years, said, "While people my age are often asked if the riders of today are better than the riders of years ago, my answer would be 'No, they are not better. There are just a lot more riders today that are so very good.'"

He went on to explain the reason this is true. Today there are so many ways a novice can get experience, through high school rodeos, college teams, and specialized training schools. Also there are schools for those who have competed but are having a consistent problem that needs to be corrected. These training grounds were not available to contestants during the earlier days. The only way they had to learn was by entering a rodeo.

Barrett also reflected, "In my era, the forties, fifties and early sixties, rodeos used primarily ranch bulls. There were

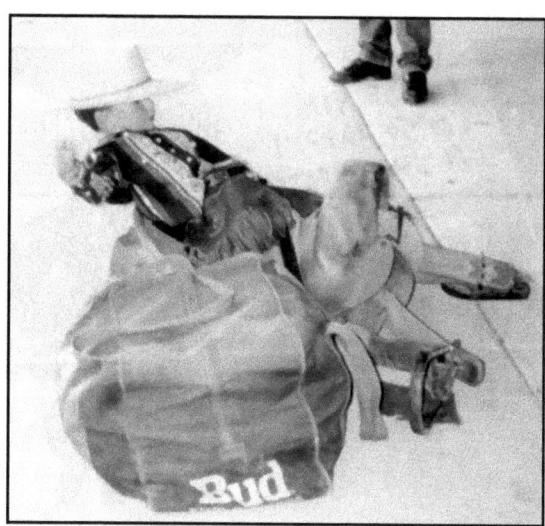

Bull and bronc riders are NEVER too young! After his dad, Grey Mapston, finished his saddle bronc ride at Cheyenne, this tiny two-year-old, Colt Mapston, took advantage of the saddle to do some practicing behind the chutes. Good form!

more Brahma bulls that had big humps and larger front ends. Bull riders then did not experience coming down on the front [the head] with tremendous force as much, like they do today. This often causes a terrible injury."

He went on to say, "The breeding of bulls has improved, and created a product we didn't have in my era. We did not have the bull being such an athlete that they have today. Then they were more 'lumbering' but today the bull is straight backed, and the Brahma has been crossed with other breeds, which allows the rider to set his rope more toward the front."

In 1992 the president of Dodge Rodeo, Jack Lowry, and Neal Gay of Mesquite Rodeo came up with the concept of a "bounty bull" program by picking a particular bull to carry the Dodge name and give additional money, $500, supplied by Texas Dodge dealers, *if* the rider who drew him rode him. Gay would pick the bull out of the Mesquite string of bulls, to be bucked either Friday or Saturday night at the Mesquite Rodeo. Of course, this would be a tough bull, one that didn't often allow a rider a full eight-second ride. The contestant to ride him would be picked at Professional Rodeo Cowboy Association headquarters from those entered in that weekend's competition. The first bull chosen was Dodge Dakota, an 1,800-pound black bull with a white face. He didn't look particularly tough, but he went twenty-four weeks before he was ridden. In fact,

Cartoon by Daryl Talbot.

he had a fan club. People would call the office at Mesquite to find out when he was going to buck each weekend. In the fall of 1992 Joe Wimberley was the man who finally rode him, and scored 89 points. The "bounty" had built up over those weeks to $17,000.[83] In his career at Mesquite, Dodge Dakota was ridden only eight times in 101 attempts.[36]

In July 1995 Cory Check, a bull rider from Eastman, Wisconsin, set a Dodge Bounty bull riding earnings record when he rode Dodge Laramie II at Mesquite. He scored 85 points and was awarded $28,500. Forty-four cowboys had been unsuccessful in riding this bull in competition prior to Check's 85 points.[36]

In the year 2000 Dodge Durango had a run of 78 wins over the cowboys trying to ride him, and the bounty reached $48,000. All the cowboys who drew Dodge Durango had bitten the dust without a qualified ride at Mesquite Rodeo.

The original Dodge Durango entered the Mesquite arena in 1997 and went unridden in sixteen trips in 1997. However, due to the bull getting crippled, a second bull was chosen, also to be called Dodge Durango, and he arrived April 4, 1998. Cody Custer did score a 91-point ride on Durango and won the eighth round at the 1999 National Finals Rodeo, but this wasn't part of the Bounty program; therefore, Custer's ride did not count in the Bounty, unfortunately for Custer.[84] The last ride to count in the Dodge Bounty program during the 2000 Mesquite season was the last weekend of September. Rusty Burford drew him, for the second time, and only lasted a couple of seconds. It is reported the average trip on the bull is 2.26 seconds.[36] Since the Dodge Bounty program was not continued in 2001 and no one collected the $48,000, Dodge Durango wins!

Many of the cowboys and champions of yesterday are still present at rodeos today. A few work the rodeo in some way, but many are merely spectators. Jim Shoulders said he went to a bull riding at Kinder, Louisiana, not long ago. It was held at a casino and they had constructed a portable arena, and he was observing the actions prior to the rodeo. There were some porta-potties behind the chutes, and near them was the sign-up table, where the riders entered the competition. When the event started the dignitaries were introduced to the crowd, including Shoulders.

"These guys don't know how to rodeo," Shoulders told the crowd. The crowd was silent, then he added, "There have been at least twenty-four to thirty guys go in the porta-cans, and no one has even tried to turn one over. And besides that, there's no pitch game going on behind the chutes, and no one was shootin' dice! No one knows how to rodeo anymore. Nowadays the guys are standing around warming up or stretching. Why, if I had done all that I would have probably been too tired to ride!"

"Big John" Williams, the bull man of the 1950s, of Garwood, Texas, continues to be involved in rodeo by selling his dummy and a brand new "state of the art" apparatus to stock contractors all over the country. This allows them to buck bulls without the need for riders, and gives bull owners a chance to observe and determine the capability of the bull to be a consistent bucker in less time. Williams' partners in this project are

Josh Pierce of Terrell, Texas, tries to hold his seat at the 1999 Cheyenne Frontier Days.—Photo by Randall A. Wagner. Courtesy of Cheyenne Frontier Days.

"Big John" Williams and partner Roger Johnson of Humansville, Missouri, display their 2000 dummy, which is so popular with stock contractors. It allows them to buck bulls using the dummy, which is remote controlled, instead of riders.
—Photo courtesy of John Williams.

Roger and Debbie Johnson of Humansville, Missouri. The apparatus is called the Remote Double J Arena Bull Dummy.

The dummy of 2000 has been improved from the 1950s style dummy. It is bright red, heavy-duty plastic material, about three-quarters of the size of a bull rider, with arms that flop, and Velcro on the head of the dummy so that a hat can be attached. The dummy still sits on an apparatus attached to the bull. The difference in this model and the 1950s variety is that the apparatus is now released by remote control.

Johnson, Williams' partner, is an engineer, primarily involved in manufacturing remote control collars for animals that are tracked by governmental agencies and other concerned animal organizations. He and Williams collaborated and designed the new style dummy and apparatus, which is so popular with today's stock contractors that Williams has back orders to fill. Jerome Davis ordered a dummy from Williams, and after using it his comment was, "It saves kids from hav-

This is Gilbert, or Adam—no it must be Gilbert Carrillo. A photo of Adam would pretty much look the same. They are twins, and both ride bulls. Nice guys, too.
—Photo by author.

ing to get on those green bulls. It's a great invention."

The Justin Sports Medicine Program has been in place for twenty years in the rodeo world. It has come a long way, thanks to John Justin and the sports medicine doctors who have committed themselves to aiding the cowboy. They have two 18-wheel trucks that travel to approximately 150 rodeos a year, out of 700 PRCA rodeos across the country.

The on-duty athletic trainer, Bill Zeigler, who drove the Justin Sports Medicine truck to the Austin/Travis County Livestock Show & Rodeo, covers twenty of those rodeos annually. His background prepares him for this position, as he was an athletic trainer in major league baseball for twenty-two years. After working part-time for Justin in his off-seasons, he quit baseball and applied for a full-time position with Justin.

The inside of the truck appears rather stark, but this was done by design. The sides are lined with vinyl seats. A medical table sits in the middle of the floor, and there is a refrigerator, stocked with ice, plus a small metal apparatus supplying moist heat. Zeigler explained they use much more ice than moist heat on cowboys with injuries. On his roster one bareback rider was scheduled to come in for treatment before the evening performance. Most nights between one and six cowboys come prior to the rodeo for assistance, said Zeigler.

It is evident that over the twenty-year span Justin has pro-

"Son, someday this'll all be yours!" Cartoon by Daryl Talbot.

vided this medical service to professional rodeo, they have learned what is important medically and what is not often utilized. According to Dr. J. Pat Evans, the most important item when preparing a bull rider for competition is tape. He said a tremendous amount of tape is used. Otherwise, most injuries taken care of in the Justin Sports Medicine facility are relatively simple ones, requiring only tape and ice.

New Millennium Cowboys

ADAM & GILBERT CARRILLO

Born October 28, 1971, in El Paso, Texas, Adam and Gilbert Carrillo are the youngest of six children. They are iden-

Cartoon by M. C. Tin Star aka Wally Badgett.

tical twins and have many things in common. They are both close to 5'5, weigh within a couple of pounds of each other, and are both right-handed.

At the age of thirteen they knew they wanted to ride bulls. The following year Roach Hedeman taught them how to ride. The twins attended Odessa College on full rodeo scholarships. Gilbert became the PRCA bull riding rookie of 1992. Both have qualified for the PRCA National Finals, but never in the same year. Gilbert went in 1992 and 1998, and Adam qualified in 1993 and 1995.

Both were contestants in the 1999 and 2000 Professional Bull Riders Finals. They have qualified for the PBR Bud Light Cup World Championships every year since 1994. Gilbert finished eighth in 1999 and Adam finished twenty-ninth.

According to recent PBR reports, the twins struggled the first part of the 2000 season. Gilbert covered just 29.2% of his Bud Light Cup bulls and Adam only 15.2%. But the tenacious two are picking up the pace. "We've been working out extremely hard, just concentrating and focusing all our ability and mental focus on riding bulls, like we used to," said Gilbert, "and it's panning out."

TERRY WILLIAMS

Terry Williams of Carthage, Texas, has been named the Stock Contractor of the Year with the Professional Bull Riders for the past four years, 1996-1999. Except for 1995, when the Sammy Andrews bull, Bodacious, was Bull of the Year, Williams has owned four different bulls that have captured the PBR Bull of the Year honor: Baby Face in 1996, Panhandle Slim in 1997; Moody Blues in 1998; and Promise Land in 1999. This is a great honor to Williams, when one realizes there are seventeen other primary stock contractors who provide stock to the PBR, plus at least ten other individuals whose bulls are bucked.

Williams has been in the cattle business in East Texas all his life and has always been around rodeo. In the late 1980s he began bucking bulls and got into the business in a serious way. He's always admired Sammy Andrews, another stock contractor, and never hesitated to ask him questions.

Williams bucks the bulls he raises at eighteen months, then again at about two years and he may send them to a small event when they are three. But he does not consider a bull ready to buck and show what he truly can do until he is about four years of age. A bull generally averages around four years as a good bucker; some may go longer. Williams is convinced that a bull's desire to buck comes directly from the heart. "The bigger his heart the better he bucks," said the sincere bull owner (and he's not talking physical size).

When asked why he thought his bulls were so good and consistent, Williams didn't hesitate. "We take care of our bulls. We feed every day, and never vary. We try never to put them at stress, especially when they are traveling. We also look for good pens to put them in when they are on the road.

If we think something is wrong we tend to it right away." Williams is always looking for more good buckers, and goes to many jackpot buckings to watch for those young bulls with potential.

Clayton, Williams' ninth-grade son, helps out with the feeding and care of the bulls. When Williams was asked if Clayton planned to go into the raising or riding of bulls, he answered, "He'll ride a few bulls, but I'd rather see a rattlesnake bite him!"

Bulls for the Twenty-first Century

RED WOLF (DODGE RAM TOUGH)

Don Kish and John Growney bought Red Wolf from Brent Gilbert, who put on old-timer rodeos. Whenever he had a bull that was too rank, he referred them to Kish. That year the 1,800-pound red bucker went to the National Finals Rodeo. He bucked off both Aaron Semas and Brent Thurman. Unfortunately, Brent Thurman got hung up and fell under the bull, and the bull's hooves hit the rider with such force that Thurman died six days later.

Because of the death of Thurman, Red Wolf became infamous. They changed his name to Dodge Ram Tough. Don Kish said, "He was wild when we first got him, but now he's good to handle and causes no problem. He just bucks hard to get the job done and he's a good bull to be around."[36]

He became the 1994 Runner-Up NFR Bull of the Year, and in 1996 he was the PRCA Bucking Bull of the Year. Royd Doyle and Jerome Davis both scored 94 points on him at the National Finals that year. Don Kish sold the bull to Terry Williams at the National Finals 1996 Bucking Sale for $20,000.

Williams began bucking the bull at Professional Bull Riding events, changing his name back to Red Wolf. He was consistently a good bucking bull. In 1999 Williams sold him to Chad Herrington for $50,000. Red Wolf had very respectable statistics for the 1999 PBR Bud Light Cup events.

Thirteen-year-old Red Wolf retired at the last performance of the 2000 Professional Bull Riders Finals, when Pete Hessman rode him for a score of 90 points.—Photo courtesy of Robbie Herrington, Herrington Cattle Company.

He was bucked out fourteen times and ridden six, with an average score of 93 points. Buck-offs were 57% of the time.

Red Wolf hasn't slowed down much. He now weighs 2,000 pounds and still has more strength and agility than expected for a bull of his size.[86] Cody Lambert, the vice president of PBR, is in charge of assigning stock to the Bud Light Cup venues. When asked to name the top three bulls he had seen in his career, Lambert said, "Bodacious, Dillinger and Red Wolf. Red Wolf is just barely below Bodacious, and he's twelve, and hasn't lost a step. If you ride him you'll get a 92 or 93 on him."

During the 2000 season of PBR this "old" bull gave four bull riders scores of over 90 points, prior to the Finals: Cuay Hudson got 91; Jaron Nunnemaker scored 91.5; Tater Porter got 90; and Cory Turnbow, 90.5.

RED WOLF'S RETIREMENT

It was the PBR Finals and it was happening in the very last go
The stage was set for bull, cowboy and owners to put us fans on a great show
Pete Hessman was the cowboy, the owners were Robbie and Chad
And the bull the greatest now and forever this sport has ever had

As the announcer told the story of the history makin' ride
The anticipation and suspense was more than anyone could hide
Then the cowboy nodded and the chute gate opened wide
And 1800 pounds of thunder and lightning burst out of that chute with pride

It was round to the right as usual, like always hard and fast
With 'Pistol Pete' scratching and clawing as the bull just gave it more has
It was a hell of a ride and will forever be locked in our hearts and heads
'bout how Pete Hessman on this very night dodged the bullet and hot lead

The show is over now and its time for the party to begin
With Cody and Robbie on stage just waiting for their old friend
The arena gate opens now and to the center trots the honored guest
He proudly makes the circle cause he knows that he's the "Best of the very Best"

There were 17,000 fans standing and yelling for the greatest bucking bull ever
Then he stopped right in the middle just to show us he was oh so clever
He walked right up to the stage where Cody and Robbie stood
As if he were trying to tell 'em the time was right and how he understood

The coliseum got deadly quiet as the bull and Robbie at each other stared
It looked as if for a few moments they were reminiscing all that they had shared
Then the bull bowed his neck and snorted and around the arena he ran
He was making one last statement ... "I'm not afraid of any man"

This was the greatest retirement party that any bull has ever had
Even with 17,000 screaming, hollering fans it was still just a little sad
Now we'll all miss this great animal who has given us so much in the past
Our hats are off to you Red Wolf ... in our memories your name will forever last.

Happy Trails

Jim Murff wrote this poem while traveling back to Texas from the PBR Finals, October 29, 2000. The signatures are Jim Murff, cowboy poet, and Robbie and Chad Herrington, owners of Red Wolf.

During the last performance of the PBR World Championship Finals, Robbie Herrington of Herrington Cattle Company retired thirteen-year-old Red Wolf. Earlier that day the bull was drawn by Pete Hessman of Dodge City, Kansas, who rode the red "senior" bull and scored *90 points!* Red Wolf has been compared to a "seventy-year-old man playing linebacker on a college football team." Cody Lambert said Red Rock never misfired, and of his 2,000 pounds, 1,800 pounds of it must have been heart.

Cody Custer, thirty-five years old, 1992 PRCA World Champion Bull Rider from Wickenburg, Arizona. Photo taken in 1994.
—Photo by Dan Hubbell.

13
COMPETITION—THE AMERICAN WAY

The rodeo cowboy enjoys "going down the road." He thrives on the competition, enjoys meeting others who have the same interests, sees the country, and gets a good geography lesson for no extra charge. But one thing has bothered the rodeo man almost since the beginning of rodeo—the prize monies. It has never been what he thought it should be.

They watch football, basketball, and baseball stars sign contracts for millions of dollars. Some even do it before they play their first professional game. Cowboys can certainly envy these other athletes, not for what they do but for the monies they receive for doing what they excel in. A cowboy works very hard to do the best he can at his sport. He works at improving his abilities and tries to learn from every experience in his competition, whether it be bull riding, roping, or steer wrestling. However, the cowboy pays his own way. He gets from rodeo to rodeo at his own expense, he pays his own entry fee, and takes care of his own room and board when traveling. If he is lucky enough to have a sponsor help him financially, that helps—but it is still a costly sport. When the prize money is tallied, that amount does not include the costs a rodeo cowboy incurs along the way.

Cowboys know there must be a better way. They have tried ever since the cowboys formed the Cowboys Turtle Association in 1936 to get better prize monies when they won. They continued trying after Bob Wegner was blackballed by the ProRodeo Cowboys Association in 1967 for forming the rodeo league, American Cowboys Association.

In the bull riding competition the George Paul Memorial Bull Riding was held in 1977, and still continues today. Then Bullnanza, held at the Lazy E Arena, Guthrie, Oklahoma, began in 1989. It was an invitation-only event. Next came the formation of Bull Riders Only (BRO) with CEO Shaw Sullivan running the show. In 1990 he formed a league that allowed bull riders to ride in a series of competitions seen on television. They were all held in large cities and were underwritten by corporate sponsors.

"Now we're talking," thought the bull riders. BRO did not require entry fees, and the monies that could be won rivaled all but the top professional rodeos. Their performances were sold out, or nearly sold out, and although these were fans from the cities, they appreciated the competitive bull riders pitted against the treacherous athletes in the pens—the bulls. It made good watching.

Cody Custer won the BRO Finals at McNichols Arena in Denver, in October 1992, by riding Copenhagen High Five for a score of 95 points. He won $16,600, including go-round money.

Sullivan wanted his bull riders to sign exclusive BRO contracts. The riders balked; they were not about to limit themselves from being able to ride at PRCA or other competitions, if they chose to do so.[87] This is where the cowboy athlete differs from athletes of other sports. Don't limit him or try to tie him down!

Shortly after this, the Professional Bull Riders (PBR) organization was formed. For a while the two competitive but friendly organizations tried to work together. By 1994 they had split and gone their separate ways.

Many bull ridings were held, and are still being held, under various independent names, across the country. Spectators attend by the droves, but some of the venues have a tough time enticing top-ranked bull riders to compete. It becomes discouraging to a crowd when they watch 100 bulls buck out, and only two or three cowboys make qualified rides.

In 1992 twenty bull riders had a meeting in a hotel in Scottsdale, Arizona, and came up with the concept of the Professional Bull Riders organization. Each bull rider put up

Everett Erickson of Hornitos, California, doesn't quite make the whistle at Cheyenne Frontier Days, 2000. —Photo by Randall A. Wagner, courtesy of Cheyenne Frontier Days.

$1,000, allowing the group to begin with $20,000. It was their goal to make a "Star Driven Sport" and to find sponsors that would put up the kind of money they felt should be available to riders. Their mission was "to promote, protect and enhance bull riding in a professional manner while creating a star driven sport." The idea was to get television and other sponsors to help financially, then they could build the organization and meet their goal. Many of the changes made by PBR came from complaints made by bull riders about what was happening in rodeos—low money, entry fees, not enough good bulls, and so on.

In 1995 Randy Bernard had graduated with an agriculture business management degree and had completed an internship with the Calgary Stampede for four and a half months. From there he went to work for the California Fair, and was a protégé of Maynard Potter, who took a town of 18,000 people and a fair that had an attendance of 35,000 people to an attendance of 435,000. As Potter's protégé Randy worked with entertainers and gained a strong background in promotion. He had been approached by Louis Cryer, commissioner to the Professional Rodeo Cowboys Association, to consider the PRCA as employment, which he was planning to pursue.

One day Tuff Hedeman and Cody Lambert were sitting in Bernard's office, at the California Fair, and noticed an airline ticket to Colorado Springs on his desk. The cowboys questioned him as to why he was going to Colorado Springs. He admitted he was going to interview with PRCA. Lambert and Hedeman suggested he consider a job with their organization, Professional Bull Riders. In 1995 Bernard became CEO of PBR.

Bernard said he chose to go with the PBR because he felt he could be more involved in the development there and be on the front line when decisions were made. Bernard's enthusiasm is obviously infectious.

Tuff Hedeman is the president of the PBR; Cody Lambert is the vice president. The board of directors consists of Jerome Davis, Troy Dunn, Michael Gaffney, Ty Murray, and Aaron Semas.

Cody Lambert is responsible for the stock used at the Bud Light Cup events. He chooses the stock to be used, cuts the deal with the stock contractors, hires the trucks, and decides which bulls are to buck in which go-rounds of each event.

If Lambert is told about an unknown bull he might want to consider, he researches the bull thoroughly to make sure he is truly a bucker. "If I use an unknown bull, especially at the Bud Light Cup level, a good proven bull goes unused." Cash awards are given for the best bulls of each event.

In an interview with Bernard in April 1999, he said, "People are not interested in watching minor league, they want to see the stars, watch the majors." The difference in PRCA and PBR is primarily that PRCA has over 11,000 con-

1999 photo of Ty Murray and his World Champion form. His balance in bull riding is remarkable. Photo by Dan Hubbell.

testants including permit holders, with 762 events. A permit holder in the PRCA organization can compete against Ty Murray, all-around champion of the world, just by paying his entry fee, which is one of the organization's primary rules. If you are a member of PRCA, no matter what your level of capability, you can compete against anyone by paying an entry fee to an ordinary rodeo. The exceptions are only for specific venues, such as the National Finals Rodeo, Wrangler ProRodeo Tour, and Houston Livestock Show & Rodeo.

Professional Bull Riders is a tiered organization. They have a minor league (Touring Pro Division) and a major league (Bud Light Cup). Any member is eligible for the minor league. The PBR major league consists of the top forty-five members of PBR, points won (100 points for a go-round win, down to 10 points for 10th place).

In 1994 there were eight events for the year. In 1998 twenty-nine nationally televised Bud Light Cup events (the major league of PBR) were held. Each event featured the top forty-five bull riders in the world, and guaranteed a $75,000 purse. Qualification for the top forty-five is based on individual rank in total monies won from the regular season.

After every fourth event in the Bud Light Cup league, the bottom five riders, in points won, are dropped from the tour and the top five money earners from the minor league are picked up. In 1999 the first cut was made January 15, and the second cut was on February 6.

Of the twenty original bull riders who met and started the PBR, several have sold their stock (Scott Mendes and Bobby DelVecchio). Brent Thurman was a member until his untimely death. Currently there are seventeen major stockholders.

The first sponsors were TNN television and Budweiser Light. The total television viewing the first years of the PBR were 12 million viewers. There are now over 90 million viewers.

The only excuses the top bull riders can have to miss a Bud Light performance are injury, with a doctor's excuse, or a family medical emergency, such as the birth of a baby or a death in the family. If any of the top bull riders do miss a Bud Light venue without the reasons given above, they are forced to sit out of competition with PBR for a year. Adriano Moraes wanted to take several months off and go visit his family in Brazil. PBR said, "No, the rules do not allow it." Therefore, he took off an entire year to be in Brazil with his family.

At the Houston Livestock Show & Rodeo in 1999 Ty Murray had ridden well and was in the finals, better known as

Cartoon by Wally Badgett.

the "short go." He told the Houston rodeo board he could not be there as there was a PBR bull riding at the same time as the short go. Because of the PBR rules, if Murray missed the event he would be forced to sit out the PBR competition for a year. Murray did not attend the short go at Houston. The Houston rodeo board was furious, and there was much in the newspapers about Murray's decision to miss the "short go." Staying at Houston would have meant good money for Murray—$12,000—and if he won the all-around, possibly another

$25,000, plus money for his commentary of the rodeo on pay-per-view television. CEO Bernard said the PBR hurt Murray on the deal, but the association knows fans deserve credibility and they do advertise the "top forty-five bull riders." If Adriano Moraes couldn't go to Brazil for two months, then Ty Murray had to be treated the same way. It's the PBR rules.

PBR is very strict with their rules. After each performance contestants are required to sign autographs in the arena for fans. If they choose not to sign autographs, the first time they refuse they are fined $500. The second time they refuse they are charged $1,000, and the third offense carries a $5,000 fine. Seldom does a rider decide not to participate, and the fans get their autographs and are able to talk with their "stars." PBR feels this is tremendously important and one of the reasons their fans are so loyal.

Melvin Zebroski, Gillette, Wyoming, keeps his seat while he spurs the big black bucker at Cheyenne, 2000.—Photo by Randall A. Wagner, courtesy of Cheyenne Frontier Days.

Competition—The American Way   249

There are 800 members in the Touring Pro Division of PBR. In the Bud Light Cup Cody Hart won the Bud Light Cup World Championship for 1999, and won $322,348 for the year. He won six regular season Bud Light events.

Ty Murray won $259,000 at the Bud Light Cup World Championship in Las Vegas in October 1999. This was Murray's third career Bud Light Cup event title.

At Bud Light Cup performances there are three judges. Most judges are PRCA-trained, but rules in PBR are somewhat different. They use the half-point system. Two judges are in the arena, and one is behind the chutes, to look for fouls. The third judge often breaks ties.

The cost of a ticket for a PBR performance is $50. "If we don't give them their money's worth, it wouldn't be right," said Bernard. Each event costs between $250,000 and $500,000 to produce.

Bull riders choose and vote on the bullfighters used for PBR events. Once the top bullfighters are picked, the one with the most votes chooses the upcoming events he wants to work. Then the second most-voted-on bullfighter chooses his events, and so on. In 1999 Joe Baumgartner was picked as first choice, with Jimmy Anderson second, then Roach Hedeman followed by Frank Newsom. In 2000 Jimmy Anderson was chosen as top bullfighter. These are truly top flight bullbaiters, and the riders feel as safe as they possibly can topping that renegade bull, with these men in the arena.

At the 2000 PBR Finals Jimmy Anderson, Rob Smets, Joe Baumgartner, and Dennis Johnson had the bullfighting duties. Flint Rasmussen, barrelman, was in charge of comic relief, and delighted the audience with his antics during each television break. Injuries were minor thanks to the expert cowboy protectors, as well as Dr. Tandy Freeman and his crew of medical personnel on hand.

In a conversation with Rob Smets, World Champion Bullfighter many times, he mentioned the bulls he has faced during his career. The best bulls of their time Smets first noted was Harry Vold's 777, during the late 1970s and early '80s, followed by Oscar, Christensen's Wilfred, Steiner's Red Lightning, and Wolfman. He said other bulls that had longevity in

Jason Legler, Loveland, Colorado, has the adrenaline flowing, as he rides the wild-eyed mount. Meanwhile, bullfighters Chatman and Hargo are ready to assist, if necessary.—Photo by Randall A. Wagner, courtesy of Cheyenne Frontier Days.

the arena, such as Red Rock, were Trick or Treat, White Water Skoal, and Wolfman.

As for fighting bulls that Smets had faced he quickly commented the best was Crooked Nose, owned by Vold. "He loved the game," grinned Smets. "He wasn't a killer. He would maul you (the bullfighter) all day, whirl around and look at you, as if to say, 'Get up, Let's do it again!'" Smets had just purchased some heifers out of Wolfman from Don Kish, stock contractor, with the hope to raise some good bucking bulls of his own.

When Jim Shoulders was asked what he thought of the PBR he said, "I think it is great! I have always said, you can't sell anything if you're not on TV. The humane element is the main thing that has kept rodeo off of television, and the calf roping is the event that bothers the animal activists the most. They don't have much trouble feeling sorry for a big old bull." Larry Mahan agrees with Shoulders' assessment of the PBR and said, "I honestly believe bull riding is the only rodeo event that can stand on its own."

On March 24, 2000, PBR suffered its first death by injury in the arena. Glen Keeley, of Nanton, Alberta, Canada, had drawn Promise Land, Terry Williams' World Champion Bucking Bull, and was looking forward to a good ride and a high score. Keeley was a fifteen-year veteran bull rider and knew what it was all about. But that doesn't always work. Halfway into the ride, Keeley got in trouble. His hand hung in the rope a split second, just long enough to pull him down under the huge bull. Promise Land bucked full force and landed on Keeley's chest with all his 2,000-pound weight. Although the rider was wearing a protective vest, some blows can't be deflected. Keeley walked out of the arena, refusing a stretcher. Dr. Tandy Freeman was there, and knew Keeley had sustained rib fractures and a broken left arm. In spite of the fact his vital signs were strong, trauma and vascular surgeons could not save him. Massive internal injuries caused his death. Although family and friends were shocked and everyone involved was devastated by the outcome, two statements continued to surface. Promise Land was only doing his job, bucking as hard as he could, and only accidentally did he step on the fallen rider. The second statement was that Glen Keeley died doing what he loved. As Keeley's brother Jayson said, "Glen went out in a blaze of glory. What else can you ask for in this world than to die doing what you love."[96]

The Saturday night performance of the PBR Finals was dedicated to Glen Keeley. With his family present, all the competing cowboys plus many cowboy friends filed past a table, in the middle of the arena, and each one dropped a bandanna, on which they had written a special note to Glen. These bandannas were to be made into a quilt and given to the Keeley family. CEO Bernard also announced that a Glen Keeley Memorial Award has been formed in honor of the deceased

M. C. Tin Star aka Wally Badgett cartoon.

bull rider and is to be given to the Canadian bull rider who wins the most money each year in the PBR. For the year 2000 it was presented to B. J. Kramps, of Crooked Creek, Alberta, who was a good friend and traveled with Keeley.

In the spring of 2000 the PBR announced the formation of the Resistol Relief Fund. Resistol pledged $1 million toward helping injured bull riders pay their bills in times of need. The fund is there to support anyone who is injured by a bull—bullfighters, photographers, gatemen, etc., in addition to the bull rider. The money Resistol put up for the project is seed money, and PBR has consented to partner with them, on this non-profit fund aimed at softening the blow of the inevitable hardships associated with rodeo's most dangerous sport. Anyone can contribute to the fund.

The Professional Bull Riders organization is thriving. It is an exciting program that has chosen to present the competition in a new and different way—although the eight-second ride remains the same. No entry fee has been charged the competitor since 1996, and the prize money is made up from gate receipts, concessions, and sponsor money. Most of the Bud Light Cup events are held on weekends, so the cowboys can be home with their families during the week. As of 2000 appearance fees are paid to all participants in each of the Bud Light Cup competitions. The PBR makes a concerted effort to make sure all bulls in a performance are good, qualified buckers and have the ability to give the rider a score high enough to win money.[99]

The PBR Bud Light Cup World Championship Finals, held in Las Vegas, October 26 through 29, 2000, was a spectacular production. Forty-five bull riders, the "pick of the crop" for the year, according to total PBR monies earned, competed in four rounds of bull riding. The fifteen riders with the most points won during the finals came back for the short go. The Thomas & Mack arena was divided into two equal bull riding pens. The first eight riders competed from one arena, then everyone moved to the second arena for the next eight contestants. It made for a fast-moving program, and both arenas were very visible from any seat in the house.

The fans of the PBR are an excited and enthused group. Sixty percent of the tickets are sold to people who live east of the Mississippi River. Although these fans might not be inclined to sit through a rodeo and watch bull riding plus six other events, you can bet your boots they'll watch bull riding, every chance they get. The PBR includes their fans in many facets of the Finals. They hold a free TeamPBR Fan Fest party, which is two hours of being able to visit and get autographs and photos with their favorite bull riders, plus entertainment. Each contestant is introduced every night at the bull riding, in a big production opening, including special effects, spotlights, and fireworks. The bull riding is followed by an After Event Party in the ballroom of the host hotel, Caesar's Palace, and fans can attend for a small cost and mingle with the cowboys. There is also a Western Gift Expo that includes many of the bull riders at various booths to sign autographs and visit with fans. On Sunday morning Cowboy Church is held in the same ballroom at Caesar's Palace. In 2000 the service was led by Jim Custer, competitor Cody Custer's dad. Over a thousand attended.

The Professional Bull Riders have been accused of competing against the Professional Rodeo Cowboys Association. The critics say PBR has taken talented bull riders out of the PRCA ranks. The 1999 National Finals bull riding competition had many new unfamiliar names, and it was evident some of the seasoned bull riders were missing. This is where the decision is made by the bull rider; after all, he does pay his own way. Whether he chooses to ride in PRCA bull riding events or PBR venues is up to him. As one cowboy said, "I'd rather get on a bull with the chance of winning as much money as possible, because you never know when you might get injured, or not be able to ride again." As of June 11, 2000, unofficially, monies won in the PBR were topped by Chris Shivers with $182,650, and Aaron Semas was standing fifteenth with $58,069. Unofficial standings from the PRCA as of June 8, 2000, had Shane Drury in first place in bull riding with $44,304 and Garth Oldfield sitting in the fifteenth position with $17,891. The decision is made by the bull rider.

What will tomorrow hold for bull riding and rodeo? It's anyone's guess. For almost a century the sport has continued to develop, improve, and entertain. Bull riding cowboys have become athletes, and so have their adversaries—the 1,800-pound, hairy, horned bull with the very bad attitude. Whatever the future holds for bull riding, you can be guaranteed that the cowboy will still try to ride the gyrating, cantankerous bucker, and the bull will continue to try his best to get that cowboy off his back. And most certainly, the fans will be there to watch when the chute gate opens and the adrenaline begins to flow!

APPENDIX

CHAMPION ALL-AROUND COWBOYS

1929	Earl Thode, Belvedere, SD
1930	Clay Carr, Visalia, CA
1931	Johnie Schneider, Livermore, CA
1932	Donald Nesbit, Snowflake, AZ
1933	Clay Carr, Visalia, CA
1934	Leonard Ward, Talent, OR
1935	Everett Bowman, Hillside, AZ
1936	John Bowman, Oakdale, CA
1937	Everett Bowman, Hillside, AZ
1938	Burel Mulkey, Salmon, ID
1939	Paul Carney, Galeton, CO
1940	Fritz Truan, Long Beach, CA
1941	Homer Pettigrew, Grady, NM
1942	Gerald Roberts, Strong City, KS
1943	Louis Brooks, Pittsburg, OK
1944	Louis Brooks, Pittsburg, OK

(The above winners were named by the Rodeo Association of America.)

1945	No one chosen
1946	No one chosen
1947	Todd Whatley, Hugo, OK

(The 1947 champion was named by the Rodeo Cowboys Association, after the season ended at the request of a national trophy donor.)

1948	Gerald Roberts, Strong City, KS
1949	Jim Shoulders, Henryetta, OK
1950	Bill Linderman, Red Lodge, MT
1951	Casey Tibbs, Fort Pierre, SD

Year	Champion
1952	Harry Tompkins, Dublin, TX
1953	Bill Linderman, Red Lodge, MT
1954	Buck Rutherford, Lenapah, OK
1955	Casey Tibbs, Fort Pierre, SD
1956	Jim Shoulders, Henryetta, OK
1957	Jim Shoulders, Henryetta, OK
1958	Jim Shoulders, Henryetta, OK
1959	Jim Shoulders, Henryetta, OK
1960	Harry Tompkins, Dublin, TX
1961	Benny Reynolds, Melrose, MT
1962	Tom Nesmith, Bethel, OK
1963	Dean Oliver, Boise, ID
1964	Dean Oliver, Boise, ID
1965	Dean Oliver, Boise, ID
1966	Larry Mahan, Brooks, OR
1967	Larry Mahan, Brooks, OR
1968	Larry Mahan, Salem, OR
1969	Larry Mahan, Salem, OR
1970	Larry Mahan, Brooks, OR
1971	Phil Lyne, George West, TX
1972	Phil Lyne, George West, TX
1973	Larry Mahan, Dallas, TX
1974	Tom Ferguson, Miami, OK
1975	(tie) Tom Ferguson, Miami, OK Leo Camarillo, Oakdale, CA
1976	Tom Ferguson, Miami, OK* Tom Ferguson, Miami, OK
1977	Tom Ferguson, Miami, OK* Tom Ferguson, Miami, OK
1978	Tom Ferguson, Miami, OK* Tom Ferguson, Miami, OK

(From 1976 through 1978 world championships were determined by the highest amount of money won at the NFR, signified by *. PRCA championships were also awarded based on total season earnings.)

Year	Champion
1979	Tom Ferguson, Miami, OK
1980	Paul Tierney, Rapid City, SD
1981	Jimmie Cooper, Monument, NM
1982	Chris Lybbert, Coyote, CA
1983	Roy Cooper, Durant, OK
1984	Dee Pickett, Caldwell, ID

1985	Lewis Feild, Elk Ridge, UT
1986	Lewis Feild, Elk Ridge, UT
1987	Lewis Feild, Elk Ridge, UT
1988	Dave Appleton, Arlington, TX
1989	Ty Murray, Stephenville, TX
1990	Ty Murray, Stephenville, TX
1991	Ty Murray, Stephenville, TX
1992	Ty Murray, Stephenville, TX
1993	Ty Murray, Stephenville, TX
1994	Ty Murray, Stephenville, TX
1995	Joe Beaver, Huntsville, TX
1996	Joe Beaver, Huntsville, TX
1997	Dan Mortensen, Manhattan, MT
1998	Ty Murray, Stephenville, TX
1999	Fred Whitfield, Hockley, TX
2000	Joe Beaver, Huntsville, TX
2001	
2002	

CHAMPION BULL RIDERS

1929	Johnie Schneider, Livermore, CA
1930	Johnie Schneider, Livermore, CA
1931	Smokey Snyder, Bellflower, CA
1932	(tie) Johnie Schneider, Livermore, CA
	Smokey Snyder, Bellflower, CA
1933	Frankie Schneider, Caliente, CA
1934	Frankie Schneider, Caliente, CA
1935	Smokey Snyder, Bellflower, CA
1936	Smokey Snyder, Bellflower, CA
1937	Smokey Snyder, Bellflower, CA
1938	Kid Fletcher, Hugo, CO
1939	Dick Griffith, Fort Worth, TX
1940	Dick Griffith, Fort Worth, TX
1941	Dick Griffith, Fort Worth, TX
1942	Dick Griffith, Fort Worth, TX
1943	Ken Roberts, Strong City, KS
1944	Ken Roberts, Strong City, KS
1945	Ken Roberts, Strong City, KS
1946	PeeWee Morris, Custer, SD
1947	Wag Blessing, Bell, CA

1948	Harry Tompkins, Dublin, TX
1949	Harry Tompkins, Dublin, TX
1950	Harry Tompkins, Dublin, TX
1951	Jim Shoulders, Henryetta, OK
1952	Harry Tompkins, Dublin, TX
1953	Todd Whatley, Hugo, OK
1954	Jim Shoulders, Henryetta, OK
1955	Jim Shoulders, Henryetta, OK
1956	Jim Shoulders, Henryetta, OK
1957	Jim Shoulders, Henryetta, OK
1958	Jim Shoulders, Henryetta, OK
1959	Jim Shoulders, Henryetta, OK
1960	Harry Tompkins, Dublin, TX
1961	Ronnie Rossen, Broadus, MT
1962	Freckles Brown, Lawton, OK
1963	Bill Kornell, Palm Springs, CA
1964	Bob Wegner, Auburn, WA
1965	Larry Mahan, Brooks, OR
1966	Ronnie Rossen, Broadus, MT
1967	Larry Mahan, Brooks, OR
1968	George Paul, Del Rio, TX
1969	Doug Brown, Silverton, OR
1970	Gary Leffew, Santa Maria, CA
1971	Bill Nelson, San Francisco, CA
1972	John Quintana, Creswell, OR
1973	Bobby Steiner, Austin, TX
1974	Don Gay, Mesquite, TX
1975	Don Gay, Mesquite, TX
1976	Don Gay, Mesquite, TX
1977	Don Gay, Mesquite, TX
1978	Butch Kirby, Alba, TX
1979	Don Gay, Mesquite, TX
1980	Don Gay, Mesquite, TX
1981	Don Gay, Mesquite, TX
1982	Charles Sampson, Los Angeles, CA
1983	Cody Snyder, Redcliff, Alberta
1984	Don Gay, Mesquite, TX
1985	Ted Nuce, Manteca, CA
1986	Tuff Hedeman, Gainesville, TX
1987	Lane Frost, Lane, OK
1988	Jim Sharp, Kermit, TX
1989	Tuff Hedeman, Bowie, TX

1990   Jim Sharp, Kermit, TX
1991   Tuff Hedeman, Bowie, TX
1992   Cody Custer, Wickenburg, AZ
1993   Ty Murray, Stephenville, TX
1994   Daryl Mills, Pink Mountain, B. C.
1995   Jerome Davis, Archdale, NC
1996   Terry West, Henryetta, OK
1997   Scott Mendes, Weatherford, TX
1998   Ty Murray, Stephenville, TX
1999   Mike White, DeKalb, TX
2000   Cody Hancock, Taylor, AZ
2001
2002

PRCA BULL OF THE YEAR

1974   Tiger, Billy Minick
1975   (tie) Tiger, Cervi Rodeo Co.
       Black 6, Tommy Steiner
1976   Panda Bear, Harry Vold Co.
1977   General Isomo, Beutler Bros. & Cervi
1978   #11, Red Lightning, Steiner
1979   No. 777, Harry Vold Rodeo Co.
1980   No. 777, Harry Vold Rodeo Co.
1981   (tie) Savage 7, Steiner & No. 105, Del Hall
1982   Savage 7, Steiner
1983   Oscar's Velvet, Christensen Bros.
1984   #105, Del Hall
1985   Cowtown, Beutler & Son
1986   Mr. T., Burns Rodeo Co.
1987   Red Rock, Growney Bros.
1988   Skoal's Pacific Bell, Western Rodeos
1989   Skoal's Pacific Bell, Western Rodeos
1990   Skoal's Pacific Bell, Western Rodeos
1991   Skoal's Outlaw Willie, Andrews Rodeo Co.
1992   Copenhagen Rocky, Western Rodeos
1993   Grasshopper, Western Rodeos Inc.
1994   Bodacious, Andrews Rodeo Co.
1995   Bodacious, Andrews Rodeo Co.
1996   Dodge Ram Tough, Growney Bros.
1997   Rapid Fire, Big Bend Rodeo Co.

1998   Skoal's King Kong, Rafter H Rodeo
1999   Skoal's King Kong, Rafter H Rodeo
2000   Skoal's Border Patrol, Flying 5 Rodeo Company
2001
2002

LINDERMAN AWARD WINNERS

(To qualify a cowboy must earn at least $1,000 in each of three separate events, at least one of which must be roughstock and one a timed event. This award began in 1966, and was named for Bill Linderman.)

1966   Benny Reynolds, Melrose, MT
1967   Kenny McLean, Okanagan Falls, B. C.
1968   Paul Mayo, Grinnell, IA
1969   Kenny McLean
1970   Phil Lyne, George West, TX
1971   Phil Lyne
1972   Phil Lyne
1973   Bob Blandford, San Antonio, TX
1974   Bob Blandford
1975   Chip Whitaker, Chambers, NE
1976   Phil Lyne, Artesia Wells, TX
1977   Chip Whitaker
1978   Chip Whitaker
1979   Chip Whitaker
1980   Steve Bland, Trent, TX
1981   Lewis Feild, Peoa, UT
1982   Tom Erikson, Innisfall, Alberta
1983   Marty Melvin, Holabird, SD
1984   Marty Melvin
1985   Tom Erikson
1986   Bob Schall, Arlee, MT
1987   Tom Erikson
1988   Lewis Feild
1989   Philip Haugen, Williston, ND
1990   Bernie Smyth, Jr., Crossfield, Alberta
1991   Casey Minton, Redwood City, CA
1992   Bernie Smyth, Jr.

1993	Casey Minton
1994	No contestant qualified
1995	Chuck Kite, Monfort, WA
1996	No contestant qualified
1997	Kyle Whitaker, Chambers, NE
1998	Kyle Whitaker
1999	Dan Erickson, LaJunta, CO
2000	Jesse Bail, Camp Crook, SD
2001	
2002	

PRCA RESISTOL ROOKIE OF THE YEAR

1956	John W. Jones, San Luis Obispo, CA
1957	Bob A. Robinson, Tuttle, ID
1958	Benny Reynolds, Melrose, MT
1959	Harry Chartiers, Melba, MT
1960	Larry Kane, Big Sandy, MT
1961	Kenny McLean, Okanagan Falls, B. C.
1962	Jim Houston, Omaha, NE
1963	Bill Kornell, Salmon, ID
1964	Jim Steen, Glenn's Ferry, ID
1965	Dan Willis, Aquila, TX
1966	Tony Haberer, Muleshoe, TX
1967	Jay Himes, Beulah, CO
1968	Bowie Wesley, Wilderado, TX
1969	Phil Lyne, George West, TX
1970	Dick Aronson, Tempe, AZ
1971	Kent Youngblood, Lamesa, TX
1972	Dave Brock, Goodland, KS
1973	Bob Blandford, San Antonio, TX
1974	Lee Phillips, Carseland, Alberta
1975	Don Smith, Kiowa, OK
1976	Roy Cooper, Durant, OK
1977	Jimmy Cleveland, Hollis, OK
1978	Dee Pickett, Caldwell, ID
1979	Jerry Jetton, Stephenville, TX
1980	Jimmy Cooper, Monument, NM
1981	John W. Jones, Jr., Moro Bay, CA
1982	Clark Hankins, Rock Springs, TX
1983	Jackie Gibbs, Ivanhoe, TX

1984   Sam Poulous, Julian, CA
1985   Joe Beaver, Victoria, TX
1986   Jim Sharp, Kermit, TX
1987   Tony Currin, Heppner, OR
1988   Ty Murray, Odessa, TX
1989   David Bailey, Talhlequah, OK
1990   Fred Whitfield, Cypress, TX
1991   Brent Lewis, Pinon, NM
1992   Rope Myers, Athens, TX
1993   Blair Burk, Durant, OK
1994   Cody Ohl, Orchard, TX
1995   Curt Lyons, Ardmore, OK
1996   Shane Slack, Idabel, OK
1997   Mike White, Lake Charles, LA
1998   Danell Tipton, Spencer, OK
1999   Cash Myers, Athens, TX
2000   Luke Branquinho, Los Alamos, CA
2001
2002

PRCA BULL RIDING ROOKIE OF THE YEAR

1982   Denny Weir, Carthage, TX
1983   Jackie Gibbs, Ivanhoe, TX
1984   Sam Poulous, Julian, CA
1985   Scott Breding, Billings, MT
1986   Jim Sharp, Kermit, TX
1987   Kevin Smith, Allen, NE
1988   David Berry, Locust Grove, OK
1989   David Bailey, Tahlequah, OK
1990   Michael Gaffney, Lubbock, TX
1991   Ty Watkins, Monahans, TX
1992   Gilbert Carrillo, El Paso, TX
1993   Shawn Egg, Hockley, TX
1994   Chad Brennan, Ellsworth, NE
1995   Curt Lyons, Ardmore, OK
1996   Tony Mendes, Reno, NV
1997   Mike White, Lake Charles, LA
1998   Danell Tipton, Spencer, OK
1999   Felipe Aragon, Tome, NM

2000
2001   Zack Brown, Yorba Linda, CA
2002

PRCA NATIONAL FINALS

NFR AVERAGE BULL RIDING CHAMPIONS

		Pts	Ridden
1959	Jim Shoulders, Henryetta, OK	1611	9/10
1960	Duane Howard, Minnewaukan, ND	1416	8/10
1961	Bernis Johnson, Cleburne, TX	1197	7/8
1962	Bob Robinson, Porterville, CA	1014	6/8
1963	Leo Brown, Czar, Alberta	1384	8/8
1964	(tie) Bob Wegner, Auburn, WA	359	6/8
	Ronnie Rossen, Broadus, MT	359	6/8
1965	Ronnie Rossen, Broadus, MT	447	7/8
1966	Bob Wegner, Auburn, WA	404	6/8
1967	Freckles Brown, Soper, OK	480	7/9
1968	George Paul, Del Rio, TX	615	8/9
1969	Bobby Berger, Halstead, KS	594	8/9
1970	Gary Leffew, Santa Maria, CA	594	9/10
1971	Bobby Berger, Halstead, KS	648	9/10
1972	Phil Lyne, George West, TX	637	9/10
1973	Marvin Paul Shoulders, Henryetta, OK	747	9/10
1974	Sandy Kirby, Greenville, TX	540	8/10
1975	Denny Flynn, Springdale, AR	631	9/10
1976	Don Gay, Mesquite, TX	558	7/10
1977	No average		
1978	Lyle Sankey, Augusta, KS	688	9/11
1979	John Davis, Homedale, ID	641	8/10
1980	Lyle Sankey, Branson, MO	695	9/10
1981	Denny Flynn, Charleston, AR	700	9/10
1982	Denny Flynn, Charleston, AR	538	7/10
1983	Rickey Lindsey, Huntsville, TX	625	8/10
1984	Glen McIlvain, Mesquite, TX	630	8/10
1985	Ted Nuce, Manteca, CA	697	9/10
1986	Lane Frost, Lane, OK	678	9/10
1987	Tuff Hedeman, Bowie, TX	637	8/10
1988	Jim Sharp, Kermit, TX	771	10/10
1989	(tie) Tuff Hedeman, Bowie, TX	709	9/10
	Jim Sharp, Kermit, TX	709	9/10

264   COWBOY UP!

1990	Norman Curry, DeBerry, TX	800	10/10
1991	Michael Gaffney, Lubbock, TX	701	9/10
1992	Jim Sharp, Stephenville, TX	570	7/10
1993	Daryl Mills, Pink Mountain, B. C.	650	8/10
1994	Adriano Moraes, Keller, TX	773	10/10
1995	Jerome Davis, Archdale, NC	736	9/10
1996	Adriano Moraes, Keller, TX	724	9/10
1997	Scott Mendes, Weatherford, TX	557	7/10
1998	Ty Murray, Stephenville, TX	491	6/10
1999	Mike White, Lake Charles, LA	518	6/10
2000	Philip Elkins, Keller, TX	665	8/10
2001			
2002			

NFR TOP BUCKING BULLS

1959	Old Speck	Beutler Bros. & Son
1960	Old Speck	Beutler Bros. & Son
1961	Baldy	Korkow & Sutton
1962	Tornado	Jim Shoulders
1963	Tornado	Jim Shoulders
1964	Tornado	Jim Shoulders
1965	Tornado	Jim Shoulders
1966	Wilfred	Christensen Brothers
1967	Missoula	Christensen Brothers
1968	Booger Bear	Mesquite Rodeo Company
1969	Droopy	Walt Alsbaugh
1970	V61	Harry Knight
1971	Andy Capp	Jim Shoulders
1972	#17	Beutler Bros. & Cervi
1973	Tiger	Billie Minnick
1974	Ringeye	Mesquite Rodeo Company
1975	#33	Harry Vold
1976	Red One	Joe Kelsey
1977	Top Hand	Bob Aber
1978	#11, Red Lightning	Steiner
1979	#105	Del Hall
1980	Ruff & Ready	Neal Gay
1981	#105	Del Hall
1982	Velvet Wipeout	Erick Goolsby
1983	Sunni's Velvet	Cervi Championship Rodeo
1984	Cowtown	Beutler & Sons

1985	Cowtown	Beutler & Sons
1986	Mr. T	Pete Burns
1987	Pacific Bell	Western Rodeos, Inc.
1988	Ivy Skoal Classic	Ivy Rodeo Co.
1989	Mr. T Copenhagen	Pete Burns
1990	Playboy Skoal	David Bailey
1991	Wolfman Skoal	Growney Bros. Rodeo Co
1992	Bodacious	Andrews Rodeo Company
1993	Copenhagen Gunslinger	David Bailey
1994	Dodge Bodacious	Andrews Rodeo Company
1995	Dodge Bodacious	Andrews Rodeo Company
1996	Skat Kat Skoal	Andrews Rodeo Company
1997	Copenhagen Cowtown II	Beutler & Gaylord
1998	Skat Kat Skoal	Andrews Rodeo Company
1999	Skoal's Yellow Jacket	Flying Five Rodeo Co
2000	Dodge Durango	Rafter G Rodeo Company
2001		
2002		

PRCA DODGE NATIONAL CIRCUIT FINALS WINNERS

CIRCUITS COMPETING

Badlands Circuit
Columbia River Circuit (CR)
First Frontier Circuit (FF)
Great Lakes Circuit (GL)
Montana Circuit (MC)
Mountain States Circuit (MS)

Prairie Circuit
Sierra Circuit
Southeastern Circuit (SE)
Texas Circuit (TX)
Turquoise Circuit
Wilderness Circuit

CIRCUIT ALL-AROUND

1989	Lewis Feild, Wilderness		1996	Brian Fulton, Badlands
1990	Joe Parsons, Turquoise		1997	Tony Curran, CR
1991	Dee Pickett, Wilderness		1998	Brad Goodrich, CR
1992	Dan Mortensen, MT		1999	Mark Garrett, Badlands
1993	Ty Murray, TX		2000	Felipe Aragon, Turquoise
1994	Ty Murray, TX		2001	
1995	Speed Williams, SE		2002	

CIRCUIT BULL RIDING

Year	Champion
1987	(tie) Brett Todd, Montana
	Tuff Hedeman, TX
1988	Lane Frost, Prairie
1989	Tuff Hedeman, TX
1990	Cody Custer, Turquoise
1991	Cody Custer, Turquoise
1992	Cody Custer, Turquoise
1993	Dan Wolfe, Mountain States
1994	Ty Murray, TX
1995	Myron Duarte, Mountain States
1996	Ted Nuce, Sierra
1997	Casey Allred, Wilderness
1998	Justin Andrade, Sierra
1999	Gregory Potter, Prairie
2000	Cory Check, Great Lakes
2001	
2002	

PROFESSIONAL BULL RIDERS

WORLD CHAMPIONS

(The PBR World Champion is determined by Bud Light Cup points.)

Year	Champion
1994	Adriano Moraes, Sao Paulo, Brazil
1995	Tuff Hedeman, Morgan Mill, TX
1996	Owen Washburn, Lordsburg, NM
1997	Michael Gaffney, Albuquerque, NM
1998	Troy Dunn, Walkerston, Qslnd, Australia
1999	Cody Hart, Walnut Bend, TX
2000	Chris Shivers, Jonesville, LA
2001	
2002	

WORLD CHAMPION EVENT WINNERS

(This is determined by the highest aggregate score after five rounds of competition at the annual event held in Las Vegas.)

1995	Troy Dunn, Queensland, Australia	$ 56,975
1996	Ronny Kitchens, Kemp, TX	130,950
1997	Troy Dunn, Queensland, Australia	158,711
1998	Reed Corder, Melvin, TX	172,200
1999	Ty Murray, Stephenville, TX	263,283
2000	Tater Porter, Kenansville, FL	274,738
2001		
2002		

ROOKIE OF THE YEAR

(This is determined by the highest number of Bud Light Cup points during a cowboy's rookie year of competition.)

1995	J. W. Hart, Gainesville, TX
1996	Ronny Kitchens, Kemp, TX
1997	Keith Adams, Fredericksburg, TX
1998	Pete Hessman, Dodge City, KS
1999	Mike White, Lake Charles, LA
2000	Jason Bennett, Grand Prairie, TX
2001	
2002	

BULL OF THE YEAR

1995	Bodacious, Sammy Andrews
1996	Baby Face, Terry Williams
1997	Panhandle Slim, Terry Williams
1998	Moody Blues, Terry Williams
1999	Promise Land, Terry Williams
2000	Dillinger, Herrington Cattle Co.
2001	
2002	

STOCK CONTRACTOR OF THE YEAR

1995	Terry Williams, Carthage, TX
1996	Terry Williams, Carthage, TX

1997	Terry Williams, Carthage, TX
1998	Terry Williams, Carthage, TX
1999	Terry Williams, Carthage, TX
2000	Chad Herrington, Mount Belview, TX
2001	
2002	

HIGH MONEY BULL, BEFORE PBR FINALS

(This is determined by money earned on a bull during the regular season.)

1995	Baby Face	Terry Williams
1996	High Voltage	Sammy Andrews
1997	Shotgun Red	Jerome Robinson
1998	Promise Land	Terry Williams
1999	Gusto	Harper/Kimberlin
2000	Moody Blues	Herrington Cattle Company
2001		
2002		

PBR BUCKING BULL OF THE FINALS
(This is determined by a vote of the four Finals judges.)

1996	Strawberry Wine	James Harper
1997	Nitro	Dan Russell
1998	Copenhagen Cash	Don Kish
1999	Promise Land	Terry Williams
2000	Promise Land	Terry Williams
2001		
2002		

PBR PRIZE MONEY INCREASE

1994	$ 660,000	1999	5,000,000
1995	2,100,000	2000	6,200,000
1996	3,500,000	2001	
1997	4,000,000	2002	
1998	4,500,000		

Appendix 269

PBR RING OF HONOR
(The PBR Ring of Honor is the ultimate badge of honor in professional bull riding, reserved for those rare individuals who not only have excelled in the arena but who have dedicated themselves unselfishly to the betterment of the sport.)

1996	Cody Lambert	1999	Lane Frost
	Ted Nuce		Jerome Robinson
1997	Don Gay		Tuff Hedeman
	Harry Tompkins	2000	Clint Branger
1998	Jerome Davis	2001	
	Jim Shoulders	2002	
	Larry Mahan		

PROFESSIONAL WOMEN'S RODEO ASSOCIATION CHAMPIONS

	ALL-AROUND	BULL RIDING
1948	Margaret Owens	Jackie Worthington
1949	Amy McGilvray	Jackie Worthington
1950	Jackie Worthington	Jackie Worthington
1951	Jackie Worthington	Rose Garrett
1952	Wanda Harper Bush	Tommie Green
1953	Jackie Worthington	Jackie Worthington
1954	Jackie Worthington	Jackie Worthington
1955	Jackie Worthington	Jackie Worthington
1956	Jackie Worthington	Jackie Worthington
1957	Wanda Harper Bush	Meta Adams
1958	Wanda Harper Bush	Meta Adams
1959	Jane Mayo	Meta Adams
1960	Faye Ann Horton Leach	Incomplete records
1961	Sherry Combs Johnson	No records
1962	Incomplete records	
1963	Wanda Harper Bush	Bill Gay
1964	Wanda Harper Bush	Karen Theriot
1965	Wanda Harper Bush	Katherine Theriot
1966	Florence Youree	Fay Ann Horton Leach
1867	Betty Dusek	Sharon McFarland
1968	Wanda Harper Bush	Sharon McFarland
1969	Wanda Harper Bush	Kerry Grimes

270 COWBOY UP!

1970	Bonnie McPherson	Bonnie McPherson
1971	No records kept	
1972	No records kept	
1973	Sheila Bussey	Sheila Bussey
1974	Sue Pirtle	Lisa Martin
1975	Jimmie Gibbs Munroe	Jan Howell
1976	Sue Pirtle	Amy Iverson
1977	Jennifer Haynes	Sue Pirtle
1978	Judy Robinson	Donna Jones
1979	Jennifer Haynes	Tonya Tucker
1980	Gloria Paulsen	Tonya Tucker
1981	Betty Gayle Cooper	Amy Iverson
1982	Betty Gayle Cooper	Sandra Harrell
1983	Betty Gayle Cooper	Donna Jones
1984	Jan Howell	Trela Miller
1985	Twyla Rutherford	Tami Matteri
1986	Nancy Peirce	Lynn Jonckowski
1987	Gayle Brittain	Penny Bales
1988	Viki Williamson	Lynn Jonckowski
1989	Ronda Harrison	Tami George
1990	Ronda Harrison	Chris Swerdoski
1991	Ronda Harrison	Reijan Amason
1992	Jeana Brooks	Tammy George
1993	Jimmi Jo Martin	Melissa Phillips
1994	J. J. Hampton	Tammy Kelly
1995	J. J. Hampton	Tammy Kelly
1996	Lisa Gasperson	Tammy Kelly
1997	Joy Gordon	Tammy Kelly
1998	Tammy Kelly	Tammy Kelly
1999	J. J. Hampton	DeDee Crawford
2000	J. J. Hampton	DeDee Crawford
2001		
2002		

NATIONAL COWBOY HALL OF FAME
Oklahoma City, Oklahoma

RODEO HALL OF FAME HONOREES

Aber, Doff
Akridge, Eddy

Akers, Ira
Altizer, Jim Bob

Ambler, Jerry
Appleton, Dave
Arnold, Carl
Askin, Bob
Austin, Tex
Barmby, Bob
Beeson, Fred
Bell, Ray
Bennett, Hugh
Beutler, Elra
Beutler, Lynn
Blackstone, Vick
Blancett, Bertha
Blevins, Earl
Boen, Ken
Bolen, Bernice Dossey
Bond, Paul
Bowman, Everett
Bowman, John
Bowman, Louis Ed
Brady, Buff
Brennan, Harry
Brooks, Louis
Brown, Freckles
Burk, Clyde
Burmeister, A. H. "Hippy"
Burrell, Cuff
Buschbom, Jack
Byers, Chester
Bynum, James
Caldwell, Lee
Camarillo, Leo
Canutt, Yakima
Carney, Paul
Carr, Clay
Carroll, J. Ellison
Christensen, Hank
Clancy, Foghorn
Clark, Bobby
Clark, Gene
Clennon, Bart
Colborn, Ava

Colborn, Everett E.
Connelly, Edith Happy
Connelly, Lex
Cooper, Jimmie B.
Cooper, Roy
Cooper, Tuffy
Copenhaver, Deb
Cornish, Cecil
Cox, Breezy
Crosby, Bob
Curtis, Andy
Curtis, Eddie
Davis, Gordon
Davis, Sonny
Decker, Jo
Decker, Tater
Dightman, Myrtis
Doubleday, Ralph R
Duvall, Roy
Elliott, Verne
Eskew, Colonel Jim
Eskew, Junior
Estes, Bobby
Feild, Lewis
Ferguson, Tom
Fletcher, Kid
Fort, Troy C.
Gale, Floyd
Gamblin, Amye
Gardner, Joe
Garrett, Sam
Gaudin, D. J. "Kajun Kidd"
Goodspeed, Buck
Goodspeed, Jess
Grammer, Henry
Greenough, Turk
Griffith, Dick
Groff, Buddy
Hancock, Bill
Hancock, Sonny
Hastings, Fox
Hastings, Mike

Haverty, Del
Hefner, Hoytt
Helfrich, Devere
Hennigh, Duane
Henson, Margie Greenough
Holcomb, Homer
Hopkins, Ethel "Ma"
Irwin, C. B.
Ivory, Buster
Ivory, Perry
Jauregui, Andy
Johnson, Ben Sr.
Johnson, Clint
Jones, Cecil
Jones, John
Kirnan, Tommy
Knight, Harry
Knight, Pete
Lambert, Mel
Lefton, Abe
Leuschner, C. O. "Dogtown Slim"
Lewallen, G. K.
Like, Jim
Linder, Herman
Linderman, Bill
Linderman, Bud
Lindsey, John
Logan, Pete
Long, Hughie
Lowry, Fred
Lucas, Tad
Lybbert, Chris
Lyne, Phil
McCarty, Eddie
McClure, Jake
McCrory, Howard
McEntire, Clark
McEntire, John
McGinnis, Vera
McGinty, Rusty
McGonagill, Clay
McLaughlin, Don

McSpadden, Clem
Mahan, Larry
Mansfield, Toots
May, Harley
Merchant, Richard
Merritt, King
Mills, George
Montana, Montie
Mulhall, Lucille
Mulkey, Burel
Mullens, Johnnie
Murray, Leo "Pick"
Murray, Ty
Nesbitt, Don
Nesbitt, Pauline
Nesmith, Tom
Oliver, Dean
Oropeza, Vincente
Orr, Alice Greenough
Pickens, Slim
Pettigrew, Homer
Pickett, Bill
Pickett, Dee
Porter, Willard H.
Privett, "Booger Red"
Pruett, Gene
Purdy, Ikua
Rambo, Gene
Randall, Glenn
Randolph, Florence
Reynolds, Benny
Richardson, Nowata Slim
Riley, Doyle
Riley, Lanham
Riley, Mitzi Lucas
Roach, Ruth
Roberds, Coke T.
Roberts, E. C.
Roberts, Gerald
Roberts, Ken
Robinson, Lee
Roddy, Jack

Rollens, Rufus
Ross, Gene
Rowell, Harry
Rowell, Maggie
Rude, Ike
Rutherford, Buck
Ryan, Paddy
Salinas, Juan
Sawyer, Fern
Schneider, Frank
Schneider, Johnie
Shaw, Everett
Shelton, Dick
Shelton, Reine Hafley
Sheppard, Chuck
Sheppard, Nancy Kelley
Shoulders, Jim
Shultz, Charley
Smith, Bill
Smith, Dale D.
Snyder, Smokey
Sorenson, Doc
Sorrels, Buckshot
Sowder, Thad
Stahl, Jesse
Steele, Fannie S.
Steiner, Buck
Steiner, Tommy
Stillings, Floyd
Stoker, J. W.
Strickland, Hugh
Strickland, Mabel
Stroud, Leonard

Sundown, Jackson
Taillon, Cy
Tegland, Howard
Thode, Earl
Tibbs, Casey
Tierney, Paul
Todd, Homer
Tompkins, Harry
Trickey, Lorena
Truan, Fritz
Truitt, Dick
Tucker, Harley
Tureman, Sonny
Veach, C. Monroe
Walker, Enoch
Ward, Leonard
Weadick, Guy
Webster, Shoat
Weeks, Billy
Weeks, Guy
Welch, Joe
Whaley, Everett "Slim"
Wharton, Ray
Whatley, Todd
White, Vivian
Whiteman, Hub
Whiteman, Jim
Whitfield, Fred
Wilcox, Don
Witmer, Nancy Bragg
Worrell, Sonny
Yoder, Phil
Zumwalt, Oral

PRORODEO HALL OF FAME HONOREES
Colorado Springs, Colorado

ALL-AROUND
Everett Bowman
Louis Brooks
Paul Carney
Clay Carr
Lewis Feild
Tom Ferguson
Bill Linderman
Phil Lyne
Larry Mahan
Ty Murray
Gene Rambo
Benny Reynolds
Gerald Roberts
Chuck Sheppard
Jim Shoulders
Casey Tibbs
Fritz Truan

SADDLE BRONC
Bobby Berger
Winston Bruce
Deb Copenhaver
Shawn Davis
Brad Gjermundson
Monty Henson
Mel Hyland
Sharkey Irwin
Clint Johnson
Pete Knight
Gene Pruett
Bill Smith
Mike Stuart
Earl Thode
Guy Weeks
Marty Wood

BAREBACK
Eddie Akridge
Joe Alexander
Jack Buschbom
Bruce Ford
Marvin Garrett
John Hawkins
Jim Houston
J.C. Trujillo
Sonny Tureman
Jack Ward

BULL RIDING
Freckles Brown
Lane Frost
Don Gay
Dick Griffith
Tuff Hedeman
George Paul
Ken Roberts
Charles Sampson
Johnie Schneider
Smokey Snyder
Harry Tompkins

STEER WRESTLING
Hugh Bennett
Ote Berry
C. R. Boucher
James Bynum
Roy Duvall
John W. Jones, Sr.
John W. Jones, Jr.
Harley May
Homer Pettigrew
Bill Pickett
Jack Roddy
Gene Ross

Cartoon by Wally Badgett.

the "short go." He told the Houston rodeo board he could not be there as there was a PBR bull riding at the same time as the short go. Because of the PBR rules, if Murray missed the event he would be forced to sit out the PBR competition for a year. Murray did not attend the short go at Houston. The Houston rodeo board was furious, and there was much in the newspapers about Murray's decision to miss the "short go." Staying at Houston would have meant good money for Murray—$12,000—and if he won the all-around, possibly another

$25,000, plus money for his commentary of the rodeo on pay-per-view television. CEO Bernard said the PBR hurt Murray on the deal, but the association knows fans deserve credibility and they do advertise the "top forty-five bull riders." If Adriano Moraes couldn't go to Brazil for two months, then Ty Murray had to be treated the same way. It's the PBR rules.

PBR is very strict with their rules. After each performance contestants are required to sign autographs in the arena for fans. If they choose not to sign autographs, the first time they refuse they are fined $500. The second time they refuse they are charged $1,000, and the third offense carries a $5,000 fine. Seldom does a rider decide not to participate, and the fans get their autographs and are able to talk with their "stars." PBR feels this is tremendously important and one of the reasons their fans are so loyal.

Melvin Zebroski, Gillette, Wyoming, keeps his seat while he spurs the big black bucker at Cheyenne, 2000.—Photo by Randall A. Wagner, courtesy of Cheyenne Frontier Days.

There are 800 members in the Touring Pro Division of PBR. In the Bud Light Cup Cody Hart won the Bud Light Cup World Championship for 1999, and won $322,348 for the year. He won six regular season Bud Light events.

Ty Murray won $259,000 at the Bud Light Cup World Championship in Las Vegas in October 1999. This was Murray's third career Bud Light Cup event title.

At Bud Light Cup performances there are three judges. Most judges are PRCA-trained, but rules in PBR are somewhat different. They use the half-point system. Two judges are in the arena, and one is behind the chutes, to look for fouls. The third judge often breaks ties.

The cost of a ticket for a PBR performance is $50. "If we don't give them their money's worth, it wouldn't be right," said Bernard. Each event costs between $250,000 and $500,000 to produce.

Bull riders choose and vote on the bullfighters used for PBR events. Once the top bullfighters are picked, the one with the most votes chooses the upcoming events he wants to work. Then the second most-voted-on bullfighter chooses his events, and so on. In 1999 Joe Baumgartner was picked as first choice, with Jimmy Anderson second, then Roach Hedeman followed by Frank Newsom. In 2000 Jimmy Anderson was chosen as top bullfighter. These are truly top flight bullbaiters, and the riders feel as safe as they possibly can topping that renegade bull, with these men in the arena.

At the 2000 PBR Finals Jimmy Anderson, Rob Smets, Joe Baumgartner, and Dennis Johnson had the bullfighting duties. Flint Rasmussen, barrelman, was in charge of comic relief, and delighted the audience with his antics during each television break. Injuries were minor thanks to the expert cowboy protectors, as well as Dr. Tandy Freeman and his crew of medical personnel on hand.

In a conversation with Rob Smets, World Champion Bullfighter many times, he mentioned the bulls he has faced during his career. The best bulls of their time Smets first noted was Harry Vold's 777, during the late 1970s and early '80s, followed by Oscar, Christensen's Wilfred, Steiner's Red Lightning, and Wolfman. He said other bulls that had longevity in

Jason Legler, Loveland, Colorado, has the adrenaline flowing, as he rides the wild-eyed mount. Meanwhile, bullfighters Chatman and Hargo are ready to assist, if necessary.—Photo by Randall A. Wagner, courtesy of Cheyenne Frontier Days.

the arena, such as Red Rock, were Trick or Treat, White Water Skoal, and Wolfman.

As for fighting bulls that Smets had faced he quickly commented the best was Crooked Nose, owned by Vold. "He loved the game," grinned Smets. "He wasn't a killer. He would maul you (the bullfighter) all day, whirl around and look at you, as if to say, 'Get up, Let's do it again!'" Smets had just purchased some heifers out of Wolfman from Don Kish, stock contractor, with the hope to raise some good bucking bulls of his own.

When Jim Shoulders was asked what he thought of the PBR he said, "I think it is great! I have always said, you can't sell anything if you're not on TV. The humane element is the main thing that has kept rodeo off of television, and the calf roping is the event that bothers the animal activists the most. They don't have much trouble feeling sorry for a big old bull." Larry Mahan agrees with Shoulders' assessment of the PBR and said, "I honestly believe bull riding is the only rodeo event that can stand on its own."

On March 24, 2000, PBR suffered its first death by injury in the arena. Glen Keeley, of Nanton, Alberta, Canada, had drawn Promise Land, Terry Williams' World Champion Bucking Bull, and was looking forward to a good ride and a high score. Keeley was a fifteen-year veteran bull rider and knew what it was all about. But that doesn't always work. Halfway into the ride, Keeley got in trouble. His hand hung in the rope a split second, just long enough to pull him down under the huge bull. Promise Land bucked full force and landed on Keeley's chest with all his 2,000-pound weight. Although the rider was wearing a protective vest, some blows can't be deflected. Keeley walked out of the arena, refusing a stretcher. Dr. Tandy Freeman was there, and knew Keeley had sustained rib fractures and a broken left arm. In spite of the fact his vital signs were strong, trauma and vascular surgeons could not save him. Massive internal injuries caused his death. Although family and friends were shocked and everyone involved was devastated by the outcome, two statements continued to surface. Promise Land was only doing his job, bucking as hard as he could, and only accidentally did he step on the fallen rider. The second statement was that Glen Keeley died doing what he loved. As Keeley's brother Jayson said, "Glen went out in a blaze of glory. What else can you ask for in this world than to die doing what you love."[96]

The Saturday night performance of the PBR Finals was dedicated to Glen Keeley. With his family present, all the competing cowboys plus many cowboy friends filed past a table, in the middle of the arena, and each one dropped a bandanna, on which they had written a special note to Glen. These bandannas were to be made into a quilt and given to the Keeley family. CEO Bernard also announced that a Glen Keeley Memorial Award has been formed in honor of the deceased

M. C. Tin Star aka Wally Badgett cartoon.

bull rider and is to be given to the Canadian bull rider who wins the most money each year in the PBR. For the year 2000 it was presented to B. J. Kramps, of Crooked Creek, Alberta, who was a good friend and traveled with Keeley.

In the spring of 2000 the PBR announced the formation of the Resistol Relief Fund. Resistol pledged $1 million toward helping injured bull riders pay their bills in times of need. The fund is there to support anyone who is injured by a bull—bullfighters, photographers, gatemen, etc., in addition to the bull rider. The money Resistol put up for the project is seed money, and PBR has consented to partner with them, on this nonprofit fund aimed at softening the blow of the inevitable hardships associated with rodeo's most dangerous sport. Anyone can contribute to the fund.

The Professional Bull Riders organization is thriving. It is an exciting program that has chosen to present the competition in a new and different way—although the eight-second ride remains the same. No entry fee has been charged the competitor since 1996, and the prize money is made up from gate receipts, concessions, and sponsor money. Most of the Bud Light Cup events are held on weekends, so the cowboys can be home with their families during the week. As of 2000 appearance fees are paid to all participants in each of the Bud Light Cup competitions. The PBR makes a concerted effort to make sure all bulls in a performance are good, qualified buckers and have the ability to give the rider a score high enough to win money.[99]

The PBR Bud Light Cup World Championship Finals, held in Las Vegas, October 26 through 29, 2000, was a spectacular production. Forty-five bull riders, the "pick of the crop" for the year, according to total PBR monies earned, competed in four rounds of bull riding. The fifteen riders with the most points won during the finals came back for the short go. The Thomas & Mack arena was divided into two equal bull riding pens. The first eight riders competed from one arena, then everyone moved to the second arena for the next eight contestants. It made for a fast-moving program, and both arenas were very visible from any seat in the house.

The fans of the PBR are an excited and enthused group. Sixty percent of the tickets are sold to people who live east of the Mississippi River. Although these fans might not be inclined to sit through a rodeo and watch bull riding plus six other events, you can bet your boots they'll watch bull riding, every chance they get. The PBR includes their fans in many facets of the Finals. They hold a free TeamPBR Fan Fest party, which is two hours of being able to visit and get autographs and photos with their favorite bull riders, plus entertainment. Each contestant is introduced every night at the bull riding, in a big production opening, including special effects, spotlights, and fireworks. The bull riding is followed by an After Event Party in the ballroom of the host hotel, Caesar's Palace, and fans can attend for a small cost and mingle with the cowboys. There is also a Western Gift Expo that includes many of the bull riders at various booths to sign autographs and visit with fans. On Sunday morning Cowboy Church is held in the same ballroom at Caesar's Palace. In 2000 the service was led by Jim Custer, competitor Cody Custer's dad. Over a thousand attended.

The Professional Bull Riders have been accused of competing against the Professional Rodeo Cowboys Association. The critics say PBR has taken talented bull riders out of the PRCA ranks. The 1999 National Finals bull riding competition had many new unfamiliar names, and it was evident some of the seasoned bull riders were missing. This is where the decision is made by the bull rider; after all, he does pay his own way. Whether he chooses to ride in PRCA bull riding events or PBR venues is up to him. As one cowboy said, "I'd rather get on a bull with the chance of winning as much money as possible, because you never know when you might get injured, or not be able to ride again." As of June 11, 2000, unofficially, monies won in the PBR were topped by Chris Shivers with $182,650, and Aaron Semas was standing fifteenth with $58,069. Unofficial standings from the PRCA as of June 8, 2000, had Shane Drury in first place in bull riding with $44,304 and Garth Oldfield sitting in the fifteenth position with $17,891. The decision is made by the bull rider.

What will tomorrow hold for bull riding and rodeo? It's anyone's guess. For almost a century the sport has continued to develop, improve, and entertain. Bull riding cowboys have become athletes, and so have their adversaries—the 1,800-pound, hairy, horned bull with the very bad attitude. Whatever the future holds for bull riding, you can be guaranteed that the cowboy will still try to ride the gyrating, cantankerous bucker, and the bull will continue to try his best to get that cowboy off his back. And most certainly, the fans will be there to watch when the chute gate opens and the adrenaline begins to flow!

Appendix

CHAMPION ALL-AROUND COWBOYS

1929	Earl Thode, Belvedere, SD
1930	Clay Carr, Visalia, CA
1931	Johnie Schneider, Livermore, CA
1932	Donald Nesbit, Snowflake, AZ
1933	Clay Carr, Visalia, CA
1934	Leonard Ward, Talent, OR
1935	Everett Bowman, Hillside, AZ
1936	John Bowman, Oakdale, CA
1937	Everett Bowman, Hillside, AZ
1938	Burel Mulkey, Salmon, ID
1939	Paul Carney, Galeton, CO
1940	Fritz Truan, Long Beach, CA
1941	Homer Pettigrew, Grady, NM
1942	Gerald Roberts, Strong City, KS
1943	Louis Brooks, Pittsburg, OK
1944	Louis Brooks, Pittsburg, OK

(The above winners were named by the Rodeo Association of America.)

1945	No one chosen
1946	No one chosen
1947	Todd Whatley, Hugo, OK

(The 1947 champion was named by the Rodeo Cowboys Association, after the season ended at the request of a national trophy donor.)

1948	Gerald Roberts, Strong City, KS
1949	Jim Shoulders, Henryetta, OK
1950	Bill Linderman, Red Lodge, MT
1951	Casey Tibbs, Fort Pierre, SD

1952	Harry Tompkins, Dublin, TX
1953	Bill Linderman, Red Lodge, MT
1954	Buck Rutherford, Lenapah, OK
1955	Casey Tibbs, Fort Pierre, SD
1956	Jim Shoulders, Henryetta, OK
1957	Jim Shoulders, Henryetta, OK
1958	Jim Shoulders, Henryetta, OK
1959	Jim Shoulders, Henryetta, OK
1960	Harry Tompkins, Dublin, TX
1961	Benny Reynolds, Melrose, MT
1962	Tom Nesmith, Bethel, OK
1963	Dean Oliver, Boise, ID
1964	Dean Oliver, Boise, ID
1965	Dean Oliver, Boise, ID
1966	Larry Mahan, Brooks, OR
1967	Larry Mahan, Brooks, OR
1968	Larry Mahan, Salem, OR
1969	Larry Mahan, Salem, OR
1970	Larry Mahan, Brooks, OR
1971	Phil Lyne, George West, TX
1972	Phil Lyne, George West, TX
1973	Larry Mahan, Dallas, TX
1974	Tom Ferguson, Miami, OK
1975	(tie) Tom Ferguson, Miami, OK Leo Camarillo, Oakdale, CA
1976	Tom Ferguson, Miami, OK* Tom Ferguson, Miami, OK
1977	Tom Ferguson, Miami, OK* Tom Ferguson, Miami, OK
1978	Tom Ferguson, Miami, OK* Tom Ferguson, Miami, OK

(From 1976 through 1978 world championships were determined by the highest amount of money won at the NFR, signified by *. PRCA championships were also awarded based on total season earnings.)

1979	Tom Ferguson, Miami, OK
1980	Paul Tierney, Rapid City, SD
1981	Jimmie Cooper, Monument, NM
1982	Chris Lybbert, Coyote, CA
1983	Roy Cooper, Durant, OK
1984	Dee Pickett, Caldwell, ID

1985	Lewis Feild, Elk Ridge, UT
1986	Lewis Feild, Elk Ridge, UT
1987	Lewis Feild, Elk Ridge, UT
1988	Dave Appleton, Arlington, TX
1989	Ty Murray, Stephenville, TX
1990	Ty Murray, Stephenville, TX
1991	Ty Murray, Stephenville, TX
1992	Ty Murray, Stephenville, TX
1993	Ty Murray, Stephenville, TX
1994	Ty Murray, Stephenville, TX
1995	Joe Beaver, Huntsville, TX
1996	Joe Beaver, Huntsville, TX
1997	Dan Mortensen, Manhattan, MT
1998	Ty Murray, Stephenville, TX
1999	Fred Whitfield, Hockley, TX
2000	Joe Beaver, Huntsville, TX
2001	
2002	

CHAMPION BULL RIDERS

1929	Johnie Schneider, Livermore, CA
1930	Johnie Schneider, Livermore, CA
1931	Smokey Snyder, Bellflower, CA
1932	(tie) Johnie Schneider, Livermore, CA
	Smokey Snyder, Bellflower, CA
1933	Frankie Schneider, Caliente, CA
1934	Frankie Schneider, Caliente, CA
1935	Smokey Snyder, Bellflower, CA
1936	Smokey Snyder, Bellflower, CA
1937	Smokey Snyder, Bellflower, CA
1938	Kid Fletcher, Hugo, CO
1939	Dick Griffith, Fort Worth, TX
1940	Dick Griffith, Fort Worth, TX
1941	Dick Griffith, Fort Worth, TX
1942	Dick Griffith, Fort Worth, TX
1943	Ken Roberts, Strong City, KS
1944	Ken Roberts, Strong City, KS
1945	Ken Roberts, Strong City, KS
1946	PeeWee Morris, Custer, SD
1947	Wag Blessing, Bell, CA

1948	Harry Tompkins, Dublin, TX
1949	Harry Tompkins, Dublin, TX
1950	Harry Tompkins, Dublin, TX
1951	Jim Shoulders, Henryetta, OK
1952	Harry Tompkins, Dublin, TX
1953	Todd Whatley, Hugo, OK
1954	Jim Shoulders, Henryetta, OK
1955	Jim Shoulders, Henryetta, OK
1956	Jim Shoulders, Henryetta, OK
1957	Jim Shoulders, Henryetta, OK
1958	Jim Shoulders, Henryetta, OK
1959	Jim Shoulders, Henryetta, OK
1960	Harry Tompkins, Dublin, TX
1961	Ronnie Rossen, Broadus, MT
1962	Freckles Brown, Lawton, OK
1963	Bill Kornell, Palm Springs, CA
1964	Bob Wegner, Auburn, WA
1965	Larry Mahan, Brooks, OR
1966	Ronnie Rossen, Broadus, MT
1967	Larry Mahan, Brooks, OR
1968	George Paul, Del Rio, TX
1969	Doug Brown, Silverton, OR
1970	Gary Leffew, Santa Maria, CA
1971	Bill Nelson, San Francisco, CA
1972	John Quintana, Creswell, OR
1973	Bobby Steiner, Austin, TX
1974	Don Gay, Mesquite, TX
1975	Don Gay, Mesquite, TX
1976	Don Gay, Mesquite, TX
1977	Don Gay, Mesquite, TX
1978	Butch Kirby, Alba, TX
1979	Don Gay, Mesquite, TX
1980	Don Gay, Mesquite, TX
1981	Don Gay, Mesquite, TX
1982	Charles Sampson, Los Angeles, CA
1983	Cody Snyder, Redcliff, Alberta
1984	Don Gay, Mesquite, TX
1985	Ted Nuce, Manteca, CA
1986	Tuff Hedeman, Gainesville, TX
1987	Lane Frost, Lane, OK
1988	Jim Sharp, Kermit, TX
1989	Tuff Hedeman, Bowie, TX

1990 Jim Sharp, Kermit, TX
1991 Tuff Hedeman, Bowie, TX
1992 Cody Custer, Wickenburg, AZ
1993 Ty Murray, Stephenville, TX
1994 Daryl Mills, Pink Mountain, B. C.
1995 Jerome Davis, Archdale, NC
1996 Terry West, Henryetta, OK
1997 Scott Mendes, Weatherford, TX
1998 Ty Murray, Stephenville, TX
1999 Mike White, DeKalb, TX
2000 Cody Hancock, Taylor, AZ
2001
2002

PRCA BULL OF THE YEAR

1974 Tiger, Billy Minick
1975 (tie) Tiger, Cervi Rodeo Co.
Black 6, Tommy Steiner
1976 Panda Bear, Harry Vold Co.
1977 General Isomo, Beutler Bros. & Cervi
1978 #11, Red Lightning, Steiner
1979 No. 777, Harry Vold Rodeo Co.
1980 No. 777, Harry Vold Rodeo Co.
1981 (tie) Savage 7, Steiner & No. 105, Del Hall
1982 Savage 7, Steiner
1983 Oscar's Velvet, Christensen Bros.
1984 #105, Del Hall
1985 Cowtown, Beutler & Son
1986 Mr. T., Burns Rodeo Co.
1987 Red Rock, Growney Bros.
1988 Skoal's Pacific Bell, Western Rodeos
1989 Skoal's Pacific Bell, Western Rodeos
1990 Skoal's Pacific Bell, Western Rodeos
1991 Skoal's Outlaw Willie, Andrews Rodeo Co.
1992 Copenhagen Rocky, Western Rodeos
1993 Grasshopper, Western Rodeos Inc.
1994 Bodacious, Andrews Rodeo Co.
1995 Bodacious, Andrews Rodeo Co.
1996 Dodge Ram Tough, Growney Bros.
1997 Rapid Fire, Big Bend Rodeo Co.

1998   Skoal's King Kong, Rafter H Rodeo
1999   Skoal's King Kong, Rafter H Rodeo
2000   Skoal's Border Patrol, Flying 5 Rodeo Company
2001
2002

LINDERMAN AWARD WINNERS

(To qualify a cowboy must earn at least $1,000 in each of three separate events, at least one of which must be roughstock and one a timed event. This award began in 1966, and was named for Bill Linderman.)

1966   Benny Reynolds, Melrose, MT
1967   Kenny McLean, Okanagan Falls, B. C.
1968   Paul Mayo, Grinnell, IA
1969   Kenny McLean
1970   Phil Lyne, George West, TX
1971   Phil Lyne
1972   Phil Lyne
1973   Bob Blandford, San Antonio, TX
1974   Bob Blandford
1975   Chip Whitaker, Chambers, NE
1976   Phil Lyne, Artesia Wells, TX
1977   Chip Whitaker
1978   Chip Whitaker
1979   Chip Whitaker
1980   Steve Bland, Trent, TX
1981   Lewis Feild, Peoa, UT
1982   Tom Erikson, Innisfall, Alberta
1983   Marty Melvin, Holabird, SD
1984   Marty Melvin
1985   Tom Erikson
1986   Bob Schall, Arlee, MT
1987   Tom Erikson
1988   Lewis Feild
1989   Philip Haugen, Williston, ND
1990   Bernie Smyth, Jr., Crossfield, Alberta
1991   Casey Minton, Redwood City, CA
1992   Bernie Smyth, Jr.

1993	Casey Minton
1994	No contestant qualified
1995	Chuck Kite, Monfort, WA
1996	No contestant qualified
1997	Kyle Whitaker, Chambers, NE
1998	Kyle Whitaker
1999	Dan Erickson, LaJunta, CO
2000	Jesse Bail, Camp Crook, SD
2001	
2002	

PRCA RESISTOL ROOKIE OF THE YEAR

1956	John W. Jones, San Luis Obispo, CA
1957	Bob A. Robinson, Tuttle, ID
1958	Benny Reynolds, Melrose, MT
1959	Harry Chartiers, Melba, MT
1960	Larry Kane, Big Sandy, MT
1961	Kenny McLean, Okanagan Falls, B. C.
1962	Jim Houston, Omaha, NE
1963	Bill Kornell, Salmon, ID
1964	Jim Steen, Glenn's Ferry, ID
1965	Dan Willis, Aquila, TX
1966	Tony Haberer, Muleshoe, TX
1967	Jay Himes, Beulah, CO
1968	Bowie Wesley, Wilderado, TX
1969	Phil Lyne, George West, TX
1970	Dick Aronson, Tempe, AZ
1971	Kent Youngblood, Lamesa, TX
1972	Dave Brock, Goodland, KS
1973	Bob Blandford, San Antonio, TX
1974	Lee Phillips, Carseland, Alberta
1975	Don Smith, Kiowa, OK
1976	Roy Cooper, Durant, OK
1977	Jimmy Cleveland, Hollis, OK
1978	Dee Pickett, Caldwell, ID
1979	Jerry Jetton, Stephenville, TX
1980	Jimmy Cooper, Monument, NM
1981	John W. Jones, Jr., Moro Bay, CA
1982	Clark Hankins, Rock Springs, TX
1983	Jackie Gibbs, Ivanhoe, TX

1984   Sam Poulous, Julian, CA
1985   Joe Beaver, Victoria, TX
1986   Jim Sharp, Kermit, TX
1987   Tony Currin, Heppner, OR
1988   Ty Murray, Odessa, TX
1989   David Bailey, Talhlequah, OK
1990   Fred Whitfield, Cypress, TX
1991   Brent Lewis, Pinon, NM
1992   Rope Myers, Athens, TX
1993   Blair Burk, Durant, OK
1994   Cody Ohl, Orchard, TX
1995   Curt Lyons, Ardmore, OK
1996   Shane Slack, Idabel, OK
1997   Mike White, Lake Charles, LA
1998   Danell Tipton, Spencer, OK
1999   Cash Myers, Athens, TX
2000   Luke Branquinho, Los Alamos, CA
2001
2002

PRCA BULL RIDING ROOKIE OF THE YEAR

1982   Denny Weir, Carthage, TX
1983   Jackie Gibbs, Ivanhoe, TX
1984   Sam Poulous, Julian, CA
1985   Scott Breding, Billings, MT
1986   Jim Sharp, Kermit, TX
1987   Kevin Smith, Allen, NE
1988   David Berry, Locust Grove, OK
1989   David Bailey, Tahlequah, OK
1990   Michael Gaffney, Lubbock, TX
1991   Ty Watkins, Monahans, TX
1992   Gilbert Carrillo, El Paso, TX
1993   Shawn Egg, Hockley, TX
1994   Chad Brennan, Ellsworth, NE
1995   Curt Lyons, Ardmore, OK
1996   Tony Mendes, Reno, NV
1997   Mike White, Lake Charles, LA
1998   Danell Tipton, Spencer, OK
1999   Felipe Aragon, Tome, NM

2000
2001   Zack Brown, Yorba Linda, CA
2002

PRCA NATIONAL FINALS

NFR AVERAGE BULL RIDING CHAMPIONS

Year	Champion	Pts	Ridden
1959	Jim Shoulders, Henryetta, OK	1611	9/10
1960	Duane Howard, Minnewaukan, ND	1416	8/10
1961	Bernis Johnson, Cleburne, TX	1197	7/8
1962	Bob Robinson, Porterville, CA	1014	6/8
1963	Leo Brown, Czar, Alberta	1384	8/8
1964	(tie) Bob Wegner, Auburn, WA	359	6/8
	Ronnie Rossen, Broadus, MT	359	6/8
1965	Ronnie Rossen, Broadus, MT	447	7/8
1966	Bob Wegner, Auburn, WA	404	6/8
1967	Freckles Brown, Soper, OK	480	7/9
1968	George Paul, Del Rio, TX	615	8/9
1969	Bobby Berger, Halstead, KS	594	8/9
1970	Gary Leffew, Santa Maria, CA	594	9/10
1971	Bobby Berger, Halstead, KS	648	9/10
1972	Phil Lyne, George West, TX	637	9/10
1973	Marvin Paul Shoulders, Henryetta, OK	747	9/10
1974	Sandy Kirby, Greenville, TX	540	8/10
1975	Denny Flynn, Springdale, AR	631	9/10
1976	Don Gay, Mesquite, TX	558	7/10
1977	No average		
1978	Lyle Sankey, Augusta, KS	688	9/11
1979	John Davis, Homedale, ID	641	8/10
1980	Lyle Sankey, Branson, MO	695	9/10
1981	Denny Flynn, Charleston, AR	700	9/10
1982	Denny Flynn, Charleston, AR	538	7/10
1983	Rickey Lindsey, Huntsville, TX	625	8/10
1984	Glen McIlvain, Mesquite, TX	630	8/10
1985	Ted Nuce, Manteca, CA	697	9/10
1986	Lane Frost, Lane, OK	678	9/10
1987	Tuff Hedeman, Bowie, TX	637	8/10
1988	Jim Sharp, Kermit, TX	771	10/10
1989	(tie) Tuff Hedeman, Bowie, TX	709	9/10
	Jim Sharp, Kermit, TX	709	9/10

264   COWBOY UP!

1990	Norman Curry, DeBerry, TX	800	10/10
1991	Michael Gaffney, Lubbock, TX	701	9/10
1992	Jim Sharp, Stephenville, TX	570	7/10
1993	Daryl Mills, Pink Mountain, B. C.	650	8/10
1994	Adriano Moraes, Keller, TX	773	10/10
1995	Jerome Davis, Archdale, NC	736	9/10
1996	Adriano Moraes, Keller, TX	724	9/10
1997	Scott Mendes, Weatherford, TX	557	7/10
1998	Ty Murray, Stephenville, TX	491	6/10
1999	Mike White, Lake Charles, LA	518	6/10
2000	Philip Elkins, Keller, TX	665	8/10
2001			
2002			

NFR TOP BUCKING BULLS

1959	Old Speck	Beutler Bros. & Son
1960	Old Speck	Beutler Bros. & Son
1961	Baldy	Korkow & Sutton
1962	Tornado	Jim Shoulders
1963	Tornado	Jim Shoulders
1964	Tornado	Jim Shoulders
1965	Tornado	Jim Shoulders
1966	Wilfred	Christensen Brothers
1967	Missoula	Christensen Brothers
1968	Booger Bear	Mesquite Rodeo Company
1969	Droopy	Walt Alsbaugh
1970	V61	Harry Knight
1971	Andy Capp	Jim Shoulders
1972	#17	Beutler Bros. & Cervi
1973	Tiger	Billie Minnick
1974	Ringeye	Mesquite Rodeo Company
1975	#33	Harry Vold
1976	Red One	Joe Kelsey
1977	Top Hand	Bob Aber
1978	#11, Red Lightning	Steiner
1979	#105	Del Hall
1980	Ruff & Ready	Neal Gay
1981	#105	Del Hall
1982	Velvet Wipeout	Erick Goolsby
1983	Sunni's Velvet	Cervi Championship Rodeo
1984	Cowtown	Beutler & Sons

1985	Cowtown	Beutler & Sons
1986	Mr. T	Pete Burns
1987	Pacific Bell	Western Rodeos, Inc.
1988	Ivy Skoal Classic	Ivy Rodeo Co.
1989	Mr. T Copenhagen	Pete Burns
1990	Playboy Skoal	David Bailey
1991	Wolfman Skoal	Growney Bros. Rodeo Co
1992	Bodacious	Andrews Rodeo Company
1993	Copenhagen Gunslinger	David Bailey
1994	Dodge Bodacious	Andrews Rodeo Company
1995	Dodge Bodacious	Andrews Rodeo Company
1996	Skat Kat Skoal	Andrews Rodeo Company
1997	Copenhagen Cowtown II	Beutler & Gaylord
1998	Skat Kat Skoal	Andrews Rodeo Company
1999	Skoal's Yellow Jacket	Flying Five Rodeo Co
2000	Dodge Durango	Rafter G Rodeo Company
2001		
2002		

PRCA DODGE NATIONAL CIRCUIT FINALS WINNERS

CIRCUITS COMPETING

Badlands Circuit
Columbia River Circuit (CR)
First Frontier Circuit (FF)
Great Lakes Circuit (GL)
Montana Circuit (MC)
Mountain States Circuit (MS)
Prairie Circuit
Sierra Circuit
Southeastern Circuit (SE)
Texas Circuit (TX)
Turquoise Circuit
Wilderness Circuit

CIRCUIT ALL-AROUND

1989	Lewis Feild, Wilderness		1996	Brian Fulton, Badlands
1990	Joe Parsons, Turquoise		1997	Tony Curran, CR
1991	Dee Pickett, Wilderness		1998	Brad Goodrich, CR
1992	Dan Mortensen, MT		1999	Mark Garrett, Badlands
1993	Ty Murray, TX		2000	Felipe Aragon, Turquoise
1994	Ty Murray, TX		2001	
1995	Speed Williams, SE		2002	

CIRCUIT BULL RIDING

1987	(tie) Brett Todd, Montana
	Tuff Hedeman, TX
1988	Lane Frost, Prairie
1989	Tuff Hedeman, TX
1990	Cody Custer, Turquoise
1991	Cody Custer, Turquoise
1992	Cody Custer, Turquoise
1993	Dan Wolfe, Mountain States
1994	Ty Murray, TX
1995	Myron Duarte, Mountain States
1996	Ted Nuce, Sierra
1997	Casey Allred, Wilderness
1998	Justin Andrade, Sierra
1999	Gregory Potter, Prairie
2000	Cory Check, Great Lakes
2001	
2002	

PROFESSIONAL BULL RIDERS

WORLD CHAMPIONS

(The PBR World Champion is determined by Bud Light Cup points.)

1994	Adriano Moraes, Sao Paulo, Brazil
1995	Tuff Hedeman, Morgan Mill, TX
1996	Owen Washburn, Lordsburg, NM
1997	Michael Gaffney, Albuquerque, NM
1998	Troy Dunn, Walkerston, Qslnd, Australia
1999	Cody Hart, Walnut Bend, TX
2000	Chris Shivers, Jonesville, LA
2001	
2002	

Appendix 267

WORLD CHAMPION EVENT WINNERS

(This is determined by the highest aggregate score after five rounds of competition at the annual event held in Las Vegas.)

Year	Winner	Earnings
1995	Troy Dunn, Queensland, Australia	$ 56,975
1996	Ronny Kitchens, Kemp, TX	130,950
1997	Troy Dunn, Queensland, Australia	158,711
1998	Reed Corder, Melvin, TX	172,200
1999	Ty Murray, Stephenville, TX	263,283
2000	Tater Porter, Kenansville, FL	274,738
2001		
2002		

ROOKIE OF THE YEAR

(This is determined by the highest number of Bud Light Cup points during a cowboy's rookie year of competition.)

1995	J. W. Hart, Gainesville, TX
1996	Ronny Kitchens, Kemp, TX
1997	Keith Adams, Fredericksburg, TX
1998	Pete Hessman, Dodge City, KS
1999	Mike White, Lake Charles, LA
2000	Jason Bennett, Grand Prairie, TX
2001	
2002	

BULL OF THE YEAR

Year	Bull, Owner
1995	Bodacious, Sammy Andrews
1996	Baby Face, Terry Williams
1997	Panhandle Slim, Terry Williams
1998	Moody Blues, Terry Williams
1999	Promise Land, Terry Williams
2000	Dillinger, Herrington Cattle Co.
2001	
2002	

STOCK CONTRACTOR OF THE YEAR

1995	Terry Williams, Carthage, TX
1996	Terry Williams, Carthage, TX

1997	Terry Williams, Carthage, TX	
1998	Terry Williams, Carthage, TX	
1999	Terry Williams, Carthage, TX	
2000	Chad Herrington, Mount Belview, TX	
2001		
2002		

HIGH MONEY BULL, BEFORE PBR FINALS

(This is determined by money earned on a bull during the regular season.)

Year	Bull	Owner
1995	Baby Face	Terry Williams
1996	High Voltage	Sammy Andrews
1997	Shotgun Red	Jerome Robinson
1998	Promise Land	Terry Williams
1999	Gusto	Harper/Kimberlin
2000	Moody Blues	Herrington Cattle Company
2001		
2002		

PBR BUCKING BULL OF THE FINALS

(This is determined by a vote of the four Finals judges.)

Year	Bull	Owner
1996	Strawberry Wine	James Harper
1997	Nitro	Dan Russell
1998	Copenhagen Cash	Don Kish
1999	Promise Land	Terry Williams
2000	Promise Land	Terry Williams
2001		
2002		

PBR PRIZE MONEY INCREASE

Year	Amount	Year	Amount
1994	$ 660,000	1999	5,000,000
1995	2,100,000	2000	6,200,000
1996	3,500,000	2001	
1997	4,000,000	2002	
1998	4,500,000		

Appendix 269

PBR RING OF HONOR
(The PBR Ring of Honor is the ultimate badge of honor in professional bull riding, reserved for those rare individuals who not only have excelled in the arena but who have dedicated themselves unselfishly to the betterment of the sport.)

1996	Cody Lambert	1999	Lane Frost
	Ted Nuce		Jerome Robinson
1997	Don Gay		Tuff Hedeman
	Harry Tompkins	2000	Clint Branger
1998	Jerome Davis	2001	
	Jim Shoulders	2002	
	Larry Mahan		

PROFESSIONAL WOMEN'S RODEO ASSOCIATION CHAMPIONS

	ALL-AROUND	BULL RIDING
1948	Margaret Owens	Jackie Worthington
1949	Amy McGilvray	Jackie Worthington
1950	Jackie Worthington	Jackie Worthington
1951	Jackie Worthington	Rose Garrett
1952	Wanda Harper Bush	Tommie Green
1953	Jackie Worthington	Jackie Worthington
1954	Jackie Worthington	Jackie Worthington
1955	Jackie Worthington	Jackie Worthington
1956	Jackie Worthington	Jackie Worthington
1957	Wanda Harper Bush	Meta Adams
1958	Wanda Harper Bush	Meta Adams
1959	Jane Mayo	Meta Adams
1960	Faye Ann Horton Leach	Incomplete records
1961	Sherry Combs Johnson	No records
1962	Incomplete records	
1963	Wanda Harper Bush	Bill Gay
1964	Wanda Harper Bush	Karen Theriot
1965	Wanda Harper Bush	Katherine Theriot
1966	Florence Youree	Fay Ann Horton Leach
1867	Betty Dusek	Sharon McFarland
1968	Wanda Harper Bush	Sharon McFarland
1969	Wanda Harper Bush	Kerry Grimes

1970	Bonnie McPherson	Bonnie McPherson
1971	No records kept	
1972	No records kept	
1973	Sheila Bussey	Sheila Bussey
1974	Sue Pirtle	Lisa Martin
1975	Jimmie Gibbs Munroe	Jan Howell
1976	Sue Pirtle	Amy Iverson
1977	Jennifer Haynes	Sue Pirtle
1978	Judy Robinson	Donna Jones
1979	Jennifer Haynes	Tonya Tucker
1980	Gloria Paulsen	Tonya Tucker
1981	Betty Gayle Cooper	Amy Iverson
1982	Betty Gayle Cooper	Sandra Harrell
1983	Betty Gayle Cooper	Donna Jones
1984	Jan Howell	Trela Miller
1985	Twyla Rutherford	Tami Matteri
1986	Nancy Peirce	Lynn Jonckowski
1987	Gayle Brittain	Penny Bales
1988	Viki Williamson	Lynn Jonckowski
1989	Ronda Harrison	Tami George
1990	Ronda Harrison	Chris Swerdoski
1991	Ronda Harrison	Reijan Amason
1992	Jeana Brooks	Tammy George
1993	Jimmi Jo Martin	Melissa Phillips
1994	J. J. Hampton	Tammy Kelly
1995	J. J. Hampton	Tammy Kelly
1996	Lisa Gasperson	Tammy Kelly
1997	Joy Gordon	Tammy Kelly
1998	Tammy Kelly	Tammy Kelly
1999	J. J. Hampton	DeDee Crawford
2000	J. J. Hampton	DeDee Crawford
2001		
2002		

NATIONAL COWBOY HALL OF FAME
Oklahoma City, Oklahoma

RODEO HALL OF FAME HONOREES

Aber, Doff
Akridge, Eddy

Akers, Ira
Altizer, Jim Bob

Ambler, Jerry
Appleton, Dave
Arnold, Carl
Askin, Bob
Austin, Tex
Barmby, Bob
Beeson, Fred
Bell, Ray
Bennett, Hugh
Beutler, Elra
Beutler, Lynn
Blackstone, Vick
Blancett, Bertha
Blevins, Earl
Boen, Ken
Bolen, Bernice Dossey
Bond, Paul
Bowman, Everett
Bowman, John
Bowman, Louis Ed
Brady, Buff
Brennan, Harry
Brooks, Louis
Brown, Freckles
Burk, Clyde
Burmeister, A. H. "Hippy"
Burrell, Cuff
Buschbom, Jack
Byers, Chester
Bynum, James
Caldwell, Lee
Camarillo, Leo
Canutt, Yakima
Carney, Paul
Carr, Clay
Carroll, J. Ellison
Christensen, Hank
Clancy, Foghorn
Clark, Bobby
Clark, Gene
Clennon, Bart
Colborn, Ava

Colborn, Everett E.
Connelly, Edith Happy
Connelly, Lex
Cooper, Jimmie B.
Cooper, Roy
Cooper, Tuffy
Copenhaver, Deb
Cornish, Cecil
Cox, Breezy
Crosby, Bob
Curtis, Andy
Curtis, Eddie
Davis, Gordon
Davis, Sonny
Decker, Jo
Decker, Tater
Dightman, Myrtis
Doubleday, Ralph R
Duvall, Roy
Elliott, Verne
Eskew, Colonel Jim
Eskew, Junior
Estes, Bobby
Feild, Lewis
Ferguson, Tom
Fletcher, Kid
Fort, Troy C.
Gale, Floyd
Gamblin, Amye
Gardner, Joe
Garrett, Sam
Gaudin, D. J. "Kajun Kidd"
Goodspeed, Buck
Goodspeed, Jess
Grammer, Henry
Greenough, Turk
Griffith, Dick
Groff, Buddy
Hancock, Bill
Hancock, Sonny
Hastings, Fox
Hastings, Mike

Haverty, Del
Hefner, Hoytt
Helfrich, Devere
Hennigh, Duane
Henson, Margie Greenough
Holcomb, Homer
Hopkins, Ethel "Ma"
Irwin, C. B.
Ivory, Buster
Ivory, Perry
Jauregui, Andy
Johnson, Ben Sr.
Johnson, Clint
Jones, Cecil
Jones, John
Kirnan, Tommy
Knight, Harry
Knight, Pete
Lambert, Mel
Lefton, Abe
Leuschner, C. O. "Dogtown Slim"
Lewallen, G. K.
Like, Jim
Linder, Herman
Linderman, Bill
Linderman, Bud
Lindsey, John
Logan, Pete
Long, Hughie
Lowry, Fred
Lucas, Tad
Lybbert, Chris
Lyne, Phil
McCarty, Eddie
McClure, Jake
McCrory, Howard
McEntire, Clark
McEntire, John
McGinnis, Vera
McGinty, Rusty
McGonagill, Clay
McLaughlin, Don

McSpadden, Clem
Mahan, Larry
Mansfield, Toots
May, Harley
Merchant, Richard
Merritt, King
Mills, George
Montana, Montie
Mulhall, Lucille
Mulkey, Burel
Mullens, Johnnie
Murray, Leo "Pick"
Murray, Ty
Nesbitt, Don
Nesbitt, Pauline
Nesmith, Tom
Oliver, Dean
Oropeza, Vincente
Orr, Alice Greenough
Pickens, Slim
Pettigrew, Homer
Pickett, Bill
Pickett, Dee
Porter, Willard H.
Privett, "Booger Red"
Pruett, Gene
Purdy, Ikua
Rambo, Gene
Randall, Glenn
Randolph, Florence
Reynolds, Benny
Richardson, Nowata Slim
Riley, Doyle
Riley, Lanham
Riley, Mitzi Lucas
Roach, Ruth
Roberds, Coke T.
Roberts, E. C.
Roberts, Gerald
Roberts, Ken
Robinson, Lee
Roddy, Jack

Rollens, Rufus
Ross, Gene
Rowell, Harry
Rowell, Maggie
Rude, Ike
Rutherford, Buck
Ryan, Paddy
Salinas, Juan
Sawyer, Fern
Schneider, Frank
Schneider, Johnie
Shaw, Everett
Shelton, Dick
Shelton, Reine Hafley
Sheppard, Chuck
Sheppard, Nancy Kelley
Shoulders, Jim
Shultz, Charley
Smith, Bill
Smith, Dale D.
Snyder, Smokey
Sorenson, Doc
Sorrels, Buckshot
Sowder, Thad
Stahl, Jesse
Steele, Fannie S.
Steiner, Buck
Steiner, Tommy
Stillings, Floyd
Stoker, J. W.
Strickland, Hugh
Strickland, Mabel
Stroud, Leonard

Sundown, Jackson
Taillon, Cy
Tegland, Howard
Thode, Earl
Tibbs, Casey
Tierney, Paul
Todd, Homer
Tompkins, Harry
Trickey, Lorena
Truan, Fritz
Truitt, Dick
Tucker, Harley
Tureman, Sonny
Veach, C. Monroe
Walker, Enoch
Ward, Leonard
Weadick, Guy
Webster, Shoat
Weeks, Billy
Weeks, Guy
Welch, Joe
Whaley, Everett "Slim"
Wharton, Ray
Whatley, Todd
White, Vivian
Whiteman, Hub
Whiteman, Jim
Whitfield, Fred
Wilcox, Don
Witmer, Nancy Bragg
Worrell, Sonny
Yoder, Phil
Zumwalt, Oral

PRORODEO HALL OF FAME HONOREES
Colorado Springs, Colorado

ALL-AROUND
Everett Bowman
Louis Brooks
Paul Carney
Clay Carr
Lewis Feild
Tom Ferguson
Bill Linderman
Phil Lyne
Larry Mahan
Ty Murray
Gene Rambo
Benny Reynolds
Gerald Roberts
Chuck Sheppard
Jim Shoulders
Casey Tibbs
Fritz Truan

SADDLE BRONC
Bobby Berger
Winston Bruce
Deb Copenhaver
Shawn Davis
Brad Gjermundson
Monty Henson
Mel Hyland
Sharkey Irwin
Clint Johnson
Pete Knight
Gene Pruett
Bill Smith
Mike Stuart
Earl Thode
Guy Weeks
Marty Wood

BAREBACK
Eddie Akridge
Joe Alexander
Jack Buschbom
Bruce Ford
Marvin Garrett
John Hawkins
Jim Houston
J.C. Trujillo
Sonny Tureman
Jack Ward

BULL RIDING
Freckles Brown
Lane Frost
Don Gay
Dick Griffith
Tuff Hedeman
George Paul
Ken Roberts
Charles Sampson
Johnie Schneider
Smokey Snyder
Harry Tompkins

STEER WRESTLING
Hugh Bennett
Ote Berry
C. R. Boucher
James Bynum
Roy Duvall
John W. Jones, Sr.
John W. Jones, Jr.
Harley May
Homer Pettigrew
Bill Pickett
Jack Roddy
Gene Ross

Appendix   275

CALF ROPING
Barry Burk
Clyde Burk
Roy Cooper
Troy Fort
Glen Franklin
Toots Mansfield
Don McLaughlin
Dean Oliver

TEAM ROPING
Jake Barnes
Leo Camarillo
Les Hirdes
Ben Johnson
John Miller
Clay O'Brien Cooper
Jim Rodriguez
Dale Smith

STEER ROPING
Guy Allen
Jim Bob Altizer
Sonny Davis
Clark McEntire
Ike Rude
Everett Shaw
Shoat Webster
Olin Young

CONTRACT PERSONNEL
Ellen Backstrom
Hadley Barrett
Bobby Clark & Gene Clark
Jo Decker
George Doak & Junior Meek
Jasbo Fulkerson
Dudley Gaudin
Tom Hadley
Chuck Henson
Homer Holcomb
Mel Lambert
Pete Logan

George Mills
Montie Montana
Jerry Olson
Chuck Parkison
Wick Peth
Wilbur Plaugher
Glenn Randall
Jimmy Schumacher
Andy Womack

NOTABLES
Malcolm Baldridge
Josie Bennett
Benny Binion
John Burke
Lex Connelly
Bob Crosby
Myron "Doc" Etienne
Eldon Evans
Bill Hervey
Buster Ivory
Cecil Jones
John Justin
Harry Knight
Tad Lucas
Clem McSpadden
Dave Stout
Cy Taillon
Bob Thain
W.R. Watt, Sr.

STOCK CONTRACTORS
Walt Alsbaugh
Gene Autry
Bob Barnes
Lynn Beutler
Henry & Robert Sr. Christensen
Everett Colborn
Leo Cremer
Verne Elliott
Neal Gay
C.B. Irwin
Andy Jauregui

Joe Kelsey
D.A. "Swanny" Kerby
Reg Kesler
Cotton Rosser
Harry Rowell
Tommy Steiner
James Sutton
Harry Vold

STOCK
Baby Doll
Baldy
Bodacious
Bullet
Come Apart
Crooked Nose
Descent
Five Minutes to Midnight
Hell's Angels

High Tide
Midnight
Miss Klamath
Old Spec
Oscar
Peanuts
Poker Chip Peake
Red Rock
Scamper
Skoal's Sippin' Velvet
Steamboat
Tipperary
Tornado

RODEO LIFETIME ACHIEVEMENT
Sonny Linger
Lefty Wilken

RODEO ORGANIZATIONS

Professional Rodeo Cowboys Association
101 ProRodeo Drive
Colorado Springs, CO 80919

American Junior Rodeo Assoc.
P. O. Box 481
Rankin, TX 79778

Canadian Professional Rodeo Association
223 2116 27th Ave, N. E.
Calgary, Alberta, Canada T2E 7A6

National High School Rodeo Assoc.
11178 N. Huron St., #7
Denver, CO 80234

National Intercollegiate Rodeo Association
2316 Eastgate N. St., #160
Walla Walla, WA 99362

National Little Britches Rodeo
1045 W. Rio Grande
Colorado Springs, CO 80906

Professional Bull Riders
#6 South Tejon St., #700
Colorado Springs, CO 80903

Women's Professional Rodeo Assoc. & Professional Women's Rodeo Association
1235 Lake Plaza Drive, #134
Colorado Springs, CO 80906

Senior ProRodeo National Old Timers Rodeo Association
P. O. Box 419
Roundup, MT 59072

International Professional Rodeo Association
2304 Exchange Ave.
Oklahoma City, OK 73108

GLOSSARY

adrenaline rush: A secretion of epinephrine from the adrenal gland which causes a high in cowboys when they are preparing themselves for a ride on a bucking bull or bronc.
All-Around Champion Cowboy: Cowboy who wins the most money for the year in more than one event.
average: Taking all the scores by one cowboy and dividing by the number of bulls he drew in that event.
blacklist: When a cowboy is not in good standing with an organization for various reasons, such as not paying dues, doing something that the organization does not approve of, etc.
Bos indicus: Cattle from India.
bovine: A cow, ox, or other animal of the genus Bos.
bucking machine: An apparatus that is motorized and has the motions of a bucking bull or a bronc.
buckjumping: An Australian word used to define bronc riding.
buck off: When a bull rider loses his balance during the ride and falls to the ground before the eight-second whistle blows.
bull-baiter: A slang word used to describe a bullfighter, someone who teases a bull.
bullock: A castrated bull, steer, or a young bull. Primarily used in Australia.
bull rope: A rope the bull rider uses to hold on to while riding; similar to the rigging used in bareback bronc riding, except it is made of rope, with usually a leather area where the riding hand is placed.
Bushmen's carnival: A gathering in Australia which is similar to a United States rodeo, where cowboys challenge one another in various horse and cattle events.
chaps: Worn by cowboys over their pants, to protect their legs, usually made of leather.
chute: Enclosed area with a gate that swings open from the side and hinges at the bull's head.
circuit: Smaller areas divided off in the U. S., so that cowboys could make rodeos in their areas and not travel so far.
competition: A rider pays an entry fee and is pitted against the other

riders who also paid entry fees. The ones with the highest judged scores win the money.

Cowboy Crisis Fund: Money set aside by PRCA, through their efforts and the efforts of various sponsors, to be used in case of injury or death to cowboys in rodeo-related accidents.

cross-bred: The breeding of animals, using more than one pure-bred strain, such as Brahma with Texas Longhorn, or Hereford with Brahma, etc.

day money: Winning the event that day and being paid for a single ride, not the entire rodeo.

draw: When all cowboys are entered at an event in a rodeo, they put all the bulls' names in a hat and at random draw names for each entry.

exhibition ride: Instead of competing against other riders, the person rides to please the crowd and is paid a set amount by the rodeo producer.

flank strap: A leather strap, lined with sheepskin, that is placed around the bull's flank and over his back. Just as the rider is ready to buck out of the chute, the strap is tightened and usually makes the bull buck better.

go-round: Most rodeos comprise several go-rounds, with one head of stock for each rider in each go-round; National Finals has ten go-rounds.

hang-up: When a cowboy gets his hand caught in his bull rope or rigging and can't dismount or get released from the handhold.

"High Life": A chemical of bisulfate of carbon, which burns or deadens the skin when applied.

jackpot bull ridings: Small bull ridings, usually at a ranch, where young, novice riders practice riding bulls. There is generally no fee and no competition.

Justin Heeler Program: A medical unit that attends rodeos in customized trucks prepared to treat injured cowboys prior to and during the rodeo.

maverick: An unbranded or orphaned range calf or colt, or a horse or steer that has escaped from the herd.

mount money: A rider is given a set amount of money to attempt to ride a bucking bronc or bull; not a competition, but an exhibition ride.

novice: A person new to an activity; a beginner.

permit holder: A rodeo cowboy is still amateur, holding a PRCA permit, until he wins $1,000 in a PRCA-sanctioned rodeo; then he is no longer eligible to hold a permit.

Persimmon Hill: The hill in Oklahoma City where the National Cowboy Hall of Fame is located.
pick-up men: Usually two cowboys, on horseback, in the arena who are supposed to ride next to a bronc at the end of their eight-second ride and assist the rider off. They also herd the broncs, bulls, and other stock used in the rodeo out of the arena, if required.
PROCOM: The computerized division of PRCA that cowboys contact to enter any PRCA-sanctioned rodeo.
protective gear: Anything used to prevent a rider from sustaining an injury, such as a face mask, a vest, a helmet, etc.
protective vest: A covering for the chest made for the specific purpose to protect the roughstock rider from any blow to that area of the body. The material used has the ability to deflect the blow and protect the rider from serious injury. It is not foolproof, and the rider can be injured in spite of it if the blow is hard enough.
pulling leather: A term used to describe a roughstock rider who touches the animal with his free hand, which automatically disqualifies the rider.
pull the rope: When a bull rider is preparing in the chute, he needs someone to tighten his bull rope so that he has a snug hold on the rope with his riding hand.
purse: The monies offered for an event or a rodeo.
quadrille: A feature in a rodeo where riders on horseback, usually a man and a woman, are a team and they perform intricate riding with a number of other teams. It is similar to square dancing on horseback, but there is no caller. Usually a producer paid the participants in this program, allowing cowboys and cowgirls to make additional money, not just what they might win in an event.
qualified ride: A cowboy who rides a saddle bronc, bareback horse, or bull until the eight-second whistle blows without touching the animal with his free hand.
range cowboys: Cowboys who make a living working on ranches, instead of rodeoing.
reride: If a saddle bronc, bareback horse, or bull does not perform fairly during the eight-second ride, or the equipment provided is faulty and breaks, the judges make the determination whether the rider should be allowed a second ride, or another head of stock, or with equipment that does not break.
ridden to a finish: In the early days of rodeo the roughstock events were not timed (eight seconds) but were judged from the time the rider got on the bull or bronc's back until it stopped bucking, or the rider fell off. Many times this went on for a long time,

causing spectators to lose interest. But more importantly, it also discouraged bulls and broncs from bucking the next time they were tried, which required new stock to be found.

rigging: A leather apparatus that fits around the bronc's belly with a handle-like hold for the rider's hand, used in the bareback riding event.

rodeo team: A group of cowboys who represent a sponsor, a school, a circuit, or a country and compete against other cowboys in rodeo events.

roughriders: A term used in Australia to define riders of bucking broncs and bulls.

roughstock: Bulls used in the bull riding event and broncs used in the saddle bronc or bareback riding events.

round-up: A term used for gathering horses or cows in a group; also used in reference to a rodeo (such as Pendleton Round-Up).

rowel: A wheel, sometimes sharp (but in bull riding not sharp) inserted into a shank of a spur.

scab riders: Riders who rode roughstock for exhibition and were paid, sometimes two or more times during a rodeo under different names. This was usually done when not enough riders showed up for an event, but still allowed the audience the opportunity to watch the cowboys riding the stock.

scratch: In roughstock refers to spurring the bull or bronc during the ride.

short go: The top fifteen (or so) after a designated number of go-rounds have one last bull, to determine the winner.

snubbers: Men used to hold an animal prepared to buck, while a rider got mounted. This was done before the days of chutes.

spurs: An apparatus that goes around the heel of the cowboy boot, made of metal, that aids the cowboy in scratching the roughstock during an event; it is not dangerous or painful to the bull or bronc, but gives a more enthusiastic animal.

stock contractors: Those who supply stock to rodeos, such as bulls and broncs, roping calves, and steers, and many times supply the hands to run the rodeo.

suicide wrap: A way of wrapping the end of a bull rope around the rider's hand, to keep him from losing his grip and loosening the rope and being bucked off.

surcingle: A girth that binds a saddle, pack, or blanket to the body of a horse.

trade out: There was a certain time in the Rodeo Cowboys

Association that a cowboy could trade with another rider, in order to make more rodeos during a period of time.

try: What determines how much a rider puts into bull riding—how much courage, heart, 110%.

turn out: If a rider draws a head of stock, and he knows the history of the animal, he may opt to not show up at a rodeo or choose not to ride him. This could be done if the stock does not have a history of bucking well and the rider does not think he can score highly on it, or if the reputation of the animal is that he has a tendency to intentionally try to hurt the rider.

waving a trip: A term used for a roper on horseback running to rope a steer. Once his rope is thrown over the steer's horns, he will try to maneuver the rope around his rump, then run his horse in such a way that the steer is tripped and falls to the ground. This is an event, but also is a method used by range cowboys when necessary to down a steer for the purpose of treating or checking it.

Wild West show: Before and after the turn of the twentieth century producers gathered cowboys, cowgirls, and oftentimes Indians to depict early-day western events, and held these spectacular presentations in various areas of the country (often the East) or other countries. The people involved were paid employees, however, and the roughstock riding and roping were exhibition; riders and ropers were not competing for prizes.

World Champion Cowboy: From 1929, records were kept and only one World Champion Cowboy was chosen in each event and the All-Around. Prior to 1929, some rodeos would advertise their events and call the winner the "World Champion"; therefore there could be several different cowboys claiming to have been the World Champion—winning at Cheyenne, or Denver, or Calgary.

wrangler: A cowboy who rode horseback and worked with horses and/or cattle, in herding them, sorting them, and/or keeping them fit.

wreck: When a rider is bucked off and does not get to safety without being tousled about by the bull.

RESOURCE MATERIALS
[Reference numbers within text refer to this list.]

1. *My 50 Years in Rodeo, Living with Cowboys, Horses and Danger* by Foghorn Clancy. The Naylor Company, San Antonio, 1952.
2. *50 Years of Rodeo* with Williams-Jobe Gibson American Legion Post No. 128, Sidney, Iowa Rodeo, 1973.
3. *Man, Beast, Dust: The Story of Rodeo* by Clifford P. Westermeier. University of Nebraska Press, Lincoln & London, 1947.
4. *Black Cowboys* by Paul W. Stewart and Wallace Yvonne Ponce. Phillips Publishing Inc., Broomfield, CO, 1986.
5. *World's Oldest Rodeo* by Danny Freeman. Published by Prescott Frontier Days, Inc., Prescott, AZ, 1988.
6. *Let 'er Buck! A History of the Pendleton Roundup* by Virgil Rupp. Published by the Pendleton Round-Up Association, Pendleton OR, 1985.
7. *A Hundred Years of Heroes: A History of the Southwestern Exposition and Livestock Show* by Clay Reynolds with Marie-Madeleine Schein. Published by Texas Christian University Press, Fort Worth, 1995.
8. *Let 'er Buck: A Story of the Passing of the Old West* by Charles Wellington Furlong, F.R.G.S. Published by G. P. Putnam's Sons, NY & London, 1923.
9. *Mr. Rodeo: The Big Bronc Years of Leo Cremer* by Patrick Dawson. Published by Cayuse Press, Livingston, MT, 1986.
10. *Rodeo Road: My Life as a Pioneer Cowgirl* by Vera McGinnis. Published by Hastings House, NY, 1974.
11. *American Rodeo: From Buffalo Bill to Big Business* by Kristine Fredriksson. Published by Texas A&M University Press, College Station, TX, 1985.
12. *Let's Go! Let's Show! Let's Rodeo!* by Shirley E. Flynn. Published by Wigwam Publishing Co., Cheyenne, WY, 1996.

13. *Cheyenne Frontier Days: "A Marker from Which to Reckon All Events"* by Milt Riske. Published by The Cheyenne Corral of Westerners International, 1984.
14. *Daddy of 'Em All: The Story of Cheyenne Frontier Days* by Robert D. (Bob) Hanesworth. Published by Flintlock Publishing Company, Cheyenne, WY, 1967.
15. *Boots and Saddles* by Imogene Beals. Published by Siloam Springs Printing, Siloam Springs, AR, 1994.
16. *Pikes Peak or Bust Rodeo: The First Fifty Years*, edited by Steve Fleming and Judi Lakin. Published by the ProRodeo Hall of Fame and Museum of the American Cowboy, through a grant from El Pomar Foundation, 1990.
17. *Cowgirls of the Rodeo* by Mary Lou LeCompte. Published by University of Illinois Press, Urbana and Chicago, IL, 1993.
18. *"Here's a Go!" Remembering Harry Rowell and the Rowell Ranch Rodeo* by Victoria Carlyle Weiland and William A. Strobel. Published by Rowell Ranch Rodeo, Inc., Hayward, CA, 1995.
19. *The Cowboy and Rodeo Evolution: A Tribute to Early Day Cowboys and to Rodeos* by Cleo Mackey. Published by Cleo Mackey Publishing, Dallas, TX, 1979.
20. *Fifty Years at the San Angelo Stock Show & Rodeo* by contributing writers Jeanette Gideon, Scott Campbell, Steve Kelton, Ross McSwain, Bill Hinnant, Dee Lackey and Elmer Kelton. Published by the Talley Press, by San Angelo Stock Show & Rodeo Foundation, San Angelo, TX, 1982.
21. *Rodeo*, photographs and text by Louise L. Serpa, notes by Larry McMurtry. Published by Aperture Foundation, Inc., New York, NY, 1994.
22. *Hoofs and Horns*, a western publication, by Hoofs & Horns Publishing Co., est. in 1931, Ethel A. Hopkins, editor.
23. *100 Years Rodeo Stock Contracting*. Published by the Professional Rodeo Stock Contracting Association. Author, Victoria Carlyle Weiland, 1997.
24. "The Remarkable Men Who Rule Rodeo," article by Paul Friggens, *Empire Magazine,* Dec. 12, 1965, *Denver Post*, Denver, CO.
25. "Eight Seconds to Judgment," article by Freeman Gregory, *Houston Livestock Show & Rodeo Magazine,* August 1998, Vol. VI, No 3.
26. *Rodeo Champions: Eight Memorable Moments of Riding, Wrestling and Roping* by Larry Pointer. University of New Mexico Press, Albuquerque, NM.

Resource Materials   285

27. *The Last Best Place: A Montana Anthology.* Edited by William Kittredge & Annick Smith. Published by the Montana Historical Society Press, 1988.
28. *Rain or Shine: A Family Memoir* by Cyra McFadden. Published by University of Nebraska Press, Lincoln, NE & London, England, 1986.
29. *The Finals: A Complete History of the National Finals*, published by the Professional Rodeo Cowboys Association. Editor, Steve Fleming, 1998.
30. *Extra Extra!* Newsletter by Rodeo Historical Society, Oklahoma City, OK, 1967-1972.
31. *The Buckboard*, Official Publication of the Rodeo Cowboys Association (1947-53), Earl Lindsey, editor-publisher.
32. *The Roundup,* magazine published monthly in the Heart of the Rodeo Country, Tulsa OK, publishers, George Ketcham, editor.
33. *Roundup,* published quarterly for honorees, donors and friends of the ProRodeo Hall of Champions, Colorado Springs (1988-1993).
34. *The Wild Bunch,* magazine by Rodeo Hall of Fame, Oklahoma City, compiled and written by Willard H. Porter.
35. *Rodeo Sports News,* publication of the Rodeo Cowboys Association.
36. *ProRodeo Sports News,* publication of the ProRodeo Cowboys Association, 1975.
37. *The Cowboys* by William H. Forbis. The Old West Series, Time-Life Books, NY. Published by Time, Inc., 1973.
38. *Who's Who in Rodeo* by Willard Porter. Powder River Book Co., Oklahoma City, OK, 1983.
39. *A Brand of its Own: The 100 Year History of the Calgary Exhibition and Stampede* by James H. Gray. Western Producer Prairie Books, Saskatoon, Saskatchewan, 1985.
40. "Rodeo 100—Looking Back" article compiled by Dr. Bruce Claussen, for the 1982 Nebraskaland Days Souvenir Program, the 100th Year Anniversary of the Buffalo Bill Rodeo.
41. "It's Been 90 Years Since the First Denver Stock Show," article by Walter Dennis, in *Quarter Horse News,* Feb. 9, 1996.
42. "Earl Anderson: 1894-1960" article compiled by Traci Hatton, for magazine *The Fence Post,* June 14, 1993.
43. "The Man of Three Centuries," article by Doug Perkins, *The Cattleman* magazine, October 1999.
44. *R-o-d-e-o Back of the Chutes* by Gene Lamb, Editor of *Rodeo Sports News,* and the *Rodeo Sports News Annual,* Official Publications of the Rodeo Cowboys Association, Inc., 1956.

45. *Calgary Stampede: The Authentic Story of the Calgary Stampede, 1912-1964* by Fred Kennedy. Published by West Vancouver Enterprises, Ltd., Vancouver, B. C., 1965.
46. *Biting the Dust: The Wild Ride and Dark Romance of the Rodeo Cowboy and the American West* by Dirk Johnson. Published by Simon and Schuster, 1994.
47. *Boston Garden Official Program*, 1933.
48. "Remarkable Rides and Riders," article by Frank Dean, *The Western Horseman*, April 1967.
49. "Ronnie Rossen, Montana Bull Rider," article by Helen Clark, *The Western Horseman*, June 1966.
50. "Richest Roughrider," Sports Section, *Newsweek* magazine, October 27, 1958.
51. "Jim Shoulders, He Put the 'Rode' in Rodeo," article by Lee Pitts, *Cowboys & Country* magazine, Spring 1995.
52. "The Suicide Circuit," Sports Section of *Time Magazine*, November 18, 1957.
53. "Rodeo's Rambling Wreck," article by Paul Friggens, *True Magazine*, August 1960.
54. "The Jim Shoulders Story—Bull Riding Preparation," and continued "Staying On and Getting Off," article in *Hoofs & Horns*, August and September 1968.
55. "Bull Nurse and Boss Hostler," article by Willard Porter, *Argosy* magazine, 1957.
56. *ProRodeo Cowboy Association Media Guide*, 1999.
57. "Picked Up in the Rodeo Arena," article by Jerry Armstrong, *The Western Horseman*, April 1966.
58. "Freckles" article by Andy Edson in *Horse & Rider All-Western Yearbook*, 1975.
59. "Brown Still Scoring," article in *Horse & Rider* magazine, December 1972.
60. "Ace Rodeo Rider Tells How He Tames VICIOUS BRONCS," article by Johnie Schneider in *Popular Science Monthly* magazine, August 1934.
61. "Denver's National Western" article by Gavin Ehringer in *Cowboys & Indians* magazine, Winter 1995.
62. "Six Seconds of a 'Ton of Mean,'" article by K. C. Compton in *Women's Sports & Fitness* magazine, July/August 1997.
63. "Ladies' Choice" article by Kendra Santos in *American Cowboy* magazine, January/February 1996.
64. Ty Murray News, official publication of the Ty Murray Fan Club, Winter 1999.

65. "The Greatest Cowboy Ever, Ty Murray, is the Michael Jordan of Rodeo—And That's No Bull," article by Skip Hollandsworth, *Texas Monthly* magazine, May 1999.
66. "Tad Lucas, World Champion," article in *The Western Horseman*, April 1965.
67. "Is Rodeo a Cruel Sport?" article by Robert M. Miller, D.V.M., in *The Western Horseman* magazine, February 1966.
68. "State of Ohio Passes Bill Outlawing Rodeo" article by Gene Pruett, in *The Western Horseman* magazine, December 1965.
69. "Big Bend Rodeo Company" article in *The Western Horseman*, July 1965.
70. "A rodeo cowboy's perfect ride ends in death," article by Skip Myslenski, *Chicago Tribune* newspaper, Sunday, August 6, 1989.
71. State of Oklahoma Citation, Lane Frost, pursuant to the motion of Representative of the House Tommy Thomas.
72. "Governor Declares July 26 Lane Frost Memorial Day," article in *Atoka (OK) Times* newspaper, July 18, 1990.
73. Texas House Resolution No. 118, printed in *Quanah (TX) Tribune-Chief* newspaper, Oct. 17, 1989.
74. National Cowgirl Hall of Fame biographies: Sue Pirtle, Jonnie Jonckowski, Jan Youren.
75. "'Rodeo Girl' real champion" article by Lynn Sim Ross, *State Journal Register*, July 29, 1980.
76. "Jan Youren, Rodeoing Grandmother," article by Rhonda Sedgwick Stearns, *National Cowgirl Hall of Fame* magazine.
77. "Jonckowski part of bull riding field," article in *Billings (MT) Gazette*, April 8, 1992.
78. "I Just Couldn't Quit," article by Jonnie Jonckowski, *Living Positive* magazine, Premier Issue, 1998.
79. "Jackie Worthington and Her Cowgirl Crew," article by Ray Davis, *The Western Horseman* magazine, March 1975.
80. Eulogy at Jack Long's Memorial Service, April 5, 2000, San Antonio, Texas, given by Porter Loring.
81. Mabel Strickland Fact Sheet. National Cowgirl Hall of Fame.
82. *ProRodeo Cowboys Association Media Guide*, 1999.
83. "Ton of Trouble," article by Bill Campbell, April 1, 1999, *Dallas Morning News*.
84. "Bounty Bulls Offer Guarantee of Big Bucks," by Ed Knocke, April 1, 1999, *Dallas Morning News*.
85. "Behind the Chutes" by Kendra Santos, October/November 1999 in *ProBull Rider*, the official magazine of the Professional Bull Riders, Vol. 5, No. 5.

86. *Professional Bull Riders Media Guide*, 2000.
87. "Where Have All the Bull Riders Gone?," article by Gavin Ehringer, *Western Horseman* magazine, November 1996.
88. *Fearless Funnymen: The History of the Rodeo Clown* by Gail Hughbanks Woerner. Published by Eakin Press, 1993.
89. "From Bull Rider to Broadcaster," article by Gavin Ehringer, *Western Horseman* magazine, January 1998.
90. "People, Places & Puns" column, in magazine, *Horse & Rider*, August 1976.
91. "Heart of a Champion," article by Charles Bene, *ProRodeo Sports News,* Sept. 16, 1998.
92. Jack Long essay, printed in *Boots & Saddle*, a San Antonio magazine.
93. *Australian Cowboys, Roughriders and Rodeos* by Jenny Hicks. Published by Angus & Robertson/Harper Collins, 2000.
94. *Fifty Years of Nebraska's Big Rodeo*, endorsed by Nebraska Bicentennial Association. Published by Rodeo Book Co., 1975.
95. American Brahman Breeders Association, www.brahman.org.
96. "In Memoriam: Glen Keeley 3/20/70 to 3/24/00" article by Kenra Santos in *Professional Bull Riders* magazine, Volume 6, No. 3, 2000.
97. "Hall of Fame, Two Clowns, Nasty Bull Join Group," article in *East Oregonian* newspaper, Pendleton, Oregon, September 12, 1978.
98. *The Billboard*, a weekly newspaper, printed in New York, primarily for the show business world. It included Broadway, vaudeville, circus, Wild West, etc., information. A column entitled "The Corral" reported rodeo contest business, contestant information, and Wild West news.
99. *Tuff Hedeman* by Brett Hoffman. Published by Daniel Collins, Fort Worth, TX, 2000.

INDEX

—A—
A-14, 197-198
Abbie, Hank, 119
Aber, Doff, 67
Ada, Oklahoma, 158
Adams, Alice, 22
Adams, Don, 116
Akers, Ira, 90
Akin, Lee, 224, 226
Al Kadir Shrine Rodeo, 89
Al Smith, 19
Albuquerque, New Mexico, 180
Alice, Texas, 149
All Girl Championship Rodeo, 69
Allen, Prairie Lilly, 173
Allen, Rex, 133
Alley, Sterling B., 176
Altizer, Blanche, 172
Amarillo, Texas, 169, 170
American Black Cowboy Association, 19
American Cowboys Association, 120, 241
American Junior Rodeo Association, 130, 185
Anderson, Earl, 17, 100-102
Anderson, Handy, 39
Anderson, Jack, 102-103, 197
Anderson, Jimmy, 249
Andrews, Don, 177, 178, 183
Andrews, Sammy, 187, 220, 235
Andrews Rodeo Company, 218, 220, 226
Angels Camp rodeo, 115
anti-rodeo bills, 120
Apple Valley, 87

Archdale, North Carolina, 215
Ardmore, Oklahoma, 87
Argosy Magazine, 110
Arkansas High School All-Around, 155
Arlington, Texas, 77
Arnold, Carl, 62
Auburn, Washington, 120
Austin, Texas, 6, 10, 16, 61, 220
Austin/Travis County Livestock Show & Rodeo, 232
Australian Cowboys, Roughriders and Rodeos, 168
Autry, Gene, 16, 48, 79

—B—
Baby Face, 235
Backstom, Sunny, 197
Bad Company Rodeo, 191, 192
Bagnell, Scotty, 49
Baker, Howard, 63
Baldridge, Malcolm, 190
Bandera, Texas, 68
Bandy, Mike, 145-147
Bar Seven rodeo, 10
Barbour, Mack, 103
Barker, Texas, 17
Barmby, Bob, 162-163
Barnes, 138, 144
Barrett, Hadley, 221, 226-227
Barrow, Richard, 8
Barry, Fred, 64
Bartram, John, 38
Bascom, Weldon, 37
Bastrop, Texas, 155

Bates, Almon, 18
Baughman, Wart, 63
Baumgartner, Joe, 249
Beals, Charley, 75, 141
Beaumont, Texas, 71, 155
Becker, Fritz, 63
Beeson, Fred, 6
Beeville, Texas, 34
Bellmon, Henry, 193
Belvedere Hotel, 65, 86
Benedictus, Tony, 49
Bennett, Hugh, 12, 30, 31, 33, 47, 141
Bennett, Josie, 12
Berger, Bobby, 172
Bernard, Randy, 243-245, 248, 249, 252
Bernard, Tim, 17, 58
Beutler Brothers & Son, 93, 110, 121, 181
Beutler, Lynn, 113
Big Sandy Valley, 12
Big Spring, Texas, 71
Billboard, The, 14
Billings, Montana, 38, 172
Billy Bob's Texas, 200
black cowboys, 19, 148, 189
Black Cowboys, 19
Black Devil, 58
Black 6, 147
Black Smoke, 124, 127
Blackfoot, Idaho, 57
Blancett, Bertha Kaepernik, 173
Blessing, Wag, 58-59, 63
Blue, 113
Blue Bell, Inc., 137
Bobby Twister, 169
Bodacious, 187, 211, 218, 220-221, 235, 237
Boettcher, Fred, 210
Bolin, Ricky, 145-147, 179-180
Bolivar, Missouri, 138
Bonner, Joe, 159
Boots & Saddles, 19
Bos indicus, 8

Boston Garden Rodeo, 21, 25, 29, 31-32, 44, 85
Boulder, Colorado, 101
bounty bull program, 227-229
Bovolupus, 14
Bowman, Ed, 6
Bowman, Everett, 12, 30, 31, 33, 34, 67
Bowman, John, 12
Brady, Buff, 54
Brahma bulls, 7-8, 17, 23, 25-26, 28, 35, 37, 55-58, 72, 73, 199, 227
Brahmer, Barney, 158
Brander sisters, 168
Branger, Clint, 220
Branson, Missouri, 145
Brasingtion, Joe, 87
Breding, Scott, 221
Breheny, Martin, 4
Brent Thurman Memorial Bull Riding, 220
Bride, Tom, 26
Bridgeport, Connecticut, 98
Broadview Hotel, 112
Brooke Army Medical Center, 202
Brooks, Louis, 68
Brown, Bobby, 147
Brown, Duncan, 87
Brown, Freckles, 87, 93, 117, 118-119, 123-125, 135, 138, 141, 149, 193
Brown, George, 32
Brown, Leo, 116, 118, 125
Bruneau, Idaho, 175
Buckboard, 81
Bud Light Cup, 215, 234, 235, 236, 244, 246, 249, 253
Budweiser Light, 246
Bull Pin Safety Release, 214
Bull Riders Only (BRO), 220, 242
BullMania, 159
Bullnanza, 242

Burden, LeRoy, 140
Burford, Rusty, 229
Burk, Clyde, 33
Burnett, Tom, 11, 14
Burns, Hal, 195, 197
Burns, Oregon, 194
Burns, Pete, 142
Burnt River Ranch, 194
Burrell, Cuff, 16, 43
Burrell, Joe, 38
Burwell, Nebraska, 11, 126
bushmen's carnivals, 27
Butler, Oklahoma, 38-39
Butram, Pat, 86
Butte, Montana, 22
Byers, Chester, 61
Bynum, James, 122, 130

—C—
C85, 188
Caesar's Palace, 254
Caldwell, Junior, 29
Calf Scramble, 134
Calgary Red, 6
Calgary Stampede, 2, 13, 24, 42, 190, 244
California Fair, 244
California Polytechnic College, 69
California Rodeo, 190
Calvert, 137
Camdenton, Missouri, 87
Canton, Oklahoma, 59
Cape Girardeau, New Jersey, 166
Cardston, Alberta, Canada, 24
Carney, Paul, 33
Carrillo, Adam, 233-235
Carrillo, Gilbert, 232, 233-235
Carroll, Howard, 118
Carson, Johnny, 84
Carthage, Texas, 145, 235
Casa Grande, Arizona, 169
Casper, Wyoming, 102, 131
Casteel, Art, 29
Cathey, Sloan, 219-220

Cathey, Wacey, 198, 219-220
Cedar Creek, Texas, 200
Central Arizona College, 189
Central Point, Oregon, 221
Cervi Championship Rodeo Company, 197
Cervi, Mike, 197
Charles, Jim, 93, 116, 118, 135
Charleston, Arkansas, 159
Chartier, Dallas, 118
Chatman, Rick, 182, 202, 203, 204, 206, 250
Check, Cory, 228
Cheyenne Frontier Days, 2, 7, 8, 13, 14, 22, 28, 77, 90, 96, 161, 173, 184, 186, 191-192, 195, 196, 197, 200, 202, 203, 204, 208, 210, 213, 225, 230, 243
Cheyenne, Wyoming, 1, 10, 29, 68
Chicago, 14, 43, 61
Chicago World's Fair, 43, 61
Chief Joseph, 115
Christensen Brothers, 72, 124
chutes, 7, 14, 22
Cimarron Dude Ranch, 97
Claassen, Steve, 214
Clancy, Foghorn, 1, 6, 10, 28
Clark, Bobby, 140
Clark, Duke, 111
Clark, Gene, 94, 140
Clayman, Larry, 182
Clemens, Bill, 48
Clemens, Mark Twain, 33
Clennon, Bart, 53
Clovis, California, 57, 193
Clyde Miller Wild West Show, 14, 99
Coffee, Leon, 159, 217
Cogger, Lou, 10, 24
Colborn and Sorensen, 57
Colborn, Everett, 12, 33, 48, 49, 53, 84, 90
Cole, C. A. "Chili," 106, 119

Cole, Chip, 106
Coleman, Texas, 124
College National Finals, 186, 215
Comanche, Texas, 142
Combs, Willard, 88
Competition, Missouri, 43
Condon, Larry, 116
Connecticut, 120
Considine, Norm, 138
Conway, Eddie, 118, 119
Cook, Art, 63
Cook, Bob, 163
Cook, Fred, 78
Cooke, Alvin, 114-115
Cooper, Felix, 45-46
Cooper, Jackie, 48, 59
Coors, 140
Coors Chute Out Rodeo Series, 140
Coors Favorite Cowboy, 140
Coors Man in a Can, 140
Copenhagen Cup, 223, 226
Copenhagen High Five, 242
Copenhagen Stinger, 183
Copenhagen-Skoal, 140
Copenhagen-Skoal Scholarship Award Program, 140
Copenhaver, Deb, 86
Corsicana, Texas, 214
Covington Middle School, 220
Cow Palace Rodeo, 68, 80, 87, 143
Cowan, Dona, 165
Cowboy Amateur Association of America (CAA), 66
Cowboy Church, 254
Cowboy Protective Association, 66
Cowboys' Steer-Riding Contest, 25-26, 29
Cowboys Turtle Association, 31-33, 34-35, 39, 42, 47-50, 59, 65, 74, 80, 81, 241; *also see* Rodeo Cowboys Association

Cowtown, New Jersey, 26-27
Cox, Dickey, 118, 119, 121, 162
Crain, Paul, 29
Cravens, Walter, 38-39
Cremer, Leo, 17, 22, 56, 57, 58, 63, 168
Creswell, Oregon, 162
Cripple Creek, Colorado, 41
Crockett, Jeff, 183
Crockett, Texas, 149
Cronkhite, John Van, 9
Crook, Colorado, 126
Crooked Creek, Alberta, Canada, 252
Crooked Nose, 250
Crosby, Bob, 12
Cross Triangle Ranch, 9
Crown Royal, 140
Crump, Pete, 93, 102, 116, 118
Cryer, Louis, 244
Culley, Matt, 55
Cullison, Bob, 93
Cummings, Warren, 11
Curtis, Eddie, 26, 31, 32
Custer, Cody, 208, 222, 229, 240, 242, 254
Custer, Jim, 254

—D—
Dallas Cowboys, 177, 178
Dallas, Texas, 90, 91, 92
Dalton, James A., 51
Daniel, Price, 134
Daniels, Lewis, Jr., 19
Darnell, Hank, 6
Daugherty, Red, 64
Davidson, Dogie, 63, 65
Davis, Carson, 215
Davis, Dr. Z. B., 8
Davis, Jerome, 215-216, 231, 236, 244
Davis, John, 177
Davis, Russell, 222

Davis, Shawn, 129
Davis, Tiffany, 215
Dearinger, Jean, 8
Decker, Tater, 185
Deer Park, Washington, 113
Del Rio, Texas, 76, 119, 130, 159
DelVecchio, Bobby, 246
Dempsey, Jack, 7
Denver, Colorado, 23, 123, 205, 242
Denver National Western Stock Show and Rodeo, 23, 117, 123, 205, 223
Dew, Jack, 37
Dewey, Oklahoma, 19
Diamond Spur Rodeo, 113
Diamond W Ranch, 200, 201
Dightman, Myrtis, 119, 148-151, 155, 189
Dillinger, 237
Doak, George, 162
Dobbs, Quail, 182
Dodge Bodacious, 187
Dodge City, Kansas, 239
Dodge Dakota, 227-228
Dodge Durango, 226, 228-229
Dodge Laramie II, 228
Dodge Magnum Power, 187
Dodge National Circuit Finals Rodeo, 140, 183, 227-228
Dodge Ram Tough, 236-239
Dodge Trucks, 140
Dollarhide, Ross, 64
Donaldson, Bob, 182
Dooley, Orie, 64-65
Dorenkamp, Jerry, 197
Dossey, Bernice, 54
Dossey, Carl, 67
Double Trouble, 58
Dougherty, Red, 141
Douglas, Tommy, 10
Doyle, Leslie, 214
Doyle, Royd, 236
Draeksler, Iva Del Jacobs, 22

Dripping Springs, Texas, 199
Droopy, 17
Drumheller, George, 4, 167
Drury, Shane, 254
Dry Ice, 224
Dublin, Ireland, 166
Dublin, Texas, 49, 53
Dunn, Bubba, 220
Dunn, Troy, 244
Dunton, Nick, 212
Dykes, Carl, 37, 39

—E—
Eastman, Wisconsin, 228
Eddis, Zebbie, 89
Edinburg, Texas, 161
Edwards, Ettie, 168
Eight Seconds, 193
"88," 65
El Paso, Texas, 185, 233
Elk City, Oklahoma, 110
Ellensburg Rodeo, 58
Elliott & McCarty, 23
Elliott, Verne, 7, 23, 55
Elroy, Texas, 200
Elvis, 81
Empire State Building, 21
Erickson, Everett, 243
Eskew, Colonel, 37, 98
Eskew, Junior, 54, 169
ESPN, 226
ESPN2, 226
ether, 70, 94
Evans, Dr. J. Pat, 177, 178, 179, 180, 183-184, 209, 233

–F–
fatalities, 12, 38-39, 87-89, 103, 113-114, 169, 183, 191-194, 199-204, 209, 219-220, 236, 251
Favor, Jack, 68

Feist, Bob, 194
Fernamburg, Dan, 29
Fifty Years at San Angelo, 28
Finley, Larry, 141
Fletcher, Frances, 44
Fletcher, George Leslie (*see* Fletcher, Kid)
Fletcher, Henry, 43
Fletcher, Kid, 36, 42, 43-45, 46
Flint Hills, 99
Flint Hills Rodeo Company, 74
Flying U Rodeo Company, 114, 199
Flynn, Denny, 155-161
Flynn, Lynn, 159
Flynn, Mike, 155
Folsom, California, 199
Fonzie, 163, 222
Ford, Bruce, 172
Fort Madison, Iowa, 131
Fort Peck Rodeo Company, 19
Fort Pierre, South Dakota, 90
Fort Smith, Arkansas, 74
Fort Worth Rodeo, 5, 9, 17, 27, 61, 62, 68, 81, 162
Fort Worth, Texas, 14, 24, 165, 166, 216
48 Hours, 173
14th Amendment, 120
Fredericks, Jerry, 74, 87
Freeman, Dr. Tandy, 209, 211-212, 214, 215, 249, 251
Frizzell, Herb, 71-72
Frost, Lane, 185, 186, 191-194
Fulkerson, Jasbo, 57, 63
Furlong, Charles Wellington, 3-4

—G—
Gable, Nan, 166
Gaffney, Michael, 219, 244
Gafford, Brida, 22
Gale, Floyd, 12
Galemba, Ed, 162
Gardenhire, Phil, 222
Garfield County Frontier Fair, 11
Garrett, Jack, 9
Garrett, Mark, 223
Garrett, Sammy, 6
Garrison, Walt, 177, 178
Garstad, Gid, 136
Garwood, Texas, 132, 229
Gaskill, Dorothy, 169
Gaudin, D. J., 90, 94, 123, *also see* Kajun Kidd
Gay, Don, 91, 133, 151-153, 154, 159, 163, 177, 178, 198, 212, 214
Gay, Neal, 81, 90, 91, 94, 135, 151, 152, 227
Gay, Pete, 152
Gene Autry's World Championship Rodeo, 49
Gentry, Kay Rossen, 127-128
George Paul Memorial Bull Riding, 159, 242
Gibson, Marie, 165
Gilbert, Brent, 236
Gillette, Wyoming, 248
Girls Rodeo Association, 169, 170, 171-172, 174
Gladewater, Texas, 162
Glen Keeley Memorial Award, 252
Glover, Dave, 119, 150
Gonzales, Rafael, 34
Gooding, Idaho, 89
Goodrich, Myrtle Compton, 22, 54
Gordon, Alvin, 37
Gordon, Nebraska, 165
Goyins, Blaine Allen, 69-70
Grand National Rodeo, 114, 163, 190
Grant, Bob, 90
Grant, Howard, 27
Gravit, Johnny, 103
Great Falls, Montana, 39
Greeley, Colorado, 136
Green, Joe, 93, 101-102, 116, 118, 119

Green, Marion, 169
Greenough, Alice, 22, 48, 168, 169
Greenough, Margie, 168-169
Greenough, Turk, 141
Griffith, Curley, 6, 9, 10, 11, 18, 59-60
Griffith, Dick, 17-18, 33, 36, 43, 48, 59-62, 65, 67, 68
Griffith, Mac, 118
Griffith, Toots, 6, 60
Grover, Colorado, 17, 100, 197, 225
Growney Brothers Rodeo Company, 163, 197, 222
Growney, John, 163, 193, 194, 197, 199, 236
Guffey, Colorado, 129
Guthrie, Oklahoma, 242
Guymon, Sandy, 44

—H—
Hall, Del, 150
Hand, Billy, 116
Hanford, California, 43
Hannon, Chick, 29
Hannon, Ray, 29
Hardin-Simmons University Rodeo Association, 71
Harding, Warren G., 60
Hare, Miles, 182, 184
Hargis, Ken, 29
Hargo, Dwayne, 202, 203, 204, 210, 250
Harley, Kim, 201
Harmon, Monroe, 76
Harris, Howard, III, 27
Harris, Howard Sr., 27
Harry Knight Rodeo Company, 162; *also see* Knight, Harry
Hart, Cody, 249
Hart, Harry, 33
Hastings, Fox, 165, 173
Hastings, Mike, 64

Hataway, Delbert, 118, 119
Hatchell, Steve, 223
Havana, Cuba, 154
Hawn, Happy Jack, 3
Hayward, California, 17, 51
Hazen, Jimmie, 63
Heacock, Steve, 37
Heard and Heard, 34
Hedden, Vanas, 147
Hedeman, Clarice, 185
Hedeman, Red, 185
Hedeman, Roach, 234, 249
Hedeman, Tuff, 174, 183-184, 185-188, 192, 211, 220-221, 244
Hefner, Hoyt, 36, 54
Heinen, Phil, 136
Helfrich, Devere, 98
Helldorado Rodeo, 37, 57
Hennigh, Duane, 88
Henryetta, Oklahoma, 95, 104, 105
Henson, Monty, 91
Herbert Hoover, 19
Herefords, 12, 23
Herman, Brian, 219
Herrington Cattle Company, 239
Herrington, Chad, 236, 238
Herrington, Robbie, 238, 239
Hessman, Pete, 237, 239
Hicks, Jenny, 168
High Life, 5-6
High School Rodeo Association, 185, 193, 214, 215
Hill, Cecil, 159
Hill, Clayton, 64
Hill, Shorty, 29, 46
Hitchcock, Horace, 64
Hobson, Al, 26
Holcomb, Homer, 40, 56, 62, 63, 137
Hollister, California, 199
Hoofs & Horns, 37, 50-51, 67, 72, 80-81, 128
Hopkins, Ma, 50-51, 80

Horner, Mildred Mix, 22, 33
Horner, Tommy, 39
Hornitos, California, 243
Houston Livestock Show & Rodeo, 65, 96, 134, 204, 246
Howard, Duane, 93
Hudson, Cuay, 237
Hughes, Florence, 165
Hugo, Colorado, 43, 44, 46, 191, 193
Humansville, Missouri, 231
Hunking, Mert, 194
Hurst, Joleen, 154
Hussar, Alberta, Canada, 41
Hutchison, Lawrence, 118

—I—
Idabel, Oklahoma, 19
Idaho Bill, 6
Intercollegiate National Bull Riding, 216
International Professional Rodeo Association, 174
International Rodeo Association, 66, 78, 81
International Trick Riding Competition, 62
Iowa Park, Texas, 11
Irish, Ned, 53
Irwin, C. B., 4
Ivory, Buster, 65, 94, 114-115, 122
Ivory, June, 132

—J—
J. C. Penney, 137
J-5, 101-102
J-H Rodeo, 87
J31, 220
Jacksboro, Texas, 172
Jackson, Jimmy, 37
James, Lowell, 119

Jasbo, 54, 63
Jauregui, Andy, 42, 89, 143
Jernigan, Beaver, 182
Jet Age, 102-103, 197
Jim Shoulders Rodeo Company, 96; *also see* Shoulders, Jim
Johnson, Bernis, 116, 150
Johnson, Carroll, 64
Johnson, Colonel W. T., 16, 21, 22, 25, 30-33, 34
Johnson, Debbie, 231
Johnson, Dennis, 249
Johnson, Roger, 231
Jonckowski, Jonnie, 172-174
Jones, Arnold, 78
Jones, Cecil, 94, 114
Jones, Henry Preston "Buck," 71-72
Jones, Mrs., 80
Jordan, Allan, 163
Judd, Johnnie, 6
Junior Bull Riding Association, 142
Justin Boots, 96, 139, 177
Justin Cowboy Crisis Fund, 139
Justin Heeler program, 177-185, 209
Justin, John, 177, 232
Justin Sports Medicine, 139, 209, 212, 232
Justin World Bull Riding Championships, 173

—K—
Kajun Kidd, 83, 84-85, 86, 90, 94, 123
Kaneb, Utah, 89
Kansas City, Missouri, 151
Keeley, Glen, 251-252
Kelly, Tammy, 174
Kelsey, Joe, 53, 114
Kemmerer, Wyoming, 131
Kemp, Miss, 168
Kenney, James, 68
Kerrville, Texas, 76

Index 297

Killough, Buck, 37
Kilpatrick, Col. John Reed, 32, 33, 48, 53
Kimberley, British Columbia, 42
Kimbro, Clyde, 139
Kinder, Louisiana, 229
Kinsley, Otho, 62
Kirby, Butch, 159, 160
Kirby, Sandy, 144, 180, 181
Kirkwood, Fay, 169
Kirnan, Tommy, 13
Kish, Don, 163, 193, 194, 236, 250
Kiss Me, 190
Kissimmee, Florida, 50
Kitchens, Ronnie, 214
Klamath Falls, Oregon, 45
Knapp, Jack, 54, 57
Knight, Harry, 33, 90, 102, 127, 131, 133, 162
Knock 'Em Out John, 216
Korkow, 133
Kornell, Bill, 41, 118, 119, 120, 136
Kramps, B. J., 252
Kreig, Vaughn, 22
Kuhn, Butch, Jr., 195
Kunktz, Tommy, 58

—L—

La Junta, Colorado, 193
LaCoste, Kelly, 182
Lake Isabella, California, 114
Lamb, Gene, 79
Lambert, Cody, 186, 192, 207, 209, 211, 212, 219, 237, 239, 244
Lambert Master Pro, 209
Lane Frost Memorial Day, 193
Laramie, Wyoming, 142, 195
Larson, Willy Gene, 200
Las Vegas, Nevada, 37, 57, 99, 123, 187, 199, 204, 217, 219, 223, 249, 253

Lavender, Sonny, 89
Lazy E Arena, 242
Lee Rider, 137
Leete, Frances "Flaxie," 44
Leffew, Gary, 119, 142, 147-148
Legler, Jason, 250
LeGrand, Buck, 9, 83, 84
Lemmel, Red, 223
Leppy, 72-73
Leslie, Wade, 194, 214, 221-222
Let 'er Buck, 3
LeTourneau, Ed, 93, 115
Levi Strauss Co., 137
Levi Strauss Perpetual Trophy, 68-69
Lewallen, G. K., 53, 65
Lewis, Raymond, 222
Lewis, Wayne, 93
Lewiston, Idaho, 58, 100
Like, Jim, 141
Liland, Bill, 26
Linder, Herman, 24, 30, 32, 33
Linderman, Bill, 137, 138
Linderman, Bud, 53
Lindsey, John, 57
Little Britches Rodeo Association, 144, 215
Little Rock, Arkansas, 149
Livermore, California, 40, 193
Logan, Pete, 94, 129
London, England, 61
Long Beach, California, 220
Long, Hughie, 26
Long, Jack, 19, 178
Long, Peggy, 22
Longmont, Colorado, 18
Loring, Porter, 68
Los Angeles, California, 134, 145-147, 188
Los Angeles International Airport, 145-147
Loveland, Colorado, 250
Lowry, Jack, 227

Lubbock, Texas, 87
Lucas, Buck, 13
Lucas, Tad, 22, 165, 166
Lunc, Ross, 37
Lund, M., 26
Lyon County Fair Rodeo, 183
Lyons, Curt, 214

—M—

Mad Scramble, 22
Madison Square Garden Rodeo, 21, 22, 30, 32, 33, 35, 38, 44, 48, 53, 59, 64, 65, 78, 84, 85, 86, 95, 97, 98, 123, 137, 168
Madland, Ken, 87-89
Magdalena, New Mexico RoundUp, 10
Mahan, Larry, 119, 122-123, 128-130, 155, 251
Major, Randy, 142
Mansfield, Toots, 48, 53, 104
Mapston, Colt, 227
Mapston, Grey, 227
Marble Falls, Texas, 58
Marietta, Oklahoma, 77
Marion, Frank, 32, 36
Markley, Bill, 73
Marks, E. H. "Emil," 17
Marsh, Luther, 26
Martin, Chuck, 59
Martin, Prosser, 7
Mason, Mike, 199
Matli, John, 9
Matthews, Bob, 37
Maxwell, Virgil, 78
May, Harley, 69, 86, 122, 123, 141
Mayetta, Kansas, 74
Maynard, Bob, 89-90, 103
Maynard, Don, 89
Mayo, Bob, 138
McCarger, Fred, 34
McCarroll, Bonnie, 165, 173

McCarty, Ed, 4, 6, 7, 8, 23, 55
McCarty, Linda, 201
McClure, Jake, 12, 31, 32
McCrory, Howard, 48
McDonald, Bryan, 141, 142
McGinnis, Vera, 164, 165, 166
McGinty, Rusty, 12, 31, 33, 34
McIllvain, Glenn, 198
McKee, Bill, 136
McLaughlin boys, 54
McLaughlin, Don, 88
McMullen, Adam, 11
McNab, Diana, 130
McNichols Arena, 242
McSpadden, Clem, 125
Mead, Kansas, 170
medical program in rodeo, 177-185
Meek, Junior, 81, 82
Mendes, Carl, 12, 63
Mendes, Scott, 246
Merchant, Richard, 30, 62
Merino, Colorado, 127
Mesquite Rodeo, 90-91, 135, 224, 227-228
Mesquite Rodeo Company, 96
Metro-Goldwyn-Mayer trophy, 166
MGM Grand, 223
Miami, Oklahoma, 165
Midland, Texas, 96
Midnight, 7
MidWinter Championship Contest, 6, 9
Mighty Mike, 103
Miller Brothers 101 Ranch Real Wild West, 14, 99
Miller, Clyde, 43-44, 99
Miller Lite, 96
Miller, Robert M., 120
Millerick, Jack, 76
Mills, George, 54, 57, 63, 65, 67, 92
Mills, Hank, 48
Mills, Polly, 54, 65

Minick, Billy, 158, 162
Minnick, Lizzy, 33
Miss Newhall, 42
Mitchell, Cheryl, 201
Mix, Tom, 2
Monte Vista, Colorado, 60, 131
Moody Blues, 235
Moomaw, Leo, 17, 58
Moon Walker, 199
Moore, Frank, 84-85
Moraes, Adriano, 246, 248
Mortensen, Brock, 214
Mortensen, Dan, 224
Mortensen, Judd, 214
Moses Lake, Washington, 221
Mosley, Bill, 170
Mosley, Dixie, see Reger, Dixie Lee
Mosley, Larry, 174
Mote, Bobby, 224
Mr. Bubbles, 158
Mr. T. Copenhagen, 195-197
Muley, 73
Mulhall, Colonel Zack, 5-6
Mulhall, Lucille, 5
Mulkey, Burel, 12, 32, 141
Muncy, Jordan, 175
Mundorf, Bill, 195
Murff, Jim, 238
Murphy, Buck, 54
Murphy, Hardy, 54
Murphy, Red, 17
Murray, Butch, 214
Murray, Joy, 214
Murray, Ty, 174, 197, 212, 213, 214-215, 244, 245, 246-248, 249
Muskogee, Oklahoma, 75
Myers, Carl C., 71

—N—

Nafzger, Carl, 118, 143, 150
Nanton, Alberta, Canada, 251
Napoleon, 164

National Cowboy Hall of Fame, 40, 135, 150, 166, 167
National Cowgirl Hall of Fame, 167, 170, 174
National Finals Rodeo, 92-93, 96, 116, 117-120, 124, 125, 127, 133, 135, 136, 137, 139, 144, 148, 150, 152, 154, 158, 163, 177, 180, 183, 186-187, 190, 193, 194, 197, 199, 200, 204, 207, 216, 218, 219, 221, 222, 223, 224, 226, 229, 236, 246, 254
National High School Rodeo Association, 185, 193, 214, 215
National Intercollegiate Rodeo Association, 68
National Rodeo Association, 45, 66
National Western Stock Show and Rodeo, see Denver
Neal Barstow ProRodeo Equipment, 212
Neal, Vern, 113
Nebraska's Big Rodeo, 11
Nelson, Alvin, 88
Nelson, Harry, 87
Nelson, Jerry, 216
Nesbitt, Jimmy, 56, 57
Nesbitt, Pauline, 22
New Mexico State Fair Rodeo, 125
New Orleans, 64
New York, 12, 14, 21, 30
Newsom, Frank, 249
No Doze, 127
Normand, Hobart, 67
North Platte, Nebraska, 24
Northwest Cowboys Association, 35, 66
Norton, Kansas, 11
Nuce, Ted, 142, 197, 198
Number 2, 89

Number 3, 101
Number Four, 135
Number 6, 114
Number 7, 58, 138
Number 11, 100, 131, 146, 158, 159-161
Number 11+, 151
Number 22, 91, 121
Number 27, 93
Number 29, 115
Number 30, 113
Number 31, 90
Number 40, 76-77, 111, 181
Number 61, 82
Number 67, 124
Number 105, 150
Number 214, 140
Nunnemaker, Jaron, 237

—O—
"O," 157
O'Byrne, Josh, 205, 224
O'Donnell, Doug, 56, 168
O'Driscoll, Ellis, 202
O-Bar, 158-159
Oakland Tribune, 17
Odessa College, 215, 234
Odessa, Texas, 19
Odgen, Idaho, 39
Official Rodeo Rules, 67
Ogallala, Nebraska, 125
Ohio, 120
Oiltown, Oklahoma, 94
Oklahoma City, Oklahoma, 113, 135
Old Black Steer, 17
Old Speck, 62, 93, 126
Old Time Cowboys' Reunion, 141
Old-Timers Rodeo, 128, 152
Oldfield, Garth, 254
Olivo, Adam, 201
Omaha, Nebraska, 60
Omak, Washington, Stampede, 49

Original Coors Folsom Championship Rodeo, 199
Osborn, Julia, 72
Osborn, Ollie, 173
Osborne, Cherrie Lee, 48
Oscar, 162-163, 222, 250
Oskaloosa, Iowa, 10
Otho Kingsley Ranch Rodeo, 55
Owens, Mitch, 33, 35
Ox Bar ranch, 175

—P—
Paisano Ranch, 34
Palestine, Illinois, 159, 160
Panhandle Slim, 235
Pardee, C. W. "Doc", 15, 164
Pardee, E., 31
Paris, Arkansas, 155
Parker, Tex, 10
Parks, Mary, 22
Patch, Jim, 63
Pattie, Jane, 145
Paul, George, 119, 130-131
Payette Valley, Idaho, 176
Peekskill, New York, 97
Peetz, Colorado, 105
Pendleton RoundUp, 2-3, 4, 35, 47-48, 81-82, 115, 116, 168, 190
Pendleton RoundUp Association, 3
Pendleton RoundUp Hall of Fame, 4, 167
Permit Bull Riding program, 141-142
Perry, Iowa, 99
Persimmon Hill, 135
Petaluma, California, 103
Peth, Wick, 127, 134, 143, 182
Pettigrew, Homer, 53, 67
Petty, Alonza, 19
Phillipsburg, Kansas, 46
Phoenix rodeo, 65, 169
Pickens, Slim, 57, 132

Pierce Estate Ranch, 134
Pierce, Josh, 230
Piper, Harold, 29
Pirtle, Sue, 174
Playboy, 217
Pocatello, Idaho, 140, 183, 189
Poison Ivy, 17
Ponca City, Oklahoma, 111
Pope, Bob, 128
Pope, Norma, 128
Porter, Tater, 237
Porter, Willard H., 111
Portland, Oregon, 87, 103, 124
Potter, Maynard, 244
Prescott, 48-50
Prescott Evening Courier, 48
Prescott Frontier Days, 1, 2, 12, 15, 23, 25, 35, 59, 78, 89
Prescott Rules, 15, 50
Presidential Rodeo, 190
Preston, Idaho, 37
prize monies, 241-254
PROCOM, 142
Professional Bull Riders (PBR), 187, 211, 212, 214, 215, 221, 234, 235, 236, 239, 242-245, 246, 248- 249, 252-254
Professional Rodeo Cowboys Association (PRCA), 140, 142, 174, 177, 186, 189, 193, 215, 216, 219, 223, 226, 227, 232, 244-245, 254
Professional Women's Rodeo Association (PWRA), 171, 172, 174
Promise Land, 235
ProRodeo Cowboys Association, 241
ProRodeo Hall of Fame, 40, 163, 167, 215, 218, 221
ProRodeo Sports News, 141, 145, 180

Providence, Rhode Island, 37
Pruett, Gene, 117, 120, 141
Pueblo, Colorado, 141

—Q—
Queen Creek, Arizona, 174
Quintana, John, 135, 162
Quirk, Frank, 38
Quirk, Louis, 38, 63, 69

—R—
Rafter G Rodeo, 226
Rafter H Rodeo, 226
Rafter J, 133
Rambo, Gene, 65, 141
Randolph, Florence, 22
Rapid City, South Dakota, 181
Rasmussen, Flint, 249
Rastus, 22
Reagan, Bob, 34
Reagan, Rocky, 34
Reagan, Ronald, 190
Real West, 151
Red Bluff, California, 103, 193, 194
Red Lightning, 146, 158, 159-161, 250
Red Lodge, Montana, 172
Red Rock, 163, 191, 193, 194, 197, 222, 250
Red Rock, Texas, 200
Red Wolf, 199, 219, 236-239
Redding, California, 193
Reger, Buddy, 169
Reger, Dixie Lee, 169-170, 172
Reger, Monty, 169
Reger, Virginia, 169
Reich, Polly, 174
Remote Double J Arena Bull Dummy, 231
Reno, Nevada, 216
Resistol Hats, 139
Resistol Relief Fund, 252-253

Resistol Rookie of the Year, 215
Reynolds, Benny, 93
Reynolds, Clive, 134
Reynolds, Fess, 58
Rinestine, Bill, 93, 116
Rio Linda, California, 145
Roach, Ruth, 165, 173
Roberts, Bill, 105, 108, 110
Roberts, E. C., 74, 99
Roberts, Gerald, 65, 79, 99, 100, 137, 138, 141
Roberts, Ken, 65, 73-74, 99, 141
Roberts, Margie, 99
Robinson, Bob, 116, 119
Robinson, Claude, 133
Robinson, Jerome, 150
Rochester, New York, 64
Rockabar, Rocky, 116
Rocky Ford, Colorado, 128
rodeo schools, 104-113, 143-145, 155, 172
Rodeo Association of America (RAA), 16, 34, 39, 44, 51, 58, 66, 81
Rodeo Ben, 39, 138
Rodeo Cowboys Association (RCA), 50, 66, 67, 78, 79, 81, 82, 86, 88, 93, 97, 120-121, 172, 226
Rodeo Foundation, 117
Rodeo Girl, 174
Rodeo Hall of Fame, 18
Rodeo Historical Society, 40
Rodeo Information Commission, 81
Rodeo Sports News, 81, 87, 120-121
Rodeo Stock Contractors, Inc. (RSC), 163
Rogers, Marvel, 19
Rogers, Roy, 53, 67
Rogers, Will, 25, 60
Romer, Bob, 182
Rookie of the Year, 139, 215, 216

Rose, Caroline Ramsey, 132
Ross, Katherine, 174
Ross, Sul, 68
Rossen, Ronnie "Punch," 93, 116, 118, 119, 120, 125-128, 147-148
Rossen, Ruby, 127
Rossen, Wayne, 127
Rosser, Cotton, 69, 133
Rowell, Harry, 17, 51, 62
Rowell Rodeo, 17, 51
Roy, Montana, 200
Rude, Ike, 62
rules, rodeo, 15, 50, 67
Runyan, Grace, 165
Russell, Dan, 197
Russell, Linda, 197
Rutherford, Buck, 87
Ryan, Duward, 37
Ryan, Paddy, 11

—S—

Sacramento, California, 162
safety gear, 205, 206-214
Saint Stephens Episcopal Church, 39
Salinas, California, 3, 51, 90
Salt Lake City, 56
Sampson, Charles, 188, 198
Sampson, Gordon Casey, 114
San Angelo rodeo, 119-120
San Angelo, Texas, 27, 37, 106, 171
San Angelus Hotel, 171
San Antonio Livestock Show & Rodeo, 133, 134
San Antonio, Texas, 133, 134, 167
San Bernardino, California, 89
San Francisco, California, 80, 163
San Francisco Cow Palace, 114
Sand Man, 226
Sandall, Hubert, 44

Sankey, Ike, 143-145
Sankey, Lyle, 143-145
Savery, Wyoming, 136
Schader, Brandon, 203
Schader, Charles "Trey," 200-203
Schlosser, Greg, 220
Schneider, Frankie, 43, 64
Schneider, Johnie, 11, 13, 40-41, 42, 43, 141
Schumacher, Jimmy, 64
Scobey, Montana, 19
Scotia, Fred, 114
Scottsdale, Arizona, 173, 242
Scrap Iron Patch, 38,
Seagle, Nathan, 39
Sears & Roebuck, 137
Sellers, Earl, 76
Sellers, Jack, 76
Semas, Aaron, 203, 218, 236, 244, 254
Senior ProRodeo Association, 115
"777," 249
Shannon, Texas, 169
Sharkey, 3-4
Sharkey, Jr., 4
Sharp, Frank, 26
Sharp, Jim, 186
Shaw, Everett, 31, 33, 119
Shaw, Roscoe, 33
Shellenberger, David, 77
Shelton, Dick, 12
Shelton, Reine Hafley, 22
Shepard, Bob, 93
Shivers, Chris, 254
Shoulders, Jim, 73, 86, 87, 88, 90, 91, 93, 94-97, 103, 104-110, 116, 118, 120, 122, 123, 125, 128, 133, 135, 138-139, 149, 151, 152, 178, 190, 229, 231, 250
Shoulders, Sharron, 95
Shultz, Guy, 6, 9
Shultz, John, 11

Sidney (Iowa) RoundUp, 23
Sidney American Legion, 45
Sidney, Iowa, 24, 45, 46, 121
Sierra Circuit, 189-190
Sikestown, Missouri, 147, 150
Silver Lake, Oregon, 194
Silver Spurs Rodeo, 190
Sirett, Kagan, 223
Sisters, Oregon, 193, 194
Skoal's King Kong, 226
Skoal's Pacific Bell, 197
Skuthorpe, Violet, 168
Sky High, 59
Sleepy, 76
Sluggett, Lari, 200
Smets, Rob, 182, 184, 249-250
Smith, Dale, 86, 88
Smith, Rose, 165, 173
Snowdrift, 114-115
Snyder, Albert Edward, (see Snyder, Smokey)
Snyder, Cody, 161
Snyder, Smokey, 12, 26, 27, 33, 41-43
Soldiers Field, 7, 13
Sonora Red, 37, 62-63
Sons of the Pioneers, 67
Soper, Oklahoma, 123
Sorrells, Buckshot, 67
Southwest Rodeo Association, 66
Southwestern Rodeo Association, 132
Spanish Fork, Utah, 193
Speedy Gonzales, 136
Spider Ranch, 78
Spillum, 57
Spinning Wheel, 37
Spokane, Washington, 89, 113, 145
sponsors, 137-141
Spot, 111-113
Spurling, Jack, 103
St. Francisville, Louisiana, 8
St. Louis, Missouri, 82, 139, 140, 157, 160

St. Paul, Oregon, 193
St. Petersburg, Florida, 167
Staneart, Marty, 195, 196
Stanley, New Mexico, 142
Stanton, Kenny, 118, 119
Star Flight, 202
Steen, Jim, 119
Steiner, Beverly, 153
Steiner, Bobby, 146, 147-148, 153-155
Steiner, Buck, 5, 16
Steiner, Joleen, 154
Steiner ranch, 155
Steiner Rodeo Company, 82, 91, 124, 133, 139, 140, 146, 147, 151, 157, 158, 159, 160
Steiner, Tommy, 16, 90, 148, 149, 153
Stephens, Frank, 12
Sterling, Colorado, 128
Stevenson, Legs, 220
Stevenson, Tanya Tucker, 176
Stewart, Clarence, 9
Stillings, Floyd, 12
Stockdale, Texas, 201
Stockton, California, 40, 43
Stokes, Homer C., 11
Stratton, Tate, 142, 206
Strickland, Mabel DeLong, 165, 167
Strong City, Kansas, 42, 73
Stroud, Leonard, 6, 9
Stryker, John, 10, 11, 24
Sturman, Kent, 214
Sublett, Red, 9, 10, 56
Sublette, Joel, 119
suicide wrap, 108
Sul Ross State University, 186
Sullivan, Odis, 89
Sullivan, Shaw, 242
Sulphur, Oklahoma, 101
Summerville, Georgia, 145
Sumner, Phil, 220
Sundown, Jackson, 124

Sunny, 198
Sunny's Velvet, 102, 197-198
Sutton Rodeos, Inc., 133, 195
Sydney, Australia, 4

—T—
Taillon, Cy, 94
Takin' Care of Business, 191, 192
Tarzan, 45-46
Taylor, Berva Don, 132
Taylor, Dan, 85-86, 114, 122, 123, 132
Taylor, Monty, 145-147
team rodeo program, 121
team roping, 159
TeamPBR Fan Fest party, 253
Teddy, 10
Teddy Roosevelt, 24
television coverage, 81, 223, 226, 246
Temple, Texas, 152
Tennessee Gas & Transmission Company, 133
Terrell, Texas, 230
Texaco, 17, 168
Texas Arts & Industrial College, 68
Texas House of Representatives, 193
Texas State Fair Rodeo, 69
The Czar, Alberta, Canada, 125
Thode, Earl, 12
Thomas & Mack Stadium, 187, 253
Thomas, Tommy, 193
Thompson, Claire Belcher, 22
Thompson, Snowy, 5
Thornton, Randy, 219
Three Hill Rodeo, 224
Three Rivers, 34
Thurman, Brent, 199-200, 217-220, 236, 246
Thurman, Brock, 217

Index 305

Thurman, Kay, 217, 219, 220
Tibbs, Casey, 63, 87, 90, 123, 141, 190
Timex, 191
TNN, 223, 226, 246
Todd, Brown, 135
Todd, Homer, 75
Tompkins, Harry, 73, 90, 93, 97-99, 103, 117, 123, 138, 141, 151
Tornado, 95, 118, 125, 134-135
Torrance County, New Mexico, 175
Touring Pro Division, 246, 249
trade out, 83, 117
Travis Air Base, 103
Treasure Island, California, 37
Tremors, 200
Trick or Treat, 250
Truan, Fritz, 33, 59
Truitt, Dick, 12, 31, 32
Tucker, Harley, 115
Tucker, Tanya, 147
Tucumcari, New Mexico, 167
Tuff Hedeman Challenge, 216
Tulsa, Oklahoma, 44, 58, 75, 94, 164, 188
Turnbow, Cory, 237
Turquoise Circuit, 189
Twin Falls, Idaho, 183
Tyler, Glenn, 64

—U—
U.S. Olympic Trials, 172
U.S. Team Roping Championship, 159
U.S. Tobacco, 140
University of Denver, 130

—V—
V61, 161-162
Valley City, North Dakota, 145
Van Nuys, California, 62

Vela, Rudy, 161
Vernon, Texas, 44
Victorville, California, 89
Vinita, Oklahoma, 83
Visalia, California, 87
Vogt, Henry, 4
Vold, Harry, 183, 188, 249, 250
Vold, Wayne, 200
Voss, Andy, 201
Voss, Skipper, 182

—W—
Waco Fair & Rodeo, 124
Waco, Texas, 6
Wahlert, Jeff, 225
Walco, 144
Wallace, Jimmy, 29
Wallace, Roy, 116
Walls, Wesley, 37
Ward, Bill, 65
Warren Cummings Livestock Commission Company, 11
Washington, D.C., 14
Waverly, New York, 64
Weadick, Guy, 2, 24
Webb, Ronny, 115
Webster, Shoat, 53
Wegner, Bob, 93, 94, 103, 116, 118, 119, 120-121, 127, 241
Weidemann, Fred, 17
Weiser, Idaho, 173
Wembley, England, 4
Wessel, Raymond, 197, 214, 218
West Fork Ranch, 172
West Klicktat Horsemen's rodeo, 72
West of the Pecos Rodeo, 89
West, Terry Don, 217, 220
West Virginia, 120
Western Gift Expo, 254
Western Horseman, 120

Western Rodeo Inc., 187, 197
Whaley, Slim, 110, 111
Wharton County, Texas, 134
Wharton, Ray, 86
Whately, Todd, 65, 87, 138
Wheatland, Wyoming, 123
White, Grace, 22
White House, 60
White Salmon, 72
White Swan, Washington, 114
White, Vivian, 22, 32, 170, 172
White Water Skoal, 250
Whiteman, Hub, 31, 67, 141
Whiteman, Jim, 63, 64
Whitley, B. J., 133
Wichita Falls, Texas, 169
Wichita, Kansas, 6, 9, 111
Wickenburg, Arizona, 240
Wilbur, Washington, 58
Wild Bunch, 18
Wild Horse Race, 97
Wild Rogue ProRodeo, 221
Wild West Show, 43
Wilfred, 250
Wilkinson, Al, 29
Willcox, Arizona, 123
Williams, Big John, 114, 132-135, 229, 231
Williams, Charlene Frnka, 132
Williams, Clayton, 236
Williams, George, 121
Williams, Johnnie, 26
Williams, Terry, 235-236, 251
Wilmer, Red, 98
Wilson, Homer, 5
Wilson, Mary Keen, 22
Wimberley, Joe, 228
Wolf, Bob, 71

Wolfman, 250
Wolfman Skoal, 194, 222
Womack, Andy, 87
women in rodeo, 69, 164-176
Women's Professional Rodeo Association (WPRA), 140, 172, 174
Woodlake, California, 114
Woods, Eddie, 141
Woods, Pat, 26
Woodstown, New Jersey, 39
Worthington, Jeanette "Jackie," 170-172
Wrangler, 96, 137-139
Wrangler Jeans Bullfight Tour, 181, 182
Wrangler ProRodeo Tour, 223, 224, 246
Wrangler Round, 183

—Y—
Yakima, Washington, 190
Yale, Bug, 12, 31
Yardley, George, 59, 68
Yavapai County Messenger, 50
"YD," 139
Yerington, Nevada, 183
Yonnick, Buttons, 38, 50, 63
Young, Jeff, 1
Young, Tot, 1
Youren, Jan, 175

—Z—
Zebroski, Melvin, 248
zebus, 168
Zeigler, Bill, 232

www.ingramcontent.com/pod-product-compliance
Lightning Source LLC
Chambersburg PA
CBHW071654160426
43195CB00012B/1465